JavaScript by Example

Modern JavaScript programming with real world web apps

Dani Akash S

BIRMINGHAM - MUMBAI

JavaScript by Example

First published: August 2017

Production reference: 1260817

Published by Packt Publishing Ltd.
Livery Place
35 Livery Street
Birmingham
B3 2PB, UK.
ISBN 978-1-78829-396-9

www.packtpub.com

Credits

Author
Dani Akash S

Reviewer
Loiane Groner

Commissioning Editor
Smeet Thakkar

Acquisition Editor
Shweta Pant

Content Development Editor
Roshan Kumar

Technical Editor
Harshal Kadam

Copy Editor
Akshata Lobo

Project Coordinator
Devanshi Doshi

Proofreader
Safis Editing

Indexer
Mariammal Chettiyar

Graphics
Jason Monteiro

Production Coordinator
Shraddha Falebhai

About the Author

Dani Akash S is a passionate, self-taught application developer who loves working on the JavaScript stack. He has worked on many JavaScript frameworks, such as React.js, React Native, Angular, Vue, Express, and Sails. He has built many web and mobile applications. In his free time, he loves to explore new technologies and contribute to open source projects on GitHub.

You can find him on his Twitter handle: @DaniAkashS

A great thanks to God for being there for me all the time.

About the Reviewer

Loiane Groner has more than 10 years of experience in developing enterprise applications. She has worked at multinational companies, such as IBM, and now works as a business analyst and developer at a financial institution. Her areas of expertise include Java, Sencha technologies (Ext JS), Angular, and hybrid mobile development with Phonegap and Ionic.

She is passionate about technology and has dedicated herself to spreading knowledge in the software development community through her blog (http://loiane.com) and as a speaker at IT conferences. She also maintains a training portal, http://loiane.training.

Loiane is also author of *Ext JS 4 First Look, Mastering Ext JS* (first and second editions), *Sencha Architect App Development* and *Learning JavaScript Structure and Algorithms* (first and second editions) and *JavaScript Regular Expressions*, all published by Packt.

If you want to keep in touch with her, you can find *Loiane* on the following social media platforms:

- **Facebook:** https://www.facebook.com/loianegroner
- **Twitter:** @loiane
- **GitHub:** https://github.com/loiane
- **Packt:** https://www.packtpub.com/books/info/authors/loiane-groner

I would like to thank my parents for giving me education, guidance, and advice for all these years and helping me to be a better human being and professional.

A very special thanks to my husband for being patient and supportive and giving me encouragement so that I keep doing what I love.

I would like to thank Packt for the amazing opportunity to write books about topics I really love. Thanks to all the people involved in the process of creating, reviewing, and publishing the books.

I also would like to thank the readers of this book, and the books that I have written for the support and feedback. Your feedback is very valuable for me to improve as an author and as a professional. Thank you very much!

www.PacktPub.com

For support files and downloads related to your book, please visit www.PacktPub.com. Did you know that Packt offers eBook versions of every book published, with PDF and ePub files available? You can upgrade to the eBook version at www.PacktPub.com and as a print book customer, you are entitled to a discount on the eBook copy. Get in touch with us at service@packtpub.com for more details. At www.PacktPub.com, you can also read a collection of free technical articles, sign up for a range of free newsletters and receive exclusive discounts and offers on Packt books and eBooks.

https://www.packtpub.com/mapt

Get the most in-demand software skills with Mapt. Mapt gives you full access to all Packt books and video courses, as well as industry-leading tools to help you plan your personal development and advance your career.

Why subscribe?

- Fully searchable across every book published by Packt
- Copy and paste, print, and bookmark content
- On demand and accessible via a web browser

Customer Feedback

Thanks for purchasing this Packt book. At Packt, quality is at the heart of our editorial process. To help us improve, please leave us an honest review on this book's Amazon page at: https://www.amazon.com/dp/1788293967. If you'd like to join our team of regular reviewers, you can e-mail us at customerreviews@packtpub.com. We award our regular reviewers with free eBooks and videos in exchange for their valuable feedback. Help us be relentless in improving our products!

I dedicate this book to my family members: my dad, Sekar, my mom, Grace Regina, and my brother Amresh, who have all helped me with everything in my life.

Table of Contents

Preface

JavaScript is a rapidly evolving language with new features being added to it annually. This book is designed to get your hands dirty by building a wide range of applications with JavaScript. This will help you build a solid foundation with JavaScript, which will help you adapt to its new and upcoming features in the future, as well as learn other modern frameworks and libraries.

What this book covers

Chapter 1, *Building a ToDo List*, starts with a simple DOM manipulation with JavaScript and work with event listeners, which will give you a good idea of how JavaScript works with the HTML in the website. You'll set up the basic development environment and build your first ToDo list app.

Chapter 2, *Building a Meme Creator*, helps you build a fun application, Meme Creator. Through this, you'll understand the canvas element, use ES6 classes, and be introduced to layouts using CSS3 flexbox. This chapter also introduces you to Webpack and setting up your own automated development environment using it.

Chapter 3, *Event Registration App*, focuses on developing a responsive Event Registration form with an appropriate form validation, which allows users to register for your upcoming event and also visually display the registration data through charts. This chapter helps you understand different methods of performing AJAX requests and how to work with dynamic data.

Chapter 4, *Real-Time Video Call App with WebRTC*, uses WebRTC to build a real-time video call and chat application in JavaScript. This chapter focuses on using the powerful web APIs available to JavaScript in the browser.

Chapter 5, *Developing a Weather Widget*, helps you build a weather widget for an application using the HTML5 custom elements. You'll learn about web components and their importance in web application development.

Chapter 6, *Building a Blog with React*, discusses React, a library for building user interfaces in JavaScript created by Facebook. You'll then build a blog using React and tools such as create-react-app and react-router.

Chapter 7, *Redux*, will deep dive into making your blog more maintainable and scalable, along with an improved user experience, using Redux to manage data across the React components.

What you need for this book

For the best experience while building the projects in this book, you will need the following:

- A Windows or Linux machine with at least 4 GB RAM memory or a Mac
- An iPhone or Android mobile device
- A fast internet connection

Who this book is for

This book is intended for web developers with a basic knowledge of HTML, CSS, and JavaScript who are looking to improve their skills and build powerful web applications.

A basic knowledge of JavaScript or any other programming language will be great. However, if you are completely new to JavaScript and programming, then you can read one of the following simple tutorials, which will help you get started with the basics of JavaScript, and you'll then be ready to read this book in no time:

- Mozilla Developer Network: https:/ / developer. mozilla. org/ en- US/ docs/ Learn/ JavaScript/ First_ steps/ What_ is_ JavaScript
- w3schools: https:/ / www. w3schools. com/ js/

Conventions

In this book, you will find a number of text styles that distinguish between different kinds of information. Here are some examples of these styles and an explanation of their meaning. Code words in text, database table names, folder names, filenames, file extensions, pathnames, dummy URLs, user input, and Twitter handles are shown as follows: "In our index.html file, our <body> element is divided into a navigation bar and div containing the contents of the website."

A block of code is set as follows:

```
loadTasks() {
  let tasksHtml = this.tasks.reduce((html, task, index) => html +=
  this.generateTaskHtml(task, index), '');
  document.getElementById('taskList').innerHTML = tasksHtml;
}
```

When we wish to draw your attention to a particular part of a code block, the relevant lines or items are set in bold:

```
function mapStateToProps() {
  return {
    // No states needed by App Component
  };
}
```

Any command-line input or output is written as follows:

```
npm install -g http-server
```

New terms and **important words** are shown in bold.

Words that you see on the screen, for example, in menus or dialog boxes, appear in the text like this: "Clicking on the **Read More** button in the home page will take you to the post details page instantly."

Warnings or important notes appear like this.

Tips and tricks appear like this.

Reader feedback

Feedback from our readers is always welcome. Let us know what you think about this book-what you liked or disliked. Reader feedback is important for us as it helps us develop titles that you will really get the most out of. To send us general feedback, simply e-mail feedback@packtpub.com, and mention the book's title in the subject of your message. If there is a topic that you have expertise in and you are interested in either writing or contributing to a book, see our author guide at www.packtpub.com/authors.

Customer support

Now that you are the proud owner of a Packt book, we have a number of things to help you to get the most from your purchase.

Downloading the example code

You can download the example code files for this book from your account at http:/ / www. packtpub. com. If you purchased this book elsewhere, you can visit http:/ / www. packtpub. com/ support and register to have the files e-mailed directly to you. You can download the code files by following these steps:

1. Log in or register to our website using your e-mail address and password.
2. Hover the mouse pointer on the **SUPPORT** tab at the top.
3. Click on **Code Downloads & Errata**.
4. Enter the name of the book in the **Search** box.
5. Select the book for which you're looking to download the code files.
6. Choose from the drop-down menu where you purchased this book from.
7. Click on **Code Download**.

Once the file is downloaded, please make sure that you unzip or extract the folder using the latest version of:

- WinRAR / 7-Zip for Windows
- Zipeg / iZip / UnRarX for Mac
- 7-Zip / PeaZip for Linux

The code bundle for the book is also hosted on GitHub at https:/ / github. com/ PacktPublishing/ JavaScript- by- Example. We also have other code bundles from our rich catalog of books and videos available at https:/ / github. com/ PacktPublishing/ . Check them out!

Errata

Although we have taken every care to ensure the accuracy of our content, mistakes do happen. If you find a mistake in one of our books-maybe a mistake in the text or the code-we would be grateful if you could report this to us. By doing so, you can save other readers from frustration and help us improve subsequent versions of this book. If you find any errata, please report them by visiting http:/ / www. packtpub. com/ submit- errata, selecting your book, clicking on the **Errata Submission Form** link, and entering the details of your errata. Once your errata are verified, your submission will be accepted and the errata will be uploaded to our website or added to any list of existing errata under the Errata section of that title. To view the previously submitted errata, go to https:/ / www. packtpub. com/ books/ content/ support and enter the name of the book in the search field. The required information will appear under the **Errata** section.

Piracy

Piracy of copyrighted material on the Internet is an ongoing problem across all media. At Packt, we take the protection of our copyright and licenses very seriously. If you come across any illegal copies of our works in any form on the Internet, please provide us with the location address or website name immediately so that we can pursue a remedy. Please contact us at copyright@packtpub.com with a link to the suspected pirated material. We appreciate your help in protecting our authors and our ability to bring you valuable content.

Questions

If you have a problem with any aspect of this book, you can contact us at questions@packtpub.com, and we will do our best to address the problem.

1
Building a ToDo List

Hi there!

We are going to be building some really interesting applications with JavaScript in this book. JavaScript has evolved from being a simple scripting language that is used for form validation in browsers to a powerful programming language that is used practically everywhere. Check out these use cases:

- Want to set up a server to handle millions of requests with a lot of I/O operations? You have Node.js with its single threaded non-blocking I/O model that can handle the heavy load with ease. Write JavaScript on the server with Node.js frameworks, such as **Express** or **Sails**.
- Want to build a large scale web application? This is an exciting time to be a frontend developer, since lots of new JavaScript frameworks, such as **React**, **Angular 2**, **Vue.js**, and so on, are available to speed up your development process and build large scale applications easily.
- Want to build a mobile app? Pick up **React Native** or **NativeScript** and you can build truly native mobile applications that work across both iOS and Android with a single codebase written in JavaScript. Not enough? Use **PhoneGap** or **Ionic** to simply create a mobile application with HTML, CSS, and JavaScript. Just like a web app!
- Want to build a desktop app? Use **Electron** to build a cross-platform native desktop application using HTML, CSS, and of course, JavaScript.
- JavaScript is also playing an important role in building **Virtual Reality** (**VR**) and **Augmented Reality** (**AR**) applications. Check out **React VR**, **A-Frame** for building WebVR experiences and **Argon.js**, **AR.js** for adding AR to your web applications.

JavaScript is also evolving rapidly. With the introduction of **ECMAScript 2015** (**ES6**), a lot of new additions came into the language that simplify a lot of work for developers, providing them with features that were previously only possible using TypeScript and CoffeeScript. Even more, features are being added to JavaScript in its new specifications (ES7 and beyond). This is an exciting time to be a JavaScript developer and this book aims at building a solid foundation so that you can adapt to any of the earlier mentioned JavaScript platforms/frameworks in the future.

This chapter is targeted at readers who know the basic concepts of HTML, CSS, and JavaScript, but are yet to learn new topics, such as ES6, Node, and so on. In this chapter, the following topics will be covered:

- **Document Object Model** (**DOM**) manipulation and event listeners
- Introduction to and the practical usage of the ES6 implementation of JavaScript
- Using Node and npm for frontend development
- Using Babel to transpile ES6 to ES5
- Setting up an automated development server with npm scripts

If you feel you are comfortable with these topics, you can jump over to the next chapter, where we will be dealing with some advanced tools and concepts.

System requirements

JavaScript is the language of the web. So, you can build web applications from any system with a web browser and a text editor. But we do need some tools for building modern complex web applications. For better development experience, it's recommended to use a Linux or Windows machine with minimum 4 GB RAM or a Mac machine. Before we start, you might want to set up some of the following applications in your system.

Text editor

First of all, you need a JavaScript-friendly text editor. Text editors are important when it comes to writing code. Depending on the features they provide, you can save hours of development time. There are some really good text editors out there with excellent languages support. We are going to be using JavaScript in this book, so I'd recommend getting one of these open source JavaScript-friendly text editors:

- Atom: `http://atom.io`
- Visual Studio Code: `http://code.visualstudio.com`

- Brackets: `http://brackets.io/`

You can also try Sublime Text: `https://www.sublimetext.com/`, which is a great text editor, but unlike the previously mentioned ones, Sublime Text is commercial and you need to pay for continued usage. There is also another commercial product WebStorm: `https://www.jetbrains.com/webstorm/`, which is a full-fledged **Integrated Development Environment** (**IDE**) for JavaScript. It comes with various tools for debugging and integration with JavaScript frameworks. You might want to give it a try sometime.

I would recommend using **Visual Studio Code** (**VSCode**) for the projects in this book.

Node.js

Here's another important tool that we will be using throughout this book, Node.js. Node.js is a JavaScript runtime built on Chrome's V8 engine. It lets you run JavaScript outside your browser. Node.js has become really popular because it lets you run JavaScript on the server and is really fast thanks to its non-blocking I/O methods.
One other excellent advantage of Node.js is that it helps create command-line tools, which can be used for various purposes, such as automation, code scaffolding, and more, many of which we will be using in this book. At the time of writing this book, the latest **Long Term Support** (**LTS**) version of Node.js is 6.10.2. I'll be using this version throughout this book. You can install the latest LTS version available at the time you are reading this book.

For Windows users

Installation on Windows is straightforward; just download and install the latest LTS version available at: `https://nodejs.org/en/`.

For Linux users

The easiest way is to install the latest LTS version through your package manager by following the instructions provided at `https://nodejs.org/en/download/package-manager/`.

For Mac users

Install Node.js using Homebrew:

- Install Homebrew from: `https://brew.sh/`
- Run the following command in terminal: `brew install node`

Once you have installed Node.js, run `node -v` in your Terminal (command prompt for Windows users) to check whether it is properly installed. This should print the current version of the node you have installed.

Google Chrome

Finally, install the latest version of Google Chrome: `https://www.google.com/chrome/` in your system. You can use Firefox or other browsers, but I will be using Chrome, so it will be easier for you to follow if you use Chrome.

Now that we have all the necessary tools installed in our system, let's get started with building our first application!

ToDo List app

Let's take a look at the application we are about to build:

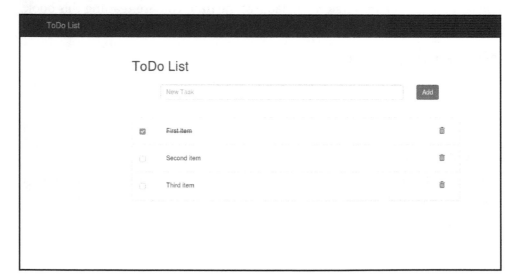

We are going to build this simple ToDo List app, which allows us to create a list of tasks, mark them as completed, and delete tasks from the list.

Let's get started by using the starter code of Chapter 1 in the book's code files. The starter code will contain three files: index.html, scripts.js, and styles.css. Open the index.html file in a web browser to see the basic design of the ToDo List app, as shown in the preceding screenshot.

The JavaScript file will be empty, in which we are going to write scripts to create the application. Let's take a look at the HTML file. In the <head> section, a reference to the styles.css file and BootstrapCDN are included, and at the end of the <body> tag, jQuery and Bootstrap's JS files are included along with our scripts.js file:

- Bootstrap is a UI development framework that helps us to build responsive HTML designs faster. Bootstrap comes with set of JavaScript codes that requires jQuery to run.

- jQuery is a JavaScript library that simplifies JavaScript functions for DOM traversal, DOM manipulation, event handling, and so on.

 Bootstrap and jQuery are widely used together for building web applications. In this book, we will be focusing more on using JavaScript. Hence, both of them will not be covered in detail. However, you can take a look at w3school's website for learning Bootstrap: https://www. w3schools.com/bootstrap/default.asp and jQuery: https://www. w3schools.com/jquery/default.asp in detail.

In our HTML file, the styles in the CSS file included last will overwrite the styles in the previous file. Hence, it's a good practice to include our own CSS files after the default framework's CSS files (Bootstrap in our case) if we plan to rewrite any of the framework's default CSS properties. We don't have to worry about CSS in this chapter, since we are not going to edit default styles of Bootstrap in this chapter. We only need to concentrate on our JS files. JavaScript files must be included in the given order as in the starter code:

```
<script src="https://code.jquery.com/jquery-3.2.1.min.js"></script>
<script
src="https://maxcdn.bootstrapcdn.com/bootstrap/3.3.7/js/bootstrap.min.js"
integrity="sha384-
Tc5IQib027qvyjSMfHjOMaLkfuWVxZxUPnCJA712mCWNIpG9mGCD8wGNIcPD7Txa"
crossorigin="anonymous"></script>
<script src="scripts.js"></script>
```

We are including the jQuery code first after which Bootstrap JS files are included. This is because Bootstrap's JS files require jQuery to run. If we include Bootstrap JS first, it will print an error in the console, saying Bootstrap requires jQuery to run. Try moving the Bootstrap code above the jQuery code and open up your browser's console. For Google Chrome, it's *Ctrl+Shift+J* on Windows or Linux and *command+option+J* on Mac. You will receive an error similar to this:

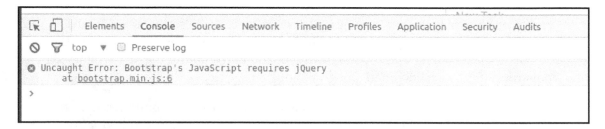

Hence, we are currently managing dependencies by including the JS files in the right order. However, in larger projects, this could be really difficult. We'll look at a better way to manage our JS files in the next chapter. For now, let's continue on to build our application.

The body of our HTML file is divided into two sections:

- Navigation bar
- Container

We usually use the navigation bar to add links to the different sections of our web app. Since we are only dealing with a single page in this app, we will only include the page title in the navigation bar.

 I have included many classes to the HTML elements, such as `navbar`, `navbar-inverse`, `navbar-fixed-top`, `container`, `col-md-2`, `col-xs-2`, and so on. They are used for styling the elements using Bootstrap. We'll discuss them in later chapters. For now, let's focus only on the functionality part.

Chrome DevTools

In the body section, we have an input field with a button to add a new task and an unordered list to list out the tasks. The unordered list will have a checkbox to mark the task as completed and a delete icon to remove the task from the list. You might notice that the first item in the list is marked completed using a strike-through line. If you inspect the element using Chrome DevTools, you will notice that it has an additional class `complete`, which adds a strike-through line on the text using CSS, which is defined in our `styles.css` file.

To inspect an element using Chrome DevTools, right-click over that element and select inspect. You can also click *Ctrl+Shift+C* on Windows or Linux, or *command+shift+C* on Mac, and then, hover the cursor over the element to see its details. You can also directly edit the element's HTML or CSS to see the changes reflected on the page. Delete the complete class from the `div` of the first item in the list. You'll see that the strike-through line has gone. The changes made directly in the DevTools are temporary and will be cleaned when the page is refreshed. Take a look at the following image for a list of tools available to inspect an element in Chrome:

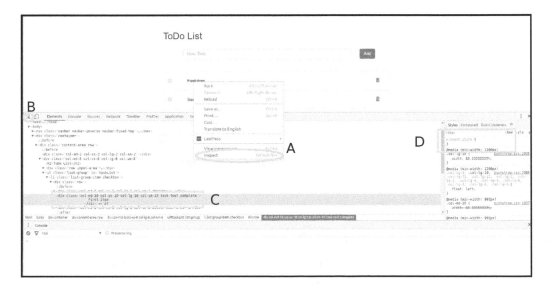

- **A**: Inspect element from right-click
- **B**: Click the cursor icon and select a different element by hovering the cursor over the element
- **C**: Directly edit the HTML of the page
- **D**: Directly edit the CSS associated with an element

One other nice feature of Chrome DevTools is that you can write `debugger` anywhere in your JavaScript code and Google Chrome will pause the execution of the script at the point in which `debugger` was called. Once the execution is paused, you can hover your cursor over the source code in sources tab and it will show the value contained in the variable in a popup. You can also type in the variable's name in the console tab to see its value.

This is the screenshot of Google Chrome debugger in action:

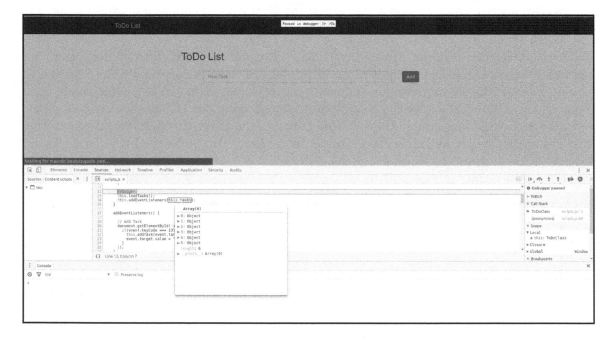

Feel free to explore the different sections of the Chrome Developer Tools to understand more about the tools it provides for the developers.

Getting started with ES6

Now that you have a good idea about the developer tools, let's start the coding part. You should already be familiar with the JavaScript ES5 syntax. So, let's explore JavaScript with the ES6 syntax in this chapter. ES6 (ECMAScript 2015) is the sixth major release of ECMAScript language specification. JavaScript is an implementation of ECMAScript language specification.

At the time of writing this book, ES8 is the latest release of JavaScript language. However, for simplicity and ease of understanding, this book only focuses on ES6. You can always learn about the latest features introduced in ES7 and beyond on the Internet easily once you grasp the knowledge of ES6.

At the time of writing this book, all the modern browsers support most of the ES6 features. However, older browsers don't know about the new JavaScript syntax and, hence, they will throw errors. To resolve such backward compatibility issues, we will have to transpile our ES6 code to ES5 before deploying the app. Let's look into that at the end of the chapter. The latest version of Chrome supports ES6; so, for now, we'll directly create our ToDo List with the ES6 syntax.

I'll explain in detail about the new ES6 syntax. If you find difficulties understanding normal JavaScript syntax and data types, do refer to the respective section in the following w3schools page: `https://www.w3schools.com/js/default.asp`.

Open up the `scripts.js` file in your text editor. First of all, we will create a class that contains the methods of our ToDo List app, and yeah! Classes are a new addition to JavaScript in ES6. It's simple to create objects using classes in JavaScript. It lets us organize our code as modules. Create a class named `ToDoClass` with the following code in the scripts file and refresh the browser:

```
class ToDoClass {
  constructor() {
    alert('Hello World!');
  }
}
window.addEventListener("load", function() {
  var toDo = new ToDoClass();
});
```

Your browser will now throw an alert saying "**Hello World!**". So here's what the code is doing. First, `window.addEventListener` will attach an event listener to the window and wait for the window to finish loading all the needed resources. Once it is loaded, the `load` event is fired, which calls the callback function of our event listener that initializes `ToDoClass` and assigns it to a variable `toDo`. While `ToDoClass` is initialized, it automatically calls the constructor, which creates an alert saying "**Hello World!**". We can further modify our code to take advantage of ES6. In the `window.addEventListener` part, you can rewrite it as:

```
let toDo;
window.addEventListener("load", () => {
  toDo = new ToDoClass();
```

```
});
```

First, we replace the anonymous callback function `function () {}` with the new arrow function `() => {}`. Second, we define the variable with `let` instead of `var`.

Arrow functions

Arrow functions are a cleaner and shorter way to define functions in JavaScript and they simply inherit the `this` object of its parent instead of binding its own. We'll see more about the `this` binding soon. Let's just look into using the new syntax. Consider the following functions:

```
let a = function(x) {
}
let b = function(x, y) {
}
```

The equivalent arrow functions can be written as:

```
let a = x => {}
let b = (x,y) => {}
```

You can see that `()` are optional, when we have to pass the only single argument to the function.

Sometimes, we just return a value in a single line in our functions, such as:

```
let sum = function(x, y) {
   return x + y;
}
```

If we want to directly return a value in our arrow function in a single line, we can directly ignore the `return` keyword and `{}` curly braces and write it as:

```
let sum = (x, y) => x+y;
```

That's it! It will automatically return the sum of x and y. However, this can be used only when you want to return the value immediately in a single line.

let, var, and const

Next, we have the `let` keyword. ES6 has two new keywords for declaring variables, `let` and `const`. `let` and `var` differ by the scope of the variables declared using them. The scope of variables declared using `var` is within the function it is defined and global if it is not defined inside any function, while the scope of `let` is restricted to within the enclosing block it was declared in and global if it is not defined inside any enclosing block. Look at the following code:

```
var toDo;
window.addEventListener("load", () => {
  var toDo = new ToDoClass();
});
```

If you were to accidentally re-declare `toDo` somewhere along the code, as follows, your class object gets overwritten:

```
var toDo = "some value";
```

This behavior is confusing and quite difficult to maintain variables for large applications. Hence, `let` was introduced in ES6. It restricts the scope of variables only within the enclosing in which it was declared. In ES6, it is encouraged to use `let` instead of `var` for declaring variables. Look at the following code:

```
let toDo;
window.addEventListener("load", () => {
 toDo = new ToDoClass();
});
```

Now, even if you accidentally re-declare `toDo` somewhere else in the code, JavaScript will throw an error, saving you from a runtime exception. An enclosing block is a block of code between two curly braces `{}` and the curly braces may or may not belong to a function.

We need a `toDo` variable to be accessible throughout the application. So, we declare `toDo` above the event listener and assign it to the class object inside the callback function. This way, the `toDo` variable will be accessible throughout the page.

> `let` is very useful for defining variables in `for` loops. You can create a `for` loop such that `for(let i=0; i<3; i++) {}` and the scope of the variable `i` will only be within the `for` loop. You can easily use the same variable name in other places of your code.

Let's take a look at the other keyword `const`. The working of `const` is the same as that of `let`, except that variables declared using `const` cannot be changed (reassigned). Hence, `const` is used for constants. However, an entire constant cannot be reassigned but their properties can be changed. For example:

```
const a = 5;
a = 7; // this will not work
const b = {
  a: 1,
  b: 2
};
b = { a: 2, b: 2 }; // this will not work
b.a = 2; // this will work since only a property of b is changed
```

While writing code in ES6, always use `const` to declare your variables. Use `let` only when you need to perform any changes (reassignments) to the variable and completely avoid using `var`.

The `toDo` object contains the class variables and functions as properties and methods of the object. If you need a clear picture of how the object is structured in JavaScript, see: `https://www.w3schools.com/js/js_objects.asp`.

Loading the tasks from data

The first thing we want to do in our application is to load the tasks dynamically from a set of data. Let's declare a class variable that contains the data for tasks along with methods needed to pre-populate the tasks. ES6 does not provide a direct way to declare class variables. We need to declare variables using the constructor. We also need a function to load tasks into the HTML elements. So, we'll create a `loadTasks()` method:

```
class ToDoClass {
  constructor() {
    this.tasks = [
        {task: 'Go to Dentist', isComplete: false},
        {task: 'Do Gardening', isComplete: true},
        {task: 'Renew Library Account', isComplete: false},
    ];
    this.loadTasks();
  }

  loadTasks() {
  }
}
```

The tasks variable is declared inside the constructor as `this.tasks`, which means the tasks variable belongs to `this` (ToDoClass). The variable is an array of objects that contain the task details and its completion status. The second task is set to be completed. Now, we need to generate an HTML code for the data. We'll reuse the code of the `<li>` element from the HTML to generate a task dynamically:

```
<li class="list-group-item checkbox">
  <div class="row">
    <div class="col-md-1 col-xs-1 col-lg-1 col-sm-1 checkbox">
     <label><input type="checkbox" value="" class="" checked></label>
    </div>
    <div class="col-md-10 col-xs-10 col-lg-10 col-sm-10 task-text
complete">
      First item
    </div>
     <div class="col-md-1 col-xs-1 col-lg-1 col-sm-1 delete-icon-area">
      <a class="" href="/"><i class="delete-icon glyphicon glyphicon-
trash"></i></a>
    </div>
  </div>
</li>
```

In JavaScript, an instance of a class is called the class object or simply object. The class objects are structured similarly to JSON objects in key-value pairs. The functions associated with a class object are called its methods and the variables/values associated with a class object are called its properties.

Template literals

Traditionally, in JavaScript, we concatenate strings using the + operator. However, if we want to concatenate multi-line strings, then we have to use the escape code \ to escape new lines, such as:

```
let a = '<div> \
    <li>' + myVariable+ '</li> \
</div>'
```

This can be very confusing when we have to write a string that contains a large amount of HTML. In this case, we can use ES6 template strings. Template strings are strings surrounded by backticks ` ` ` ` instead of single quotation marks ' '. By using this, we can create multi-line strings in an easier way:

```
let a = `
<div>
    <li> ${myVariable} </li>
</div>
`
```

As you can see, we can create DOM elements in a similar way; we type them in HTML without worrying about spaces or multi-lines. Because whatever formatting, such as tabs or new lines, present inside the template strings is directly recorded in the variable. And we can declare variables inside the strings using ${ }. So, in our case, we need to generate a list of items for each task. First, we will create a function to loop through the array and generate the HTML. In our `loadTasks()` method, write the following code:

```
loadTasks() {
  let tasksHtml = this.tasks.reduce((html, task, index) => html +=
  this.generateTaskHtml(task, index), '');
  document.getElementById('taskList').innerHTML = tasksHtml;
  }
```

After that, create a `generateTaskHtml()` function inside `ToDoClass`, with the code:

```
generateTaskHtml(task, index) {
 return `
  <li class="list-group-item checkbox">
   <div class="row">
    <div class="col-md-1 col-xs-1 col-lg-1 col-sm-1 checkbox">
     <label><input id="toggleTaskStatus" type="checkbox"
     onchange="toDo.toggleTaskStatus(${index})" value="" class=""
     ${task.isComplete?'checked':''}></label>
    </div>
    <div class="col-md-10 col-xs-10 col-lg-10 col-sm-10 task-text
${task.isComplete?'complete':''}">
     ${task.task}
   </div>
    <div class="col-md-1 col-xs-1 col-lg-1 col-sm-1 delete-icon-area">
     <a class="" href="/" onClick="toDo.deleteTask(event, ${index})"><i
     id="deleteTask" data-id="${index}" class="delete-icon glyphicon
     glyphicon-trash"></i></a>
    </div>
   </div>
  </li>
 `;
```

}

Now, refresh the page, and wow! Our application is loaded with tasks from our `tasks` variable. That should look like a lot of code at first, but let's look into it line by line.

 In case the changes aren't reflected when you refresh the page, it's because Chrome has cached the JavaScript files and is not retrieving the latest one. To make it retrieve the latest code, you will have to do a hard reload by pressing *Ctrl+Shift+R* on Windows or Linux and *command+Shift+R* on Mac.

In the `loadTasks()` function, we declare a variable `tasksHtml` with a value that is returned by the callback function of the array `reduce()` method of the `tasks` variable. Each array object in JavaScript has some methods associated with it. `reduce` is one such method of JS array that applies a function to each element of the array from left to right and applies the values to an accumulator so that the array gets reduced to a single value and then it returns that final value. The `reduce` method accepts two parameters; first is the callback function, which is applied to each element of the array, and the second one is the initial value of the accumulator. Let's look at our function in normal ES5 syntax:

```
let tasksHtml = this.tasks.reduce(function(html, task, index, tasks) {
  return html += this.generateTaskHtml(task, index)
}.bind(this), '');
```

- The first parameter is the callback function, whose four parameters are `html`, which is our accumulator, `task`, which is an element from the tasks array, index, which gives the current index of the array element in the iteration, and `tasks`, which contains the entire array on which the reduce method is applied on (we don't need the entire array inside the callback function for our use case, so the fourth parameter is ignored in our code).
- The second parameter is optional, which contains the initial value of the accumulator. In our case, the initial HTML string is an empty string `''`.
- Also, note that we have to `bind` the callback function with `this` (which is our class) object so that the methods of `ToDoClass` and the variables are accessible within the callback function. This is because, otherwise, every function will define its own `this` object and the parent's `this` object will be inaccessible within that function.

What the callback function does is it takes the empty `html` string (accumulator) first and concatenates it with the value returned by the `generateTaskHtml()` method of `ToDoClass`, whose parameters are the first element of the array and its index. The returned value, of course, should be a string, otherwise, it will throw an error. Then, it repeats the operation for each element of the array with an updated value of the accumulator, which is finally returned at the end of the iteration. The final reduced value contains the entire HTML code for populating our tasks as a string.

By applying ES6 arrow functions, the entire operation can be achieved in a single line as:

```
let tasksHtml = this.tasks.reduce((html, task, index) => html +=
this.generateTaskHtml(task, index), '');
```

Isn't that simple! Since we are just returning the value in a single line, we can ignore both the `{}` curly braces and `return` keyword. Also, arrow functions do not define their own `this` object; they simply inherit the `this` object of their parents. So we can also ignore the `.bind(this)` method. Now, we have made our code cleaner and much simpler to understand using arrow functions.

Before we move on to the next line of the `loadTasks()` method, let's look at the working of the `generateTaskHtml()` method. This function takes two arguments--an array element task in the tasks data and its index and returns a string that contains the HTML code for populating our tasks. Note that we have included variables in the code for the checkbox:

```
<input id="toggleTaskStatus" type="checkbox"
onchange="toDo.toggleTaskStatus(${index})" value="" class=""
${task.isComplete?'checked':''}>
```

It says that "on change of checkbox's status", call `toggleTaskStatus()` method of the `toDo` object with the index of the task that was changed. We haven't defined the `toggleTaskStatus()` method yet, so when you click the checkbox on the website now, it will throw an error in Chrome's console and nothing special happens in the browser window. Also, we have added a conditional operator `()?:` to return a checked attribute for the input tag if the task status is complete. This is useful to render the list with a prechecked check box if the task is already complete.

Similarly, we have included `${task.isComplete?'complete':''}` in the `div` that contains the task text so that an additional class gets added to the task if the task is complete, and CSS has been written in the `styles.css` file for that class to render a strike-through line over the text.

Finally, in the anchor tag, we have included `onClick="toDo.deleteTask(event,`
`${index})"` to call the `deleteTask()` method of the `toDo` object with parameters--the
click event itself and the index of the task. We haven't defined the `deleteTask()` method
yet, so clicking on the delete icon is going to take you to the root of your file system!

 `onclick` and `onchange` are some of HTML attributes that are used to call
JavaScript functions when the specified event occurs on the parent
element on which the attributes are defined. Since these attributes belong
to HTML, they are case insensitive.

Now, let's look at the second line of the `loadTasks()` method:

```
document.getElementById('taskList').innerHTML = tasksHtml;
```

We just replaced the HTML code of the DOM element with the ID `taskList` with our
newly generated string `tasksHTML`. Now, the ToDo List is populated. Time to define the
two new methods of the `toDo` object, which we included in our generated HTML code.

Managing task status

Inside `ToDoClass`, include the two new methods:

```
toggleTaskStatus(index) {
  this.tasks[index].isComplete = !this.tasks[index].isComplete;
  this.loadTasks();
}
deleteTask(event, taskIndex) {
  event.preventDefault();
  this.tasks.splice(taskIndex, 1);
  this.loadTasks();
}
```

The first method, `toggleTaskStatus()`, is used to mark a task as completed or
incomplete. It is called when a checkbox is clicked (`onChange`) with the index of the task,
which was clicked as the parameter:

- Using the task's index, we assign the task's `isComplete` status as the negation of
  its current status not using the `(!)` operator. Hence, the completion status of the
  tasks can be toggled in this function.
- Once the `tasks` variable is updated with new data, `this.loadTasks()` is called
  to re-render all the tasks with the updated value.

The second method, `deleteTask()`, is used to delete a task from the list. Currently, clicking the delete icon will take you to the root of the file system. However, before navigating you to the root of the file system, a call to `toDo.deleteTask()` is made with the click `event` and task's `index` as the parameters:

- The first parameter `event` contains the entire event object that contains various properties and methods about the click event that just happened (try `console.log(event)` inside the `deleteTask()` function to see all the details in Chrome's console).
- To prevent any default action (opening a URL) from happening once, we click the delete icon (the `<a>` tag). Initially, we need to specify `event.preventDefault()`.
- Then, we need to remove the task element of the array that was deleted from the `tasks` variable. For that, we use the `splice()` method, which deletes a specified number of elements from an array from a specified index. In our case, from the index of the task, which needs to be deleted, delete only a single element. This removes the task to be deleted from the `tasks` variable.
- `this.loadTasks()` is called to re-render all the tasks with the updated value.

Refresh the page (*hard reload* if needed) to see how our current application works with the new code. You can now mark a task as completed and can delete a task from the list.

Adding new tasks to the list

We now have the options to toggle a task status and to delete a task. But we need to add more tasks to the list. For that, we need to use the text box provided in the HTML file to allow users to type in new tasks. The first step will be adding the `onclick` attribute to the add task `<button>`:

```
<button class="btn btn-primary" onclick="toDo.addTaskClick()">Add</button>
```

Now, every button click will call the `addTaskClick()` method of the `toDo` object, which is not yet defined. So, let's define it inside our `ToDoClass`:

```
addTaskClick() {
  let target = document.getElementById('addTask');
  this.addTask(target.value);
  target.value = ""
}
addTask(task) {
  let newTask = {
    task,
```

```
    isComplete: false,
  };
  let parentDiv = document.getElementById('addTask').parentElement;
  if(task === '') {
   parentDiv.classList.add('has-error');
  } else {
   parentDiv.classList.remove('has-error');
   this.tasks.push(newTask);
   this.loadTasks();
  }
 }
}
```

Reload Chrome and try adding a new task by clicking the **Add** button. If everything's fine, you should see a new task get appended to the list. Also, when you click the **Add** button without typing anything in the input field, then it will highlight the input field with a red border, indicating the user should input text in the input field.

 See how I have divided our add task operation across two functions? I did a similar thing for the loadTask() function. In programming, it is a best practice to organize all the tasks into smaller, more generic functions, which will allow you to reuse those functions in the future.

Let's see how the addTaskClick() method works:

- addTaskClick() function doesn't have any request parameters. First, to read the new task's text, we get the <input> element with the ID addTask, which contains the text needed for the task.
  using document.getElementById('addTask'), and assign it to target variable. Now, the target variable contains all the properties and methods of the <input> element, which can be read and modified (try console.log(target) to see all the details contained in the variable).
- The value property contains the required text. So, we pass target.value to the addTask() function, which handles adding a new task to the list.
- Finally, we reset the input field to an empty state by setting target.value to an empty string ' '.

That's the event handling part for the click event. Let's see how the task gets appended to the list in the addTask() method. The task variable contains the text for the new task:

- Ideally, the first step in this function is to construct the JSON data that defines our task:

```
let newTask = {
  task: task,
  isComplete: false
}
```

- Here's another ES6 feature object literal property value shorthand; instead of writing {task: task} in our JSON object, we can simply write {task}. The variable name will become the key and the value stored in the variable becomes the value. This will throw an error if the variable is undefined.

- We also need to create another variable parentDiv to store the object of the parent <div> element of our target <input> element. It's useful because, when the task is an empty string, we can add the has-error class to the parent element parentDiv.classList.add('has-error'), which by Bootstrap's CSS, renders a red border to our <input> element. This is how we can indicate to the user that they need to enter a text before clicking the **Add** button.

- However, if the input text is not empty, we should remove the has-error class from our parent element to ensure the red border is not shown to the user and then simply push our newTask variable to the tasks variable of our class. Also, we need to call loadTasks() again so that the new task gets rendered.

Adding tasks by hitting Enter button

Well, this is one way of adding tasks, but some users prefer adding tasks directly by hitting the *Enter* button. For that, let's use event listeners to detect the *Enter* key press in the <input> element. We can also use the onchange attribute of our <input> element, but let's give event listeners a try. The best way to add event listeners to a class is to call them in the constructor so that the event listeners are set up when the class is initialized.

So, in our class, create a new function addEventListeners() and call it in our constructor. We are going to add event listeners inside this function:

```
constructor() {
  ...
  this.addEventListeners();
}
  addEventListeners() {
```

```
document.getElementById('addTask').addEventListener('keypress', event =>
{
    if(event.keyCode === 13) {
      this.addTask(event.target.value);
      event.target.value = '';
    }
  });
}
```

And that's it! Reload Chrome, type in the text, and hit *Enter*. This should add tasks to our list just like how the add button works. Let's go through our new event listener:

- For every keypress happening in the <input> element with the ID addTask, we run the callback function with the event object as the parameter.
- This event object contains the keycode of the key that was pressed. For the *Enter* key, the keycode is 13. If the key code is equal to 13, we simply call the this.addTask() function with the task's text event.target.value as its parameter.
- Now, the addTask() function handles adding the task to the list. We can simply reset <input> back to an empty string. This is a great advantage of organizing every operation into functions. We can simply reuse the functions wherever they're needed.

Persisting data in the browser

Now, functionality-wise, our ToDo List is ready. However, on refreshing the page, the data will be gone. Let's see how to persist data in the browser. Usually, web apps connect with APIs from the server-side to load data dynamically. Here, we are not looking into server-side implementation. So, we need to look for an alternate way to store data in the browser. There are three ways to store data in the browser. They are as follows:

- cookie: A cookie is a small information that is stored on the client-side (browser) by the server with an expiry date. It is useful for reading information from the client, such as login tokens, user preferences, and so on. Cookies are primarily used on the server-side and the amount of data that can be stored in the cookie is limited to 4093 bytes. In JavaScript, cookies can be managed using the document.cookie object.
- localStorage: HTML5's localStorage stores information with no expiry date and the data will persist even after closing and opening the web page. It provides a storage space of 5 MB per domain.

- sessionStorage: sessionStorage is equivalent to that of localStorage, except that the data is only valid per session (the current tab that the user is working on). The data expires when the website is closed.

For our use case, localStorage is the best choice for persisting task data. localStorage stores data as key-value pairs, while the value needs to be a string. Let's look at the implementation part. Inside the constructor, instead of assigning the value to this.tasks directly, change it to the following:

```
constructor() {
  this.tasks = JSON.parse(localStorage.getItem('TASKS'));
   if(!this.tasks) {
    this.tasks = [
        {task: 'Go to Dentist', isComplete: false},
        {task: 'Do Gardening', isComplete: true},
        {task: 'Renew Library Account', isComplete: false},
    ];
  }
...
}
```

We are going to save our tasks in localStorage as a string with 'TASKS' as its key. So when the user opens the website for the first time, we need to check whether any data is present in localStorage with the key 'TASKS'. If no data is present, it will return null, which means this is the first time a user is visiting the website. We need to use JSON.parse() to convert the data retrieved from localStorage from a string to an object:

- If no data is present in localStorage (user visiting the site for the first time), we shall prepopulate some data for them using the tasks variable. The best place to add the code to persist task data in our application will be the loadTasks() function because it is called every time a change in tasks is made. In the loadTasks() function, add an additional line:

  ```
  localStorage.setItem('TASKS', JSON.stringify(this.tasks));
  ```

- This will convert our tasks variable to string and store it in localStorage. Now, you can add tasks and refresh the page, and the data will be persisted in your browser.
- If you want to empty localStorage for development purposes, you can use localStorage.removeItem('TASKS') to delete the key or you can use localStorage.clear() to completely remove all the data stored in localStorage.

Everything in JavaScript has an inherent Boolean value, which can be called truthy or falsy. The following values are always falsy - `null`, `""` (empty string), `false`, `0` (zero), `NaN` (not a number), and `undefined`. Other values are considered truthy. Hence, they can be directly used in conditional statements like how we used `if(!this.tasks)  {}` in our code.

Now that our application is complete, you can remove the contents of the `<ul>` element in the `index.html` file. The contents will now be directly populated from our JavaScript code. Otherwise, you will see the default HTML code flash in the page when the page is loaded or refreshed. This is because our JavaScript code executes only after all the resources are finished loading due to the following code:

```
window.addEventListener("load", function() {
  toDo = new ToDoClass();
});
```

If everything works fine, then congratulations! You have successfully built your first JavaScript application and you have learned about the new ES6 features of JavaScript. Oh wait! Looks like we forgot something important!

 All the storage options discussed here are unencrypted and, hence, should not be used for storing sensitive information, such as password, API keys, authentication tokens, and so on.

Compatibility with older browsers

While ES6 works with almost all modern browsers, there are still many users who use older versions of Internet Explorer or Firefox. So, how are we going to make our application work for them? Well, the good thing about ES6 is that all it's new features can be implemented using the ES5 specification. This means that we can easily transpile our code to ES5, which will work on all modern browsers. For this purpose, we are going to use Babel: `https://babeljs.io/`, as the compiler for converting ES6 to ES5.

Remember how, in the beginning of our chapter, we installed Node.js in our system? Well, it's finally time to use it. Before we start compiling our code to ES5, we need to learn about Node and the npm.

Node.js and npm

Node.js is a JavaScript runtime built on Chrome's V8 engine. It lets developers run JavaScript outside of the browser. Due to the non-blocking I/O model of Node.js, it is widely used for building data-intensive, real-time applications. You can use it to build backend for your web application in JavaScript, just like PHP, Ruby, or other server-side languages.

One great advantage of Node.js is that it lets you organize your code into modules. A module is a set of code used to perform a specific function. So far, we have included the JavaScript code one after another inside the `<script>` tag in the browser. But in Node.js, we can simply call the dependency inside the code by creating the reference to the module. For example, if we need to jQuery, we can simply write the following:

```
const $ = require('jquery');
```

Or, we can write the following:

```
import $ from 'jquery';
```

The jQuery module will be included in our code. All the properties and methods of jQuery will be accessible inside the `$` object. The scope of `$` will be only within the file it is called. So, in each file, we can specify the dependencies individually and all of them will be bundled together during compilation.

But wait! For including `jquery`, we need to download the `jquery` package that contains the required module and save it in a folder. Then, we need to assign `$` the reference of the file in the folder containing the module. And as the project grows, we will be adding a lot of packages and refer ring the modules in our code. So, how are we going to manage all the packages. Well, we have a nice little tool that gets installed along with Node.js called the **Node Package Manager** (**npm**):

- For Linux and Mac users, npm is similar to one of these: `apt-get`, `yum`, `dnf`, and `Homebrew`.
- For Windows users, you might not be familiar with the concept of package management yet. So, let's say you need jQuery. But you don't know what dependencies are needed for jQuery to run. That's where package managers come into play. You can simply run a command to install a package (`npm install jquery`). The package manager will read all the dependencies of the target package and install the target along with its dependencies. It also manages a file to keep track of installed packages. This is used for easily uninstalling the package in the future.

Even though Node.js allows require/import of modules directly into the code, browsers do not support require or import functionality to directly import a module. But there are many tools available that can easily mimic this functionality so that we can use import/require inside our browsers. We'll use them for our project in the next chapter.

npm maintains a `package.json` file to store information regarding a package, such as its name, scripts, dependencies, dev dependencies, repository, author, license, and so on. A package is a folder containing one or more folder or files with a `package.json` file in its root folder. There are thousands of open source packages available in npm. Visit `https://www.npmjs.com/` to explore the available packages. The packages can be modules that are used on the server-side or browser-side and command-line tools that are useful for performing various operations.

npm packages can be installed locally (per project) or globally (entire system). We can specify how we want to install it using different flags, as follows:

- If we want to install a package globally, we should use the `--global` or `-g` flag.
- If the package should be installed locally for a specific project, use the `--save` or `-S` flag.
- If the package should be installed locally and it is only used for development purposes, use the `--save-dev` or `-D` flag.
- If you run `npm install <package-name>` without any flags, it will install the package locally but will not update the `package.json` file. It is not recommended to install packages without the `-S` or `-D` flags.

Let's install a command-line tool using npm called `http-server`: `https://www.npmjs.com/package/http-server`. It is a simple tool that can be used to serve static files over an `http-server` just like how files are served in Apache or Nginx. This is useful for testing and developing our web applications, since we can see how our application behaves when it's served through a web server.

Command-line tools are mostly recommended to install globally if they are going to be used only by ourselves and not by any other developer. In our case, we are only going to be using the `http-server` package. So, let's install it globally. Open your Terminal/command prompt and run the following command:

```
npm install -g http-server
```

If you are using Linux, some times you might face errors such as permission denied or unable to access file, and so on. Try running the same command as administrator (prefixed with `sudo`) for installing the package globally.

Once the installation is complete, navigate to the root folder of our ToDo List app in your terminal and run the following command:

http-server

You will receive two URLs and the server will start running, as follows:

- To view the ToDo List app on your local device, open the URL starting with 127 in your browser
- To view the ToDo List app on a different device connected to your local network, open the URL starting with 192 on the device's browser

Every time you open the application, `http-server` will print the served files in the terminal. There are various options available with `http-server`, such as -p flag, which can be used to change the default port number 8080 (try `http-server -p 8085`). Visit the http-server: `https://www.npmjs.com/package/http-server`, npm page for documentation on all available options. Now that we have a general idea of the npm packages, let's install Babel to transpile our ES6 code to ES5.

 We will be using Terminals a lot in our upcoming chapters. If you are using VSCode, it has an inbuilt terminal, which can be opened by pressing *Ctrl+`* on Mac, Linux, and Windows. It also supports opening multiple terminal sessions at the same time. This can save you lot time on switching between windows.

Setting up our development environment with Node and Babel

Babel is a JavaScript compiler, which is used to transpile JavaScript code from ES6+ to normal ES5 specification. Let's set up Babel in our project so that it automatically compiles our code.

There will be two different JS files in our project after setting up Babel. One is ES6, which we use to develop our app, and another will be the compiled ES5 code, which is going to be used by the browser. So, we need to create two different folders in our project root directory, namely, `src` and `dist`. Move the `scripts.js` file into the `src` directory. We are going to use Babel to compile the scripts from the `src` directory and store the result in the `dist` directory. So, in `index.html`, change the reference of `scripts.js` into `<script src="dist/scripts.js"></script>` so that the browser will always read the compiled code:

1. To use npm, we need to create `package.json` in our project's root directory. Navigate to the project root directory in your terminal and type:

   npm init

2. First, it will ask your project's name, type in a name. For other questions, either type in some values or just hit *Enter* to accept default values. These values will be populated in the `package.json` file, which can be changed later.

3. Let's install our development dependencies by running the following command in the terminal:

   npm install -D http-server babel-cli babel-preset-es2015 concurrently

4. This command will create a `node_modules` folder and install the packages inside it. Now, your `package.json` file will have the preceding packages in its `devDependencies` parameter and your current folder structure should be:

```
.
├── dist
├── index.html
├── node_modules
├── package.json
├── src
└── styles.css
```

If you are using git or any other version control system in your project, add `node_modules` and the `dist` folder to `.gitignore` or a similar file. These folders need not be committed to version control and must be generated when needed.

Time to write scripts to compile our code. Inside the `package.json` file, there will be a parameter called `scripts`. By default, it will be the following:

```
"scripts": {
  "test": "echo \"Error: no test specified\" && exit 1"
},
```

`test` is one of the default commands for npm. When you run `npm test` in the terminal, it will automatically execute the script inside the test key's value in the terminal. As the name suggests, `test` is used for executing automated test cases. Some other default commands are `start`, `stop`, `restart`, `shrinkwrap`, and so on. These commands are very useful to run scripts when developing server-side applications with Node.js.

However, during frontend development, we may need more commands like the default commands. `npm` also allows us to create our commands to execute arbitrary scripts. However, unlike default commands (such as `npm start`), we cannot execute our own commands by running `npm <command-name>`; we have to execute `npm run <command-name>` in the terminal.

We are going to set up npm scripts so that running `npm run build` will generate a working build for our application with the compiled ES5 code and running `npm run watch` will spin up a development server, which we are going to use for development.

Change the contents of scripts section into the following:

```
"scripts": {
  "watch": "babel src -d dist --presets=es2015 -ws",
  "build": "rm -rf dist && babel src -d dist --presets=es2015",
  "serve": "http-server"
},
```

Well, that looks like a lot of scripts! Let's go through them one by one.

First, let's check out the `watch` script:

- The function of this script is to start `babel` in the watch mode so that every time we make any change in our ES6 code inside `src` directory, it will automatically be transpiled into ES5 code inside the `dist` directory along with source maps, which is useful for debugging the compiled code. The watch mode will keep on continuing the process in the terminal until the execution is terminated (hitting *Ctrl+C*).

- Execute `npm run watch` in the terminal from your project's root directory. You can see that Babel has started compiling the code and a new `scripts.js` file will be created inside the `dist` folder.

- The `scripts.js` file will contain our code in the ES5 format. Open up `index.html` in Chrome and you should see our application running normally.

Here's how it works. Try running `babel src -d dist --presets=es2015 -ws` directly in the terminal. It will throw an error saying `babel` is not installed (the error message may vary depending on your operating system). This is because we haven't installed Babel globally. We only installed it within our project. So, when we run `npm run watch`, npm will look for the binaries for Babel inside the project's `node_modules` folder and execute the command using those binaries.

Delete the `dist` directory, and create a new script inside `package.json`--`"babel"`: `"babel src -d dist"`. We are going to use this script for learning how Babel works:

- This script tells Babel *compile all the JS files inside the* `src` *directory and save the resulting files inside* `dist` *directory*. The `dist` directory will be created if it is not present. Here, the `-d` flag is used to tell Babel that it needs to compile files inside the entire directory.
- Run `npm run babel` in the terminal and open up our new `scripts.js` file inside the `dist` directory. Well, the file is compiled, but unfortunately, the result is also in ES6 syntax, so the new `scripts.js` file is an exact copy of our original file!
- Our goal is to compile our code to ES5. For that, we need to instruct Babel to use some presets during compilation. Look at our `npm install` command, we have installed a package called `babel-preset-es2015` for this purpose.
- In our Babel script, add the option `--presets=es2015` and execute `npm run babel` again. This time the code will be compiled to ES5 syntax.
- Open up our application in the browser, add `debugger` inside our constructor, and reload. We have a new problem; the sources will now contain the code in ES5 syntax, which makes it harder to debug our original code.
- For this, we need to enable source maps using the `-s` flag that creates a `.map` file, which is used to map the compiled code back to the original source. Also, use the `-w` flag to put Babel in the watch mode.

And now our script will be the same as the one used in the `watch` command. Reload the application with the debugger and you can see that the sources will contain our original code even though it is using the compiled source.

Wouldn't it be nice if running a single command would also start up our development server using `http-server`. We cannot use `&&` to concatenate two commands that run simultaneously. Since `&&` will execute the second command, only after the first one completes.

We have installed another package called `concurrently` for this purpose. It is used for executing multiple commands together. Syntax for using `concurrently` is as follows:

```
concurrently "command1" "command2"
```

When we execute `npm run watch`, we need to run both the current `watch` script and the `serve` script. Change the `watch` script into the following:

```
"watch": "concurrently \"npm run serve\" \"babel src -d dist --
presets=es2015 -ws\"",
```

Try running `npm run watch` again. Now, you have a fully functional development environment, which will automatically serve the files as well as compile the code as you make changes to your JS code.

Shipping the code

Once development is done, for shipping the code if you use version control, add the `node_modules` and `dist` folder to the ignore list. Otherwise, send your code without the `node_modules` or `dist` folder. Other developers can simply run `npm install` to install dependencies and read the scripts inside the `package.json` file to build the project when needed.

Our `npm run build` command will remove the `dist` folder present inside the project folder and create a new `dist` folder with the latest build of JS code.

Summary

Congratulations! You have built your first JavaScript application with the new ES6 syntax. You have learned the following concepts in this chapter:

- DOM manipulation and event listeners in JavaScript
- ECMAScript 2015 (ES6) syntax of JavaScript
- Chrome Developer Tools
- The workings of Node and npm
- Using Babel to transpile the ES6 code to ES5 code

In our current npm setup, we have simply created a compile script to transform our code into ES5. There are lots of other tools available to automate more tasks, such as minification, linting, image compression, and so on. We will use one such tool called Webpack in our next chapter.

2
Building a Meme Creator

As the chapter name suggests, we are going to build a fun application in this chapter--a **Meme Creator**. Everyone loves memes! But that's not the only reason we are building a Meme Creator. We are going to explore a few new things that are going to change the way you build web applications. Let's see what's in store:

- Introduction to **CSS3 flexbox**. A new way to create responsive layouts on the web.
- Using the **Webpack** module bundler to convert all your dependencies and code to static assets.
- Using **HTML5 canvas** for drawing graphics on the fly with JavaScript.
- Creating a solid production build that is fully optimized, minified, and versioned.

Previously, you successfully built a ToDo List app while learning the new ES6 features of JavaScript. At the end of the chapter, you learned how to use Node and npm for web development. We have covered only the basics. We are yet to realize the full potential of using npm in our project. That's why, in this project, we are going to experiment with a powerful module bundler called Webpack. Before we begin with our experiment to build a fully automated development environment, let's set a few things up.

Initial project setup

Create a new folder for our Meme Creator application. Open up the folder in VSCode or any other text editor you are using for this project. Navigate to the folder in your terminal and run `npm init`. Just as we did in the previous chapter, fill in all the details asked for in the terminal, then hit *Enter* on Windows or *return* on Mac, and you will have your `package.json` file in the project root.

From the code files you downloaded for this book, open up the starter files folder for Chapter 2. You will see an `index.html` file. Copy and paste it into your new project folder. That's all for the starter files provided with this chapter, because there is not going to be a default CSS file. We are going to build the UI from scratch!

Create the files and folders we are going to use in this chapter. The folder structure should be as follows:

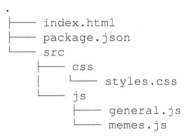

```
.
├──── index.html
├──── package.json
└──── src
      ├──── css
      │     └──── styles.css
      └──── js
            ├──── general.js
            └──── memes.js
```

For now, leave the JS files empty. We are going to work on the `styles.css` file. Open up `index.html` in your browser (try using the `http-server` package we installed globally in the previous chapter). You should see an awkward looking page with some default Bootstrap styles applied using Bootstrap's classes. We are going to turn that page into a Meme Creator app, which looks as follows:

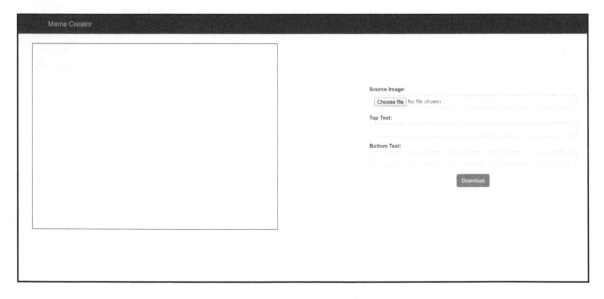

This web app is also going to be responsive. So, on your mobile devices, it should look as follows:

That blank box is going to be our canvas, which will preview the memes created with this app. Now that you have an idea of how the application will look, we'll start working on our `styles.css` file.

Responsive designing with flexbox

If you look into the `index.html` file of our previous chapter, you will see that there are classes, such as `col-md-2`, `col-xs-2`, `col-lg-2`, `col-sm-2`, and so on. They are Bootstrap's grid classes. The previous chapter's layout was designed using the Bootstrap grid system. The system divides the page into rows and 12 columns and allocates a specific number of columns to each `div` in a row depending on the screen size.

There are four different screen sizes:

- Desktop (md)
- Tablets (sm)
- Phones (xs)
- Large desktops (lg)

However, we are not going to use Bootstrap grids in this chapter. We are going to be using a new layout mode introduced in CSS3 called the flexbox. Flexbox or flexible box, as it sounds, provides a box model for creating layouts.

 Flexbox is a new layout system, which is actively being implemented by the browser vendors. Support is almost complete; it's time to adopt this standard in projects. A few problems still exist, such as IE 11 only having partial flexbox support and older versions of IE do not support flexbox. Visit https://caniuse.com/ to check details on browser support for flexbox.

Flexbox - a quick introduction

In the flexbox layout system, you declare a parent `div` with a CSS property `display: flex`, which allows you to control how you want to position its children elements.

Once you declare `display: flex`, the `div` element becomes a flexbox with two axes. The **Main axis** along with the content are placed with the **Cross axis**, which is perpendicular to the Main axis. You can use the following CSS properties in the parent flexbox to change the position of child elements (*flex items*):

- **flex-direction**: Create the Main axis either horizontally (row) or vertically (column)
- **justify-content**: Specify how flex items are placed on the Main axis
- **align-items**: Specify how flex items are placed on the Cross axis
- **flex-wrap**: Specify how to handle flex items when there is not enough space to display them in a single row

You can also apply some flex properties to flex items, such as:

- **align-self**: Specify how to place the specific flex item on the Cross axis
- **flex**: The relative size of the flex item with respect to other flex items (if you have two items with `flex: 2` and `flex: 1` respectively, the first one will be twice the size of the second one)

All those should sound confusing, but the easiest way to understand flexbox is to use online flexbox playgrounds. Google some flexbox playgrounds available online to experience how different properties of flexbox work. One such playground can be found at `http://flexboxplayground.catchmyfame.com/`.

To learn flexbox, refer to the following pages:

- Mozilla Developer Network: `https://developer.mozilla.org/en-US/docs/Learn/CSS/CSS_layout/Flexbox`
- W3Schools: `https://www.w3schools.com/css/css3_flexbox.asp`
- Flexbox Froggy (a game for learning flexbox): `https://flexboxfroggy.com/`

 At the time of writing this book, the latest version of Safari browser 10.1 is having problems with the **flex-wrap** property, which is fixed in nightly builds. If you are using the same or an earlier version of the Safari browser, I'd recommend using Chrome for this chapter.

Designing the Meme Creator

In our `index.html` file, our `<body>` element is divided into a navigation bar and `div` containing the contents of the website. The `div.body` element is further divided into `div.canvas-area` and `div.input-area`.

Navigation bar

The first part of our document's body is the navigation bar `<nav>`. The navigation bar usually contains the primary set of links for navigation in a website. Since we are building only a single page in this chapter, we can leave the navbar with only our page title.

The navigation bar is styled using Bootstrap. The class `.navbar` styles the respective element as the primary navigation bar of the page. The `.navbar-inverse` class adds a dark color to the navigation bar and the `.navbar-fixed-top` class attaches the navigation bar to the top of the screen using a fixed position. The contents of the navigation bar are wrapped inside a Bootstrap container (`div.container`). The page title is written inside `div.navbar-header` as an anchor tag with the class `.navbar-brand`, which instructs Bootstrap that this is the brand name/title of the application.

 The Bootstrap navigation bar is highly customizable. To learn more about this topic, refer to W3Schools' Bootstrap tutorial: `https://www.w3schools.com/bootstrap/` or Bootstrap's official documentation: `http://getbootstrap.com/getting-started/`.

Content area

The navigation bar occupies a fixed position on top of the screen. Hence, it will overlap with the page's content. Open up `styles.css` and add the following code:

```
body {
    padding-top: 65px;
}
```

This will add padding to the entire body section so that the navbar will not overlap with our content. Now, we need to convert our primary content area `div.body` to a flexbox:

```
.body {
    display: flex;
    flex-direction: row;
    flex-wrap: wrap;
    justify-content: space-around;
}
```

This will convert our `div.body` element into a flexbox that organizes its contents as a row (`flex-direction`) and wraps the contents to new rows if space is not available for entire rows (`flex-wrap`). Also, the contents will be surrounded by equal margin spaces horizontally (`justify-content`).

Guess what? We are done! Our primary layout is already complete! Switch to Chrome, hard-reload, and see that the contents are now aligned horizontally. Open up the responsive design mode; for mobile devices you will see that the row is automatically wrapped into two rows to display the content. Without flexbox, this would have taken thrice the amount of code to achieve the same layout. Flexbox greatly simplifies the layout process.

Now that our primary layout is complete, let's add some styles to individual elements, such as:

- Making `.canvas-area` twice the size of the `.input-area`
- Adding a black border to the canvas element
- Center-aligning the canvas and the form inputs in their respective areas
- Also, we need to add a margin to both `.canvas-area` and `.input-area` so that there will be space between them when the row is wrapped

To achieve these styles, add the following CSS to your `styles.css` file:

```css
.canvas-area {
    flex: 2;
    display: flex;
    align-items: center;
    justify-content: center;
    margin: 10px;
}
.img-canvas {
    border: 1px solid #000000;
}
.input-area {
    flex: 1;
    display: flex;
    flex-direction: column;
    align-items: center;
    justify-content: center;
    margin: 10px;
}
```

The canvas area is still quite small, but we'll handle its size from our JavaScript code. So, now, we don't need to worry about the size of the canvas.

We are almost done with our styles, except that the form inputs are now in different sizes. This happens because Bootstrap's `.form-input` styles tell the respective `div` to occupy the entire width of its parent `div`. However, when we add `align-items: center` in our style, we are telling the parent `div` to assign a limited width so that the contents are not overlapped and are then centered inside the flexbox. So, the width of each element now differs based on its contents.

To overcome this problem, we simply need to specify a fixed width to the `.form-input` class. Also, let's add some extra top margin to the download button. Add the following lines at the end of your `styles.css` file:

```css
.form-group {
  width: 90%;
}
.download-button {
  margin-top: 10px;
}
```

Now we are done building the UI for our Meme Creator using flexbox. It's time to move on to the most important topic in this chapter.

Due to its ease of use and a huge amount of features, the flexbox layout system is also being adopted in mobile application development. React Native uses flexbox to create a UI for Android and iOS apps. Facebook has also released open source libraries, such as yoga and litho, to use flexbox in native Android and iOS apps.

Webpack module bundler

It's finally time to set up our fully-featured development environment. You'll probably be wondering what Webpack is and what's it got to do with a development environment. Or perhaps, you are familiar with tools such as gulp or grunt and are wondering how Webpack is different from them.

If you have used gulp or grunt before, they are task runners. They execute a specific set of tasks to compile, transform, and minify your code. There is also a tool called **Browserify**, which lets you use require() in browsers. Usually, a development environment with gulp/grunt involves executing various commands using different sets of tools, such as Babel, Browserify, and so on, in a specific order to generate our desired output code. But Webpack is different. Unlike task runners, Webpack doesn't run a set of commands to build the code. Instead, it acts as a module bundler.

Webpack goes through your JavaScript code and looks for import, require, and so on to find files dependent on it. Then, it loads the files into a dependency graph and, in turn, finds those files, dependencies. This process goes on until there are no more dependencies. Finally, it bundles the dependency files together with the initial file into a single file using the dependency graph it built. This functionality is very useful in modern JavaScript development, where everything is written as a module:

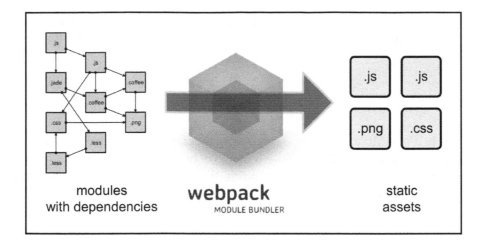

modules with dependencies — **webpack** MODULE BUNDLER — static assets

Webpack is being adopted as the bundler of popular modern frameworks, such as React, Angular, and Vue. It is also a good skill to have on your resume.

Modules in JavaScript

Remember the ToDo List app we built in the previous chapter? We used npm to install Babel to transform our ES6 code to ES5. Navigate to the `ToDo List` folder and open up the `node_modules` folder. You will find a huge list of folders containing various packages! Even though you installed only four packages, npm has traced out all the dependencies of the required packages and installed them along with the actual packages.

We only used those packages as dev-dependencies to compile our code. So, we didn't know how those packages are built. Those packages are built as modules. A module is an independent piece of reusable code that returns a value. The value can be an object, function, `string`, `int`, and so on. Modules are widely used for building large applications. Node.js comes with support for exporting and importing JavaScript modules which are currently unavailable in the browser.

Let's see how we can create a simple module in JavaScript:

```
function sum (a, b) {
  return a+b;
}
```

Consider the earlier mentioned function that returns a sum of two numbers. We are going to convert that function into a module. Create a new file `sum.js` and write the function as follows:

```
export function sum (a, b) {
  return a+b;
}
```

That's all! You just need to add an `export` keyboard before the variable or object you would like to export and it will become a module which can be used in a different file. Imagine you have a file called `add.js`, where you need to find the sum of two numbers. You can import the `sum` module as follows:

```
// In file add.js at the same directory as sum.js
import { sum } from './sum.js';

let a = 5, b = 6, total;
total = sum(a, b);
```

You can ignore the extension `.js` if you are importing a JavaScript file and use `import { sum } from './sum'`. You can also use the following:

```
let sum = (a, b) => return a+b;
module.exports = { sum };
```

Then, import it, as follows:

```
const sum = require('./sum');
```

`module.exports` and the `require` keyword has been used by Node.js for importing and exporting JavaScript modules even since before ES6 was introduced. However, ES6 has a new module syntax using the keywords `import` and `export`. Webpack supports all types of imports and exports. For our project, we'll stick with ES6 modules.

Consider the following file `sides.js`, which contains the number of sides of geometrical figures in more than one module:

```
export default TRIANGLE = 3;
export const SQUARE = 4;
export const PENTAGON = 5;
export const HEXAGON = 6;
```

To import all of them into our file, you can use the following:

```
import * as sides from './sides.js';
```

Now, all the exported variables/objects from the `sides.js` file will be accessible inside the `sides` object. To get the value of `TRIANGLE`, just use `sides.LINE`. Also, note that `TRIANGLE` is marked default. A `default` export is useful when there are multiple modules in the same file. Type in the following:

```
import side from './sides.js';
```

Now, `side` will contain the value of the default export `TRIANGLE`. So, now `side = 3`. To import other modules along with the default module, you can use the following:

```
import TRIANGLE, { SQUARE, PENTAGON, HEXAGON } from './sides.js';
```

Now, if you want to import a module that is present inside the `node_modules` folder, you can ignore the relative file path (`./` part) completely and just type `import jquery from 'jquery';`. Node.js or Webpack will automatically find the nearest `node_modules` folder from the file's parent directories and automatically search for the required package. Just make sure you have installed the package using `npm install`.

That pretty much covers the basics of using modules in JavaScript. Now it's time to learn about the role of Webpack in our project.

Bundling modules in Webpack

To start using Webpack, let's first write some JavaScript code. Open up your `memes.js` file and `general.js` file. Write the following code in both files, which simply prints the respective filenames in the console:

```
// inside memes.js file
console.log('Memes JS file');
// inside general.js file
console.log('General JS File');
```

Usually, while building multiple page web applications that have a large number of HTML files, it's common to have a single JavaScript file that has code that requires being run on all the HTML files. We are going to use the `general.js` file for this purpose. Even though our Meme Creator has a single HTML file, we'll use the `general.js` file to include some common code and include the code for Meme Creator in the `memes.js` file.

Why don't we try importing the `general.js` file inside our `memes.js` file? Since `general.js` is not exporting any modules, simply type in the following code in your `memes.js` file:

```
import './general';
```

Include a `script` tag with reference to `memes.js` file at the end of the `<body>` element in your `index.html` file and see the result in Chrome. If all goes well, you should see an error in Chrome's console saying: **Unexpected token import**. This means that something didn't go well for Chrome. Yup! Chrome doesn't know how to use the `import` keyword. To use `import`, we need Webpack to bundle both the `general.js` and `meme.js` file together and serve it as a single file to Chrome.

Let's install Webpack as a dev dependency for our project. Run the following command in the terminal:

```
npm install -D webpack
```

Webpack is now installed as a dev dependency to our project. Webpack is also a command-line tool similar to Babel. To run Webpack, we need to use `npm` scripts. In your `package.json` file, below the test script, create the following script:

```
"webpack": "webpack src/js/memes.js --output-filename dist/memes.js",
```

Now run the following command in your terminal:

```
npm run webpack
```

A new `memes.js` file will be created under the `dist/js/` directory. This file contains both the `general.js` and `memes.js` files bundled together. Open up the new JavaScript code in VSCode; you should see a large amount of code. No need to panic at this stage; that is the code used by Webpack to manage the scopes and properties of the bundled files. It's something we don't have to worry about at this point. If you scroll to the end of the file, you will see the `console.log` statements that we had written in both of our original files. Edit your script tag in `index.html` to include the new file, as follows:

```
<script src="./dist/memes.js"></script>
```

Now, reload the page in Chrome and you should see that the console statements from both the files are executed inside the `memes.js` file. We have successfully imported a JavaScript file inside our code. In our previous project, we set up the development environment so that the code will be compiled and served automatically whenever a change is made in the source file. To do ES6 to ES5 compilation and other tasks, we need to install a lot of packages and must give a lot of instructions to Webpack. For this purpose, create `webpack.config.js` in your project root folder and write the following code:

```
const webpack = require('webpack');

module.exports = {
  context: __dirname,
  entry: {
```

```
    general: './src/js/general.js',
    memes: './src/js/memes.js',
  },
  output: {
    path: __dirname + "/dist",
    filename: '[name].js',
  },
}
```

Remove all the options passed to Webpack in `package.json`. Now, your script inside `package.json` should look as follows:

```
"webpack": "webpack"
```

Since we haven't passed any arguments to Webpack, it will look for the `webpack.config.js` file inside the directory from which it was executed. It will now read the configuration from the file we just created. The first line in our config file is to import Webpack using `require('webpack')`. We are still using Node.js to execute our code, so we should use `require` in our Webpack config file. We just need to export our configuration in this file as a JSON object. In the `module.exports` object, Here's what each property is used for:

- `context`: Is used to specify the absolute path from which the path of files in the entry section needs to be resolved. Here, `__dirname` is a constant that will automatically include the absolute path of the current directory.
- `entry`: Is used to specify all the files that need to be bundled using Webpack. It accepts string, array, and a JSON object. If you need Webpack to bundle a single entry file, just specify the file's path as a string. Otherwise, use array or object.
  - In our case, we specify input files as objects in the form of `[name]`: `[path_of_the_file]`.
  - This [name] will be used in naming the output bundle of each file.
- `output`: In the output, we need to specify the absolute path of the output directory, `dist` in our case, and the filename, which is `[name]`, we specified in the entry section, followed by the file-extension `[name].js`.

Run `npm run webpack` in the terminal. You should see two new files created in the `dist` directory: `general.js` and `memes.js`, which contain the bundled code from each of their respective source files. The `memes.js` file will include the code from the `general.js` file, so it's enough to include only the `memes.js` file in your HTML.

Now that we have written the configuration for bundling our code, we'll use this configuration file to transform the ES6 syntax to ES5. In Webpack, transformations are applied when the file is imported. To apply transformations, we need to use loaders.

Loaders in Webpack

Loaders are used for applying transformations to files before importing and bundling them. In Webpack, using different third-party loaders, we can transform any file and import it into our code. This goes for files written in other languages, such as TypeScript, Dart, and so on. We can even import CSS and images into our JS code. First, we'll use loaders to transform ES6 into ES5.

In the memes.js file, add the following code:

```
class Memes {
  constructor() {
    console.log('Inside Memes class');
  }
}

new Memes();
```

This is a simple class using ES6 that has a console.log statement inside the constructor. We will use Webpack and babel-loader to transform this ES6 code to ES5 form. To do so, install the following packages:

```
npm install -D babel-core babel-loader babel-preset-env babel-preset-es2015
```

In your webpack.config.js file, add the following code below the output property:

```
module: {
  rules: [
    {
      test: /\.js$/,
      exclude: /(node_modules)/,
      use: {
        loader: 'babel-loader',
        options: {
          presets: ['env', 'es2015'],
        }
      }
    }
  ],
},
```

This is how we should add a loader in Webpack. We need to create an array of rules inside the module section. The rule contains an array of configuration objects for the loaders. In our configuration, it will test the file to see whether it matches the regular expression `.js$`, that is, check whether the file is a JavaScript file using its extension. We have excluded the `node_modules` directory so that only our code will be evaluated for transformation.

If the imported file is a JavaScript file, Webpack will use `babel-loader` with the provided options. Here, in `options`, we instruct Babel to use `env` and `es2015` presets. The `es2015` preset will transpile the ES6 code into the ES5 format.

`env` preset is more special. It is used for transpiling any ES version of javascript to the version supported by a specific environment (such as specific versions of Chrome and Firefox). If no configuration is provided, as in our earlier mentioned code, then it will make the JavaScript code (even ES8) work in almost all environments. More information on this preset can be found at `https://github.com/babel/babel-preset-env`.

 Since we are only going to use ES6 in this book, the `es2015` preset is enough for all the projects. However, if you want to learn ES7 and beyond in the future, do learn the working of the `env` preset.

Similarly, let's bundle our CSS code using Webpack. Bundling CSS code with Webpack has many advantages. Some of them are as follows:

- Use only the required CSS code for each web page by importing it in respective JavaScript files. This will lead to easier and better dependency management and reduced file sizes per page.
- Minification of CSS files.
- Automatically add vendor-specific prefixes easily using autoprefixer.
- Easily compile stylesheets written using Sass, Less, Stylus, and so on to normal CSS.

There are even more advantages as to why you need to bundle your CSS code using Webpack. So, let's start by bundling our `styles.css` file and then Bootstrap's files. Install the following dependencies for implementing our loader for CSS:

```
npm install -D css-loader style-loader
```

In our Webpack configuration, add the following object to the rules array:

```
{
  test: /\.css$/,
  use: [ 'style-loader', 'css-loader' ]
},
```

We are installing two loaders to bundle CSS files:

1. The first one is `css-loader`. It resolves all the imports and `url()` using Webpack. It then returns the complete CSS file.
2. `style-loader` will add the CSS to the page so that the styles are active on the page.
3. We need to run `css-loader` first, followed by `style-loader`, which uses the output returned by `css-loader`. To do that, we have written the following:
   - For a CSS file: `test: /\.css$/`
   - Use the following loaders: `use: ['style-loader', 'css-loader']`. Webpack executes the loaders in a last to first order. So, first, `css-loader` will be executed and its output will be passed over to `style-loader`.
4. Open up your `general.js` file and add the following line at the beginning of the file:

   ```
   import '../css/styles.css';
   ```

Also, remove the `<link>` attribute used to include the CSS file in your `index.html` page. Here's the trick: the CSS file will be imported into the `general.js` file, which will in turn be imported into the `memes.js` file, which is the only file you need to include in `index.html`.

We are going to create a large `webpack.config.js` file. If you face any problems, refer to the final `webpack.config.js` file we are creating at either: `https://goo.gl/Q8P4ta` or the book's code files under the `chapter02\webpack-dev-server` directory.

Now is the time to see our application. Execute `npm run webpack` in your terminal and open up the website that only has a single `memes.js` file included in Chrome. You should see the exact page with no changes. All the dependencies are bundled into a single file-- except Bootstrap!

Bundling Bootstrap in Webpack

Time to bundle our final dependency into Webpack. Bootstrap consists of three parts. The first is Bootstrap's CSS file, followed by jQuery and Bootstrap's JavaScript file, which is dependent on jQuery. The last two files were ignored in this chapter's index.html file, since we weren't using them. But, since we are bundling our dependencies with Webpack, let's just bring all of them together. For the first step, install our dependencies (these are not dev dependencies; hence, -S is used instead of -D):

```
npm install -S jquery bootstrap@3
```

Bootstrap is written using **Less** instead of CSS. **Less** is a CSS pre-processor that extends CSS with more features, such as variables, mixins, and functions. To import Bootstrap's less file using Webpack, we need another loader:

```
npm install -D less less-loader
```

This will install the less compiler and loader into our node_modules. Now, in our rules, modify the CSS rules into:

```
{
  test: /\.(less|css)$/,
  use: [ 'style-loader', 'css-loader', 'less-loader' ]
},
```

This will add less-loader as the first option as a loader whenever CSS or a less file is detected by Webpack. Now, try npm run webpack. This time, you will get an error in the terminal saying "*You may need an appropriate loader to handle this file type*" for the fonts that are used by Bootstrap. Since Bootstrap is dependent on a lot of fonts, we need to create a separate loader to include them in our bundle. For this purpose, install the following:

```
npm install -D file-loader url-loader
```

And then include the following object in your rules array:

```
{
  test: /\.(svg|eot|ttf|woff|woff2)$/,
  loader: 'url-loader',
  options: {
    limit: 10000,
    name: 'fonts/[name].[ext]'
  }
},
```

This will tell Webpack if the file size is smaller than 10 KB. Then, simply inline the file into JavaScript as a data URL. Otherwise, move the file into the fonts folder and create a reference in JavaScript. This is useful to reduce a network overhead if the file is smaller than 10 KB. `url-loader` requires `file-loader` to be installed as a dependency. Once again, execute `npm run webpack` and, this time, your Bootstrap less file will be bundled successfully and you will be able to view your website in the browser.

 This may look like a lot of work for a few CSS and JS files. But, when you are working on large-scale applications, these configurations can save hours of development work. The biggest advantage of Webpack is that you can write the configuration for one project and use it for other projects. So, most of the work we do here will be done only once. We'll simply copy and use our `webpack.config.js` file in other projects.

As I mentioned earlier, we didn't use Bootstrap's JS files in our application. However, we might need to use them for our applications in the future. Bootstrap requires jQuery to be available in global scope so that it's JavaScript files can be executed. However, Webpack does not expose the JavaScript variables it has bundled unless it is explicitly specified to expose them.

To make jQuery available in the global scope throughout our web application, we need to use a Webpack plugin. Plugins are different from loaders. We'll see more about plugins in a moment. For now, add the following code after the module property of Webpack:

```
module: {
  rules: [...],
},
plugins: [
  new webpack.ProvidePlugin({
    jQuery: 'jquery',
    $: 'jquery',
    jquery: 'jquery'
  }),
],
```

In our `general.js` file, include the following line to import all the Bootstrap JavaScript files into our web app:

```
import 'bootstrap';
```

This line will import Bootstrap's JavaScript files from the `node_modules` folder. You have now successfully bundled Bootstrap using Webpack. There is just one more loader that is commonly used – `img-loader`. There are scenarios when we include images in CSS and JavaScript. Using Webpack, we can automatically bundle the images while compressing the size of larger images during bundling.

To bundle images, we need to use `img-loader` and `url-loader` together. First, install `img-loader`:

```
npm install -D img-loader
```

Add the following object to your rules list:

```
{
  test: /\.(png|jpg|gif)$/,
  loaders: [
    {
      loader: 'url-loader',
      options: {
        limit: 10000,
        name: 'images/[name].[ext]'
      }
    },
    'img-loader'
  ],
},
```

Now, execute `npm run webpack` and open up the website again. You have all your dependencies bundled inside a single JavaScript file `memes.js` and you are ready to go.

 Sometimes, the `img-loader` binaries might fail during building depending on your operating system. In the latest version of Ubuntu, this is due to a missing package that can be downloaded and installed from: `https://packages.debian.org/jessie/amd64/libpng12-0/download`. In other operating systems, you have to manually find out why the build failed. If you cannot resolve the `img-loader` issue, do try to use a different loader or simply remove `img-loader` and only use `url-loader` for images.

Plugins in Webpack

Unlike loaders, plugins are used to customize the Webpack build process. There are a lot of plugins that are built into Webpack. They can be accessed by `webpack.[plugin-name]`.

We can also write our own functions as plugins.

 For more information on webpack's plugin system, refer to `https://webpack.js.org/configuration/plugins/`.

Webpack dev server

So far, we have created the Webpack configuration to compile our code, but it will be easier if we can serve the code as we did using `http-server`. `webpack-dev-server` is a small server written using Node.js and Express, which is used to serve the Webpack bundle. To use `webpack-dev-server`, we need to install it's dependencies and update our npm scripts:

```
npm install -D webpack-dev-server
```

Add the following line to the npm scripts:

```
"watch": "webpack-dev-server"
```

Using the `npm run watch`, we can now serve the files over a server on our localhost. `webpack-dev-server` does not write the bundled files to the disk. Instead, it will automatically serve them from memory. One great feature of `webpack-dev-server` is that it is able to do `HotModuleReplacement`, which will replace a part of code that has been changed without even reloading the page. To use `HotModuleReplacement`, add the following configurations to your Webpack configuration file:

```
entry: {...},
output: {...},
devServer: {
  compress: true,
  port: 8080,
  hot: true,
},
module: {..},
plugins: [
  ...,
  new webpack.HotModuleReplacementPlugin(),
],
```

Currently, `webpack-dev-server` is serving files from the root. But we need files to be served from the `dist` directory. To do that, we need to set `publicPath` in our output configuration:

```
output: {
  ...,
  publicPath: '/dist/',
},
```

Delete your `dist` folder and run the `npm run watch` command. Your web app will now print a few extra messages in the console. These are from `webpack-dev-server`, which is listening for any file changes. Try changing a few lines in your CSS file. Your changes will be immediately, reflected without having to reload the page! This is very useful to see style changes immediately as soon as the code is saved. `HotModuleReplacement` is widely used in modern JavaScript frameworks, such as React, Angular, and so on.

We are still missing `source-maps` in our code for debugging. To enable `source-maps`, Webpack provides a simple configuration option:

```
devtool: 'source-map',
```

There are different types of source-maps that can be generated by Webpack depending on the time taken to generate them and the quality. Refer to this page for more information: `https://webpack.js.org/configuration/devtool/`.

This will only add source maps to the JS files. To add `source-maps` to CSS files, which also contains Bootstrap's less files, change the CSS rules to the following:

```
{
  test: /\.(less|css)$/,
  use: [
    {
      loader: "style-loader"
    },
    {
      loader: "css-loader",
      options: {
        sourceMap: true
      }
    },
    {
      loader: "less-loader",
      options: {
        sourceMap: true
      }
    }
```

```
        ]
    },
```

This rule will tell `less-loader` to add `source-maps` to the files compiled by it and pass it to `css-loader`, which will also pass the source maps to `style-loader`. Now, both your JS and CSS files will have source maps, making it easy to debug the application in Chrome.

If you have been following along, your Webpack configuration file should now look like the code in the following URL: `https://goo.gl/Q8P4ta`. Your `package.json` file should look like: `https://goo.gl/m4Ib97`. These files are also included in the book's code inside the `chapter02\webpack-dev-server` directory.

 We have used a lot of different loaders with Webpack, each of them having their own configuration options, many of which we did not discuss here. Do visit those packages, npm or GitHub pages to learn more about their configuration and customize them as per your requirements.

The upcoming section is optional. If you want to build the Meme Creator app, you can skip the next section and start with the development. The Webpack configuration you have now will be totally fine. However, the next section is important to learn more about Webpack and use it in production, so do come back to read about it later!

Optimizing Webpack builds for different environments

While working on large scale applications, there are usually different types of environments created for the application to run, such as development, testing, staging, production, and so on. Each environment has different configurations for the application and is useful for development and testing by different groups of people in the team.

For example, imagine you have an API for payments in your app. During development, you will have sandbox credentials and, for testing, you have different credentials, and finally, for production, you have the actual credentials needed by the payment gateway. So, the application needs to use three different credentials for three different environments. It is also important not to commit sensitive information into your version control system.

So, how are we going to pass the credentials to the app without writing them in the code? That's where the concept of environment variables come in. The operating system will provide the values during compile time so that the build can be generated with values from different environment variables in different environments.

The process of creating environment variables is different for each operating system and it's a tedious task to maintain these environment variables for each project. So, let's simplify the process by using an `npm` package to load our environment variables from a `.env` file from our project root folder. In Node.js, you can access the environment variables in the `process.env` object. Here's how you can read variables from `.env` file:

1. The first step is to install the following package:

   npm install -D dotenv

2. Once this is done, create a `.env` file in your project root directory with the following lines:

   ```
   NODE_ENV=production
   CONSTANT_VALUE=1234567
   ```

3. This `.env` file contains three environment variables and their values. You should add the `.env` file to your `.gitignore` file if you are using Git or include it in the ignore list of your version control system. It's also a good practice to create the `.env.example` file, which tells other developers what kind of environment variables are needed by the application. You can commit the `.env.example` file to your version control system. Our `.env.example` file should look as follows:

   ```
   NODE_ENV=
   CONSTANT_VALUE=
   ```

These environment variables can be read by Node.js, but they can't be read by our JavaScript code. So, we need Webpack to read these variables and provide them as global variables to the JavaScript code. It is recommended to keep the letters of the environment variable names in capital letters so that you can easily identify them.

We are going to use `NODE_ENV` for detecting the environment type and to tell Webpack to generate an appropriate build for that environment, and we need to use other two environment variables in our JS code. In your `webpack.config.js` file, in the first line, include the following code:

```
require('dotenv').config()
```

This will use the `dotenv` package we just installed and load the environment variables from the `.env` file in our project's root directory. Now, the environment variables are accessible inside the Webpack configuration file in the `process.env` object. First, let's set up a flag to check whether the current environment is production. Include the following code after the `require('webpack')` line:

```
const isProduction = (process.env.NODE_ENV === 'production');
```

Now, `isProduction` will be set to true when `NODE_ENV` is set to production. To include the other two variables in our JavaScript code, we need to use `DefinePlugin` in Webpack. Inside the plugins array, add the following configuration object:

```
new webpack.DefinePlugin({
  ENVIRONMENT: JSON.stringify(process.env.NODE_ENV),
  CONSTANT_VALUE: JSON.stringify(process.env.CONSTANT_VALUE),
}),
```

`DefinePlugin` will define the constants at compile time, so you can change your environment variables depending on your environment and it will be reflected in the code. Make sure you stringify any value you pass to `DefinePlugin`. More information about this plugin can be found at: `https://webpack.js.org/plugins/define-plugin/`.

Now, inside your `memes.js` file's constructor, try `console.log(ENVIRONMENT, CONSTANT_VALUE);` and reload Chrome. You should see their values printed out in the console.

Since we set up a flag using the `isProduction` variable, we can use this variable to do various optimizations to the build only when the environment is production. Some of the common plugins used for optimizations in production builds are as follows.

Creating .env file in Windows

Windows do not allow you to create a `.env` file directly from the windows explorer since it will not allow file names starting with a dot. However, you will be able to create it from VSCode easily. First, open the project folder in VSCode using the menu option **File | Open Folder...[Ctrl+K Ctrl+O]** as shown in the following screenshot:

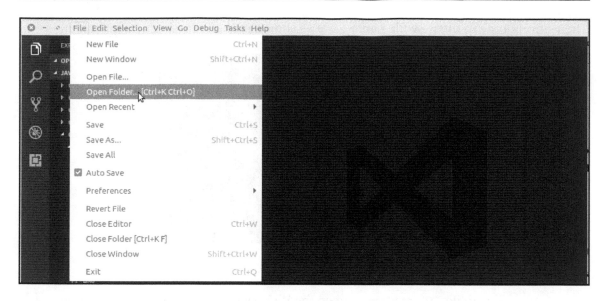

Once you have opened the folder, click on the **Explorer** icon on the top left corner of the VSCode (or press *Ctrl+Shift+E*) to open the explorer panel. In the explorer panel, click on the New File button as shown in the following screenshot:

Then simply type in the new file name `.env` as shown in the following screenshot:

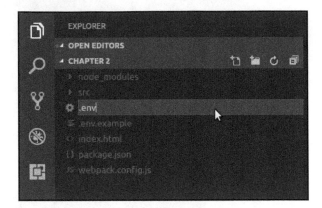

Hit *Enter* to create the `.env` file and start editing it.

 `.env` files are read only when the Webpack-dev-server starts. So, if you make any changes to the `.env` files, you will have to kill the running Webpack-dev-server instance in the Terminal and restart it so that it will read the new values in `.env` files.

UglifyJsPlugin

This is a plugin that is used for compressing and minifying JavaScript files. This greatly reduces the size of the JavaScript code and increases the loading speed for end users. However, using this plugin during development will cause Webpack to slow down, since it adds an extra step to the build process (expensive task). Hence, UglifyJsPlugin is usually used only on production environments. To do so, add the following lines at the end of your Webpack configuration:

```
if(isProduction) {
  module.exports.plugins.push(
    new webpack.optimize.UglifyJsPlugin({sourceMap: true})
  );
}
```

This will push UglifyJSPlugin to the plugins array if the environment is set to production. More information regarding UglifyJsPlugin can be found at: https://webpack.js.org/plugins/uglifyjs-webpack-plugin/.

PurifyCSSPlugin

When building web applications, there will be a lot of styles that are defined in CSS but are never used in HTML. `PurifyCSSPlugin` will go through all the HTML files and remove any unnecessary CSS styles that we have defined before bundling the code. To use `PurifyCSSPlugin`, we need to install the `purifycss-webpack` package:

```
npm install -D purifycss-webpack
```

After that, import the plugin to your Webpack configuration file and use it as specified in the following code:

```
const PurifyCSSPlugin = require('purifycss-webpack');
constglob = require('glob');

module.exports = {
  ...
  plugins: [
    ...
    new PurifyCSSPlugin({
      paths: glob.sync(__dirname + '/*.html'),
      minimize: true,
    }),
  ],
}
```

`glob` is an inbuilt module in Node.js. We specify the paths of HTML using `glob.sync`, which resolves the regular expression into all the HTML files inside the specified directory. `PurifyCSSPlugin` will now use these HTML files to purify our styles. The `minimize` option will minify CSS along with purification. More information regarding `PurifyCSSPlugin` can be found at: `https://github.com/webpack-contrib/purifycss-webpack`.

> `PurifyCSSplugin` is useful but it might cause problems with Bootstrap animations and some other plugins. Make sure you test it well before using it.

ExtractTextPlugin

In production, it is recommended to extract all your CSS code into a separate file. This is because CSS files need to be included at the beginning of the page so that page styles will be applied to HTML while it is loading. However, since we are bundling CSS together with JavaScript, we are including it at the end of the page. When the page is loading, it will look like a plain document till the CSS files are loaded.

ExtractTextPlugin is used to overcome this problem. It will extract all the CSS files in JS code into separate files with the same name as the JS file it was bundled together with. We can now include that CSS file at the top of our HTML file, which makes the styles be loaded first. As usual, the first step is to install the package:

```
npm install -D extract-text-webpack-plugin
```

After this, we need to create a new instance of ExtractTextPlugin, which we are going to use with our CSS files. Since we are also using less from Bootstrap, our configuration file should look as follows:

```
...
const extractLess = new ExtractTextPlugin({
  filename: "[name].css",
});

module.exports = {
  ...
  module: {
    rules: [
      ...
      {
        test: /\.(less|css)$/,
        use: extractLess.extract({
          use: [
            {
              loader: 'css-loader',
              options: {
                sourceMap: true
              }
            },
            {
              loader: 'less-loader',
              options: {
                sourceMap: true
              }
            }
          ],
          fallback: 'style-loader',
```

```
        })
      },
    ]
  },
  ...
  plugins: [
    ...
    extractLess,
    new PurifyCSSPlugin({
      paths: glob.sync(__dirname + '/*.html'),
      minimize: true,
    }),
    ...
  ]
}
```

We have created an instance of `ExtractTextPlugin` as `extractLess`. Since we are using `PurifyCSSPlugin`, make sure you include the `extractLess` object before we create an instance `PurifyCSSPlugin` in the plugins array.

More information regarding `PurifyCSSPlugin` can be found at: `https://github.com/webpack-contrib/purifycss-webpack`.

Once you have added `ExtractTextPlugin`, Webpack will generate two files for each JavaScript file if the JavaScript file imports CSS. You will have to include the CSS files separately in your HTML. In our case, for `memes.js`, it will generate `memes.js` and `memes.css` in the `dist` directory, which needs to be included separately in the HTML file.

`ExtractTextPlugin` will not work properly with Webpack `HotModuleReplacement` for CSS files. Hence, it's best to include `ExtractTextPlugin` only in production.

Cache busting

To use caching with the static resources produced by Webpack, it's a good practice to append the filenames of the static resources with hashes. **[chunkhash]** will generate a content-dependent hash, which should be appended to the filename that acts as the cache buster. Whenever the content of the file changes, the hash will change, which will lead to new filenames and, hence, regenerating the cache.

Only production builds need cache busting logic. Development builds do not need these configurations. Hence, we need to generate hashed filenames only at production. Also, we must generate a `manifest.json` file that contains the new filenames of the generated resources that must be inlined into the HTML file. Configurations for cache busting are as follows:

```
const fileNamePrefix = isProduction? '[chunkhash].' : '';

module.exports = {
  ...
  output: {
    ...
    filename: fileNamePrefix + '[name].js',
    ...
  }
}
```

This will add a hash prefix to the filenames in production. However, `webpack.HotModuleReplacementPlugin()` does not work well with **[chunkhash]**, so `HotModuleReplacementPlugin` should not be used in our production environment. To generate the `manifest.json` file, add the following function as an element to the plugins array:

```
function() {
  this.plugin("done", function(status) {
    require("fs").writeFileSync(
      __dirname + "/dist/manifest.json",
      JSON.stringify(status.toJson().assetsByChunkName)
    );
  });
}
```

Or it's better to add it next to `UglifyJSPlugin`, which gets executed only in production. This function will use the `fs` module in Node.js to write the generated files as a JSON file. For more information regarding this topic, refer to: `https://webpack.js.org/guides/caching/`.

Clean dist folder before generating a new build

Since we generate lot of builds with different hashed filenames, it is a good practice to delete the `dist` directory before running each build. `clean-webpack-plugin` does just that. It cleans the `dist` directory before new files are bundled. To use `clean-webpack-plugin`, run the following command inside the project root folder to install the plugin: :

```
npm install -D clean-webpack-plugin
```

Then, add the following variables to your Webpack configuration file:

```
const CleanWebpackPlugin = require('clean-webpack-plugin');
const pathsToClean = [
 'dist'
];
const cleanOptions = {
 root: __dirname,
 verbose: true,
 dry: false,
 exclude: [],
};
```

Finally, add `new CleanWebpackPlugin(pathsToClean, cleanOptions)` to your production plugins. Now, every time the production build is generated, the old `dist` folder will be deleted and a new folder will be created with the latest bundled files. More information regarding this plugin can be found at: `https://github.com/johnagan/clean-webpack-plugin`.

Source maps in production

Source maps provide us with an easy way to debug our compiled code. Browsers don't load source maps until the development tool is opened. Hence, performance-wise source maps don't cause any harm. However, if you need the original source code to be protected, then removing source maps is a good idea. You can also use private source maps by setting `sourceMappingURL` at the end of each bundled file to a restricted URL that can be used only by a trusted source (for example, source maps can be accessed only by developers within the company's domain):

```
//# sourceMappingURL: http://protected.domain/dist/general.js.map
```

The complete Webpack configuration file with all the earlier mentioned optimizations will look as: `https://goo.gl/UDuUBu`. The dependencies used in this configuration can be found at: `https://goo.gl/PcHpZf`. These files are also included in this book's code files under the `Chapter02\webpack production optimized` directory.

We have just tried of lot of community created plugins and loaders for Webpack. Remember that there is more than one way to perform these tasks. So, be sure to check out a lot of new plugins/loaders created over time. This repository contains a curated list of Webpack resources: `https://github.com/webpack-contrib/awesome-webpack`. Since we are using flexbox in the Meme Creator, some old browsers support flexbox with `vendor-prefixes`. Try adding vendor prefixes to your CSS using `postcss/autoprefixer`: `https://github.com/postcss/autoprefixer`.

Building the Meme Creator

We just built a nice little development environment using Webpack. It's time to put it into action. If you have done the production optimizations, make sure you have created the `.env` file in the project root folder and your `NODE_ENV` environment variable inside that file is not `production`. Simply set the value of `NODE_ENV=dev` while we are working on the application. We are going to build the Meme Creator now. Make sure you have included the `memes.js` and `memes.css` files (if you used `ExtractTextPlugin`) from the `dist` directory in your `index.html` file.

Open up the `memes.js` file in your text editor and keep `webpack-dev-server` running (`npm run watch`). Our first step is to create a reference to all the required DOM elements in variables in our class. We can then use the references to modify the elements later, from inside the class. Also, whenever we are creating a reference to DOM elements, it is good to have the variable names start with $. This way, we can easily know which variables contain values and which ones contain references to the DOM elements.

webpack-dev-server will print the URL in the console which you should open using Chrome to see your application. The URL will be http://localhost:8080/

Remember how in the previous chapter, we used `document.getElementById()` to search through the DOM elements? JavaScript also has a better alternative that makes querying DOM elements simpler: the `document.querySelector()` method. The former allowed us to search a document only using `Id`, but `querySelector` allows us to query the document using `id`, `class`, and even the element's name. For example, if you need to select the following:

```
<input id="target" class="target-input" type="text"/>
```

You can use one of the following:

```
document.querySelector('#target');
document.querySelector('.target-input');
document.querySelector('input#target.target-input');
```

All of these will return the first element matching the query criteria. If you want to select multiple elements, you can use document.querySelectorAll(), which returns an array of references to all the matching DOM elements. In our constructor, write the following code:

```
this.$canvas = document.querySelector('#imgCanvas');
this.$topTextInput = document.querySelector('#topText');
this.$bottomTextInput = document.querySelector('#bottomText');
this.$imageInput = document.querySelector('#image');
this.$downloadButton = document.querySelector('#downloadMeme');
```

Now we have a reference to all the required DOM elements in our class. Currently, our canvas is small; we didn't specify its size using CSS because we need the page to be responsive. If users visits the page from a mobile device, we don't want to show a horizontal scrollbar because the canvas has gone out of the screen due to its size. Hence, we will use JavaScript to create the canvas height and width depending on the screen size. We need to calculate the device width first. Add the following code above the Memes class (not inside the class):

```
const deviceWidth = window.innerWidth;
```

This will calculate the device's width and store it in a constant deviceWidth. Inside the class, create the following function:

```
createCanvas() {
  let canvasHeight = Math.min(480, deviceWidth-30);
  let canvasWidth = Math.min(640, deviceWidth-30);
  this.$canvas.height = canvasHeight;
  this.$canvas.width = canvasWidth;
}
```

 References to DOM elements contain the entire target element as a JavaScript object. It can be used in the same way we handle normal class objects. Modifications to references will be reflected in the DOM.

This will create a rectanglar canvas with height 480 and width 640 if the device's screen is large enough. Otherwise, it will create a square canvas with width deviceWidth-30. Refer to the image of the Meme Creator you saw earlier. The canvas will be rectangular for desktops and will become a square area with margin for mobile devices.

`Math.min(x, y)` will return the smallest of two numbers `x` and `y`. We reduced the width by `30` because we need to have space for the margins. Add `this.createCanvas()` inside the constructor and view the page in Chrome (Webpack will have reloaded the page for you). Try the responsive design mode to see how the canvas appears on mobile devices. Height and width are applied only when the page is loaded for the first time; hence, refresh the page when you are checking different devices.

Our canvas area is ready; let's look at a few things about the new `<canvas>` element in HTML. Canvas is a container for graphics. We can use JavaScript to write graphics on the canvas element. Canvas has several methods for drawing, such as paths, shapes, text, and images. Also, rendering graphics in canvas is faster than using DOM elements. One more advantage of canvas is that we can convert the canvas content into an image. In real-world applications, where you have server-side APIs, you can use the server to render the images and text for the memes. But, since we are not going to use server-side in this chapter, canvas is our best option.

 Visit the **Mozilla Developer Network** (**MDN**) page: `https://developer.`
`mozilla.org/en-US/docs/Web/API/Canvas_API/Tutorial` for more information regarding the canvas element.

Here is the strategy for the Meme Creator:

- The canvas element just renders the graphics to its bitmap when instructed. We cannot detect any graphics that were previously drawn on it. This leaves us no option but to clear the canvas every time a new text or image is entered into the Meme Creator and render the whole canvas again.
- We need event listeners to add text to the meme whenever the user is typing in the **Top Text** or **Bottom Text** input boxes.
- Bottom Text is a compulsory field. The user cannot download the meme unless it is filled.
- The user can select images of any size. If he selects a huge image, it shouldn't break our page layout.
- The **Download** Button should work like a download button!

Event handling

We now have an idea for building the Meme Creator. Our first step is to create a function that renders the meme to the canvas. Inside the Memes class, create a function createMeme() that is going to contain our primary canvas renderer. For now, leave the function with a simple console statement:

```
createMeme() {
  console.log('rendered');
}
```

Remember, we need to render the entire canvas every time a change happens. So, we need to attach event listeners to all the input elements. You can also use HTML event attributes such as onchange we used in the previous ToDo List app. But event listeners let us handle more than one event for an element. Hence, they are widely preferred. Also, since we are using Webpack to bundle the code, we cannot access the JavaScript variables or objects inside our HTML directly! This requires a little Webpack configuration change and it might not be needed at all. We will discuss this topic in detail in the next chapter.

First, we need to call createMeme whenever a text is entered into the TopTextInput and BottomTextInput areas. So, we need to attach an event listener that listens to the keyup event on these input boxes. Create the event listener function:

```
addEventListeners() {
  this.$topTextInput.addEventListener('keyup', this.createMeme);
  this.$bottomTextInput.addEventListener('keyup', this.createMeme);
}
```

Open Chrome and try typing in the text boxes while keeping the console open. You should see rendered being printed in the console every time you type a word. There is actually a better way to attach event listeners if you want to attach the same event listener to multiple elements. Simply use the following:

```
addEventListeners() {
  let inputNodes = [this.$topTextInput, this.$bottomTextInput,
this.$imageInput];

  inputNodes.forEach(element => element.addEventListener('keyup',
this.createMeme));
}
```

This code does the following:

- It creates an array of reference objects to all the target input elements (`inputNodes`)
- Use the `forEach()` method to loop through each element in the array and attach an event listener to it
- By using the ES6 fat arrows, we achieved it in a single line without having to worry about binding the `this` object to the callback function

We have also added `$imageInput` in `inputNodes`. This element is not going to be affected much with the `keyup` event, but we need this to be monitored when a user uploads a new image. Also, if the user copies and pastes text into the text inputs without pressing any keyboard buttons, we need to handle the change. Both of these scenarios can be handled using the `change` event. Add the following line to the `addEventListeners()` function:

```
inputNodes.forEach(element => element.addEventListener('change',
this.createMeme));
```

Whenever the user types in some text or uploads a new image, the `this.createMeme()` method will be automatically called.

Rendering an image in the canvas

The first step to render something to the canvas is to use the `CanvasRenderingContext2D` interface to get the 2D rendering context for the target `<canvas>` element. Inside our `createMeme()` function, create a context to the canvas element:

```
let context = this.$canvas.getContext('2d');
```

The `context` variable will now hold the object of the `CanvasRenderingContext2D` interface. To make rendering a little more efficient, we'll add a condition to render only when a user has selected an image. We can do this by checking whether the reference to the image input has any files in it. We should start the rendering process only when there is a file selected in the input. To do so, check whether the input element contains any file objects:

```
if (this.$imageInput.files && this.$imageInput.files[0]) {
  console.log('rendering');
}
```

Now, try typing some text into the input field. You should get an error in the console saying: **Cannot read property 'getContext' of undefined**.

```
⊗ ▶Uncaught TypeError: Cannot read property 'getContext' of undefined
        at HTMLInputElement.createMeme (memes.js:26)
⊗ ▶Uncaught TypeError: Cannot read property 'getContext' of undefined
        at HTMLInputElement.createMeme (memes.js:26)
```

At this moment, you should be asking the following questions:

- Didn't we define `this.$canvas` to hold reference to our canvas element in our constructor?
- We are getting the context object from our canvas reference `this.$canvas`. But how could `this.$canvas` be undefined?
- Aren't we doing everything right?

To find the answers, we need to use the Chrome DevTools to figure out what went wrong in our code. Add the `debugger;` keyword right before the line causing the error (the line we define our context variable). Now, reload Chrome and start typing. Chrome's debugger will have now paused the page execution and the sources tab will highlight the line in which the Chrome debugger has paused the execution:

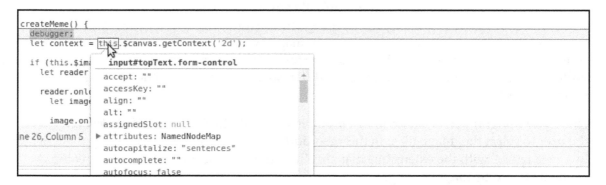

The execution of the code is now paused. This means all the variables will now contain their values during execution. Hover your cursor over the `this` keyword in the line next to `debugger;`. Surprisingly, placing the cursor over this object will highlight the top Input text field in your website! Also, the information popup will also show this object containing reference to `input#topText.form-control`. Here is the problem: the `this` object no longer has reference to the class but has reference to a DOM element. We defined the `$canvas` variable inside the class; hence, `this.$canvas` is now undefined. We faced a similar problem with binding the `this` object in the previous project. Can you guess where we went wrong?

It's the line where we attached event listeners to our input elements in our `addEventListeners()` function. Since we are using ES6 fat arrows here, you might be wondering why `this` didn't automatically inherit its value from the parent. It's because, this time, we are sending `this.createMeme` as a parameter to the `addEventListener()` method of the target element. Hence, that input element becomes the new parent for inheriting the `this` object. To overcome this problem, change `this.createMeme` to `this.createMeme.bind(this)`, or for a cleaner syntax, add the following code as the first line of our `addEventListeners()` function:

```
this.createMeme = this.createMeme.bind(this);
```

Now, `this.createMeme` can be used normally anywhere inside our `addEventListeners()` function. Try typing some text into the input boxes. This time, there shouldn't be any errors. Now, select an image from the source image input. Try typing some text. This time, you should see *rendering* text printed in the console. We are going to write the rendering code inside this `if` condition so that the meme renders only when an image is selected.

One more thing! If you click the image input, it shows all the files in the disk. We only need the user to select the image files. In this case, add the `accept` attribute to the input element in `index.html` with the extensions that are allowed for the user to select. The new input element should be the following:

```
<input type="file" id="image" class="form-control"
accept=".png,.jpg,.jpeg">
```

Reading a file using JavaScript

To read the selected image, we are going to use `FileReader`, which allows JavaScript to *asynchronously* read the contents of a file (either from a file or raw data). Note the term asynchronously; it means JavaScript will not wait for the `FileReader` code to complete execution. JavaScript will start the execution of the next line while `FileReader` is still reading the file. This is because JavaScript is a single-threaded language. It means all the operations, event listeners, functions, and so on, are executing in a single thread. If JS has to wait for the completion of `FileReader`, then the entire JavaScript code will be paused (just like how debugger pauses the execution of the script), since everything is running in a single thread.

To avoid this from happening, JavaScript does not simply wait for the event to complete, but runs the event simultaneously while executing the next lines of code. There are different ways in which we can handle asynchronous events. Generally, an asynchronous event is given a callback function (some lines of code that needs to be executed after the event is completed) or the asynchronous code will fire an event when the execution is complete and we can write a function to execute when that event is triggered. ES6 has a new way of dealing with asynchronous events, called Promises.

We will see more about using Promises in the next chapter. `FileReader` will fire a `load` event when it's finished reading the file. `FileReader` also comes with the `onload` event handler to handle the `load` event. Inside the `if` statement, create a new `FileReader` object and assign it to variable reader using the `FileReader()` constructor. Here's how we are going to handle the asynchronous `FileReader` logic: write the following code inside the `if` statement (remove the previous `console.log` statement):

```
let reader = new FileReader();

reader.onload = () => {
  console.log('file completly read');
};

reader.readAsDataURL(this.$imageInput.files[0]);
console.log('This will get printed first!');
```

Now, try selecting an image in Chrome. You should see two statements printed in the console. This is what we have done in the previous code:

- We created a new instance of `FileReader` in the reader variable
- We then specified what the reader should do in the `onload` event handler
- Then, we passed the file object of the selected image to the reader object

As you might have guessed, JavaScript will execute `reader.readAsDataURL` first and find that it is an asynchronous event. So, while the `FileReader` is running, it will execute the next `console.log()` statement.

Once the `FileReader` has completed reading the file, it will fire the `load` event, which will call the corresponding `reader.onload` event handler. Now, the `console.log()` statement inside the `reader.onload` method will be executed. `reader.result` will now contain the image data.

We need to create an `Image` object using the result from `FileReader`. Create a new instance of the image using the `Image()` constructor (we should now write the code inside the `reader.onload` method):

```
reader.onload = () => {
  let image = new Image();

  image.onload = () => {

  };

  image.src = reader.result;
}
```

As you can see, dynamically loading an image source is also an asynchronous event and we need to use the `onload` event handler provided by the `Image` object.

Once we have the image loaded, we need to resize the canvas to the image's size. To do that, write the following code inside the `image.onload` method:

```
image.onload = () => {
  this.$canvas.height = image.height;
  this.$canvas.width = image.width;
}
```

This will now resize the canvas to the size of the image. Once we have the canvas resized, our first step is to erase the canvas. The canvas object has the `clearRect()` method, which can be used to clear a rectangular area in the canvas. In our case, the rectangular area is the entire canvas. To clear the entire canvas, we need to use `clearRect()` with our canvas's context object, which is the `context` variable we created earlier. After that, we need to load the image into the canvas. Write the following code inside the `image.onload` method right after assigning the canvas dimensions:

```
context.clearRect(0, 0, this.$canvas.height, this.$canvas.width);
context.drawImage(image, 0, 0);
```

Now, try selecting an image. The image should be displayed in the canvas. This is what the previous code does:

- Clear a rectangular area in the canvas starting from the top-left coordinates (0,0), that is, the *first two parameters* of the clearRect() method and then create a rectangle with its height and width equal to that of the canvas, that is, the last two parameters of the clearRect() method. This effectively clears the entire canvas.

- Draw an image onto the canvas using the image stored in the image object starting from the coordinates (0,0). Since the canvas has the same dimensions as the image, the image will cover the entire canvas.

Rendering text on the canvas

We have an image now, but we are still missing the top text and bottom text. Here are a few things we need as the text property:

- The font size should be responsive to the size of the image
- The text should be center-aligned
- The text should have margin space at the top and bottom of the image
- The text should have a black stroke so that it can be seen clearly over the image

For our first step, we need the font size to be responsive. If the user selects either a large image or a small one, we need to have a relative font size. Since we have the canvas height and width, we can use that to get a font size that is 4% of the average of the image height and width. We can center align the text using the textAlign property.

Also, we need to specify a baseline using the textBaseline property. It is used to position the text at the specified location. First, the canvas creates a baseline at the location we specify for the text. Then, it will write the text above, below, or over the baseline based on the value supplied to textBaseline. Write the following code inside the image.onload method:

```
let fontSize = ((this.$canvas.width+this.$canvas.height)/2)*4/100;
context.font = `${fontSize}pt sans-serif`;
context.textAlign = 'center';
context.textBaseline = 'top';
```

We have specified the font to be 4% of the average of the canvas height and width and set the font style to sans-serif. Also, by setting textBaseline to top, the baseline will be on top of the text, that is, the text will be rendered below the baseline.

Canvas does not have an option to apply stroke to the text. Hence, to create a white text with black stroke, we need to create two different texts, a black stroke text and a white fill text, with the line width of the stroke text being slightly bigger than the fill text, and place them one over another. This might sound like a complex task to do, but it's actually simple.

This is how a stroke text looks:

This is how a fill text looks (in a gray background):

Create styles for the stroke text and fill text:

```
// for stroke text
context.lineWidth = fontSize/5;
context.strokeStyle = 'black';

// for fill text
context.fillStyle = 'white';
```

Get the value for the top text and bottom text from the input fields:

```
const topText = this.$topTextInput.value.toUpperCase();
const bottomText = this.$bottomTextInput.value.toUpperCase();
```

This will get the value from the input fields and automatically convert the text to uppercase letters. Finally, to render the text at the top and bottom of the canvas, we need to do the following:

```
// Top Text
context.strokeText(topText, this.$canvas.width/2,
this.$canvas.height*(5/100));
context.fillText(topText, this.$canvas.width/2,
this.$canvas.height*(5/100));

// Bottom Text
context.strokeText(bottomText, this.$canvas.width/2,
this.$canvas.height*(90/100));
context.fillText(bottomText, this.$canvas.width/2,
this.$canvas.height*(90/100));
```

Consider `context.strokeText()`. This is how the text gets rendered:

- The first parameter of the `strokeText` method, `topText` contains the text to be rendered.
- The second and third parameters contain the location where the text should start rendering. Along the x axis, the text should start rendering from the middle of the canvas (`this.$canvas.width/2`). The text will be center aligned and along the y axis from a height that is 5% from the top of the canvas (`this.$canvas.height*(5/100)`). The text will be rendered.

This is exactly where we need the top text of the meme. For the bottom text, increase the height to 90% from the top. The stroke text with black stroke will be below the fill text. Sometimes, 'M' will have additional strokes over the text. This is because the place where two lines meet is not properly rounded. To do so, add the following line after the line specifying `fillStyle`:

```
context.lineJoin = 'round';
```

Now, quickly switch to Chrome, select an image, and type some text! You have your very own Meme Creator! For reference, it should work like this:

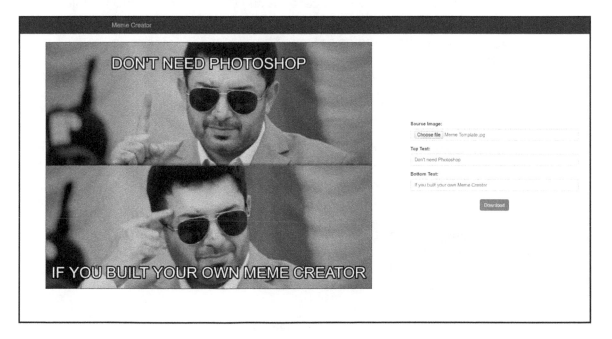

Now, to download the meme, we need to convert the canvas into an image and attach the image as the attribute to the download button. Create a new function `downloadMeme()` inside the `Memes` class. In the `addEventListeners()` function, add the following line:

```
this.$downloadButton.addEventListener('click',
this.downloadMeme.bind(this));
```

Now, inside the `downloadMeme()` function, add the following code:

```
const imageSource = this.$canvas.toDataURL('image/png');
let att = document.createAttribute('href');
att.value = imageSource.replace(/^data:image\/[^;]/,
'data:application/octet-stream');
this.$downloadButton.setAttributeNode(att);
```

Now, clicking the download button will convert the canvas into an image and let the browser download it. This is how the previous code works:

- First, the canvas is converted into a 64-bit encoded png URL using the `toDataURL('image/png')` method and is stored in the `imageSource` constant.
- Create another constant `att` that contains an HTML `'href'` attribute object.
- Now, change the value of the `att` object to the image URL stored in `imageSource` while changing the mime type from `data:image` to `data:application/octet-stream`. This step is necessary because most browsers display images directly instead of downloading them. By changing the mime type to `octet-stream` (used for binary files), we can trick the browser into thinking the file is not an image and, hence, download the file instead of viewing it.
- Finally, assign the `att` object as an attribute of `$downloadButton`, which is an anchor tag with the `download` attribute. The value of the `download` attribute will be the default name of the downloaded image.

 In the `imageSource.replace()` method, a regular expression is used for changing the mime type of the image. We will discuss more on using regular expressions in the next chapter. To know more about regular expressions, visit the following MDN page: `https://developer.mozilla.org/en/docs/Web/JavaScript/Guide/Regular_Expressions`.

Before downloading the meme from the Meme Creator, we need to validate the form so that there must be an image selected and, at least, the bottom text box is filled in order to download the meme. We need to add the form validation code in the downloadMeme() function above the code to download the file:

```
if(!this.$imageInput.files[0]) {
  this.$imageInput.parentElement.classList.add('has-error');
  return;
}
if(this.$bottomTextInput.value === '') {
  this.$imageInput.parentElement.classList.remove('has-error');
  this.$bottomTextInput.parentElement.classList.add('has-error');
  return;
}
this.$imageInput.parentElement.classList.remove('has-error');
this.$bottomTextInput.parentElement.classList.remove('has-error');
```

The previous code will check for an image and text in the bottom text input box and stop downloadMeme() from continuing execution using the return keyword. Once an empty field has been found, it will add the .has-error class to the input's parent div, which, according to Bootstrap, highlights the input in a red border (we used it previously in the ToDo list app).

You might not get the highlight, because we are using PurifyCSSPlugin with Webpack, which filters out all the unwanted styles by referring index.html. Since the .has-error class is not present in index.html initially, its style definition is also removed from the bundled CSS. To overcome this problem, add all the classes you would like to add dynamically to a hidden div element in the page. Add the following line to our index.html file just above the <script> tag:

```
<div class="has-error" style="display: none;"></div>
```

Now, the style definitions for .has-error will be included in the bundle and form validation will add a red border to the empty fields.

Making a canvas responsive to show large images

If the user selects a large image (for example, an image the size of the screen), it will cause the layout to break. To prevent this from happening, we need to zoom out our canvas when large images are selected. We can zoom in or zoom out our canvas element by controlling its height and width in CSS. In the Memes class, create the following function:

```
resizeCanvas(canvasHeight, canvasWidth) {
  let height = canvasHeight;
```

```
    let width = canvasWidth;
    this.$canvas.style.height = `${height}px`;
    this.$canvas.style.width = `${width}px`;
    while(height > Math.min(1000, deviceWidth-30) && width > Math.min(1000,
deviceWidth-30)) {
        height /= 2;
        width /= 2;
        this.$canvas.style.height = `${height}px`;
        this.$canvas.style.width = `${width}px`;
    }
}
```

This is how `resizeCanvas()` works:

- This function will initially apply the height and width of the canvas in CSS to its actual height and width (so that the zoom level of the previous image is not remembered).
- Then, it will check whether the height and width are either greater than the minimum of 1000px or `deviceWidth-30` (we already defined the `deviceWidth` constant).
- If the canvas size is greater than the given condition, we reduce the height and width by half and then assign the new values to the canvas's CSS (this will zoom out the canvas).
- Since it is a while loop, the operation is repeated until the canvas size goes below the condition, thus, effectively zooming out the canvas and preserving the page layout.

Simply call `this.resizeCanvas(this.$canvas.height, this.$canvas.width)` inside the `image.onload` method after the code to render text in the canvas.

 `height /= 2` is a shorthand used for `height = height / 2`. This is applicable for other arithmetic operators, such as +, −, *, and %.

Summary

Good work! You have built a Meme Creator that will now convert your images into memes. More importantly, you have a great development environment that will make app development with JavaScript even easier. Let's review the things you have learned in this chapter:

- A short introduction to the flexbox layout system in CSS
- An introduction to JavaScript modules
- Module bundling with Webpack
- Production optimizations to improve performance for users
- Using HTML5 canvas with JavaScript to draw graphics on a website

We learned quite a lot in this chapter. Especially about Webpack. It might seem a little overwhelming, but it is very useful in the long run. In the next chapter, we are going to see how to write modular code and reuse it across the application, which is now possible due to Webpack.

3
Event Registration App

Hopefully, you had a lot of fun creating memes and sharing them with your friends! You successfully built a Meme Creator in the previous project using HTML5 canvas. You also used flexbox to design the page layout and learned a few things regarding ES6 modules.

The most important part of the previous chapter was the development environment we created with Webpack. It lets us develop applications faster with `HotModuleReplacement`, create an optimized production build with single file assets and reduced code size, and also hides the original source code from the user, while we can use source maps to debug the original code.

Now that we have module support, we can use it to create modular functions, which will allow us to write reusable code that can be used across different parts of the project or can also be used with a different project. In this chapter, you are going to build an Event Registration app while learning the following concepts:

- Writing ES6 modules
- Form validation with JavaScript
- Working with dynamic data (data loaded from the server)
- Making AJAX requests using fetch
- Working with asynchronous functions using Promises
- Creating charts using Chart.js

Event - JS meetup

Here is the scenario for our project:

You are organizing a JavaScript meetup in your locality. You have invited people from schools, colleges, and offices, who are all interested in JavaScript. You need to create a website for attendees to register for the event. The website should have the following functionalities:

- A form to help users register for the event
- A page that shows statistics on the number of users interested in the event as a chart
- An about page with event details and the location of the event embedded as a Google Map

Also, most of the people will be using mobile phones to register for the event. So, the application should be fully responsive.

This is how the app should look on mobiles:

Initial project setup

To get started with the project, open up the starter files for Chapter 3 in VSCode. Create a .env file with the values from the .env.example file. Assign the following values to each environment variable:

- NODE_ENV=dev: Should be set to production when generating a build.
- SERVER_URL=http://localhost:3000: We will soon have a server running in this URL.
- GMAP_KEY: We are going to use the Google Maps API in this project. You need to generate your unique API key to use Google Maps. See: https://developers.google.com/maps/documentation/javascript/get-api-key to generate your API key and add the key to this environment variable.

Earlier in Chapter 2, *Building a Meme Creator*, I mentioned that you cannot access your JavaScript variables inside HTML when the modules are bundled with Webpack. In Chapter 1, *Building a ToDo List*, we used the HTML attribute to call a JavaScript function. This might look useful, but it will also expose our object structure to users (I'm referring to other developers visiting your page). Users can get a clear idea of how the ToDoClass class is structured by inspecting the object using Chrome DevTools. This should be prevented while building large-scale applications. Hence, Webpack does not allow variables to be present in the global scope.

Some plugins will need variables or objects to be present in the global scope (like the Google Maps API we are going to use). For this purpose, Webpack provides an option to expose some selected objects as libraries to the global scope (inside HTML). See the webpack.config.js file in the starter files. In the output section, I have added library: 'bundle', which means if we add the export keyword to any function, variable or object, they will be accessible inside the bundle object in the global scope. We will see how to use it while adding Google Maps to our app.

Now that we have the environment variables ready, open up the terminal in the project root folder and run npm install to install all the dependencies. Once the dependencies are installed, hit npm run watch in the terminal to start the Webpack dev server. You can now see the page in the localhost URL printed by Webpack in the console (http://localhost:8080/). Take a look at all the pages.

Adding styles to the page

At the moment, the page is responsive, since it is built with Bootstrap. However, we still need to add a few style changes to the form. It is currently very large on desktop screens. Also, we need to align the title to the center of the page. Let's add styles for the index.html page.

To align the form and its title to the center of the page, in the styles.css file (src/css/styles.css), add the following code (make sure the Webpack dev server is running):

```
.form-area {
  display: flex;
  flex-direction: column;
  align-items: center;
  justify-content: center;
}
```

The styles will be reflected immediately on the page, since HotModuleReplacement is enabled in Webpack (no more reloading!). Now, add some margin to the title and set a minimum width for the form:

```
.title {
  margin: 20px;
}
.form-group {
  min-width: 500px;
}
```

Now the form will have a minimum width of 500px. However, we are facing another problem! Since the form will always have 500px, it will go out of the screen on mobile devices (mobile users are our primary audience). We need to use media queries to overcome this problem. Media queries allow us to add CSS depending on the type of medium the page is viewed on. In our case, we need to change min-width on mobiles. To query mobile devices, add the following style below the previous styles:

```
@media only screen and (max-width: 736px) {
  .form-group {
    min-width: 90vw;
  }
}
```

This will check whether the device width is less than 736px (usually, mobiles fall under this category), and then add min-width of 90vw. vw stands for the viewport width. 90vw means 90% of the size of the width of the viewport (here, the viewport is the screen).

More information on using media queries can be found on this w3schools page: https://www.w3schools.com/css/css_rwd_mediaqueries.asp.

I have used a loading indicator image on the index.html and status.html pages. To specify a size for the image without breaking its original aspect ratio, use max-width and max-height as follows:

```
.loading-indicator {
  max-height: 50px;
  max-width: 50px;
}
```

See the status page. The loading indicator size will be reduced. We have added the necessary styles for our application. Now, it's time to make it work using JavaScript.

Validating and submitting the form using JavaScript

HTML Forms are the most important part of web applications, where user input is recorded. In our JS Meetup app, we got a nice looking form built with the help of Bootstrap. Let's explore what the form contains using the index.html file. The form contains four compulsory fields:

- **Name**
- **Email Address**
- **Phone Number**
- **Age**

And it also contains three optional fields (two of whose values are preselected):

- The user's profession
- His experience level in JavaScript
- Comments on what he expects to learn from this event

Since profession and experience level options are preselected with a default value, they aren't marked as compulsory to the user. But, during validation, we need to consider them as compulsory fields. Only the comments field is optional.

Here's how our form should work:

- The user fills up all the form details and clicks **Submit**
- The form details will be validated and if any required fields are missing, it will highlight the fields with a red border
- If the form values are valid, it will then proceed to submit the form to the server
- Once the form is submitted, the user will receive a notification that the form has been submitted successfully and the form entries will be cleared

JavaScript was initially used as a language for doing form validation in HTML. Over the course of time, it has evolved into a full-fledged web application development language. Web applications built with JavaScript make a lot of requests to the server to provide dynamic data to the user. Such network requests are always asynchronous and need to be handled properly.

HTML forms

Before we implement our form validation logic, let's look into the normal workings of the form. Click **Submit** in the current form. You should get a blank page with a message saying **Cannot POST /register**. That is Webpack dev server's message saying there are no routes configured for /register with the POST method. This is because, in index.html, the form is created with the following attributes:

```
<form action="/register" method="post" id="registrationForm">
```

This means the form's action when the **Submit** button is clicked to send data to the /register page with the POST method. While making network requests, GET and POST are two commonly used HTTP methods or verbs. The GET method cannot have a request body, so all the data is transmitted via URL as query parameters. However, the POST method can have a request body, where data can be sent as form data or a JSON object.

 There are different HTTP methods used for communicating with the server. Check out the following REST API Tutorial page for more information on HTTP methods: http://www.restapitutorial.com/lessons/httpmethods.html.

Currently, the form sends data in the form of form data using the POST method. In your index.html file, change the form method attribute to get and reload the page (the Webpack dev server does not automatically reload changes to HTML files). Now, click submit. You should see a similar blank page, but the form details are now being sent on the URL itself. The URL will now look as follows:

```
http://localhost:8080/register?username=&email=&phone=&age=&profession=scho
ol&experience=1&comment=
```

All the fields are empty except profession and experience, since they are preselected. The form values are added at the end of the route /register, followed by a ? symbol, which specifies the next text is the query parameter and the form values are separated using the & symbol. Since a GET request sends data in the URL itself, it is not suitable for sending confidential data, such as login details or the user details that we are going to send in this form. Hence, the POST method is chosen to do a form submit. Change the method to post in your index.html file.

Let's see how to inspect data that is sent using the POST request. Open Chrome DevTools and select the **Network** tab. Now type in some details in your form and click **submit**. You should see a new entry in your network requests list with the name register. If you click on it, it will open a new panel with the request details. The request data will be present in the headers tab in the Form Data section. Refer to the following screenshot:

Chrome DevTools has a lot of tools for working with network requests. We are only using it to inspect our sent data. But there is a lot more stuff you can do with it. As per the preceding image, you can see the form values I have typed in my form in the form data section in the **Headers** tab.

 Visit the following Google Developers page: `https://developers.google.com/web/tools/chrome-devtools/` to learn more on using Chrome DevTools.

Now you have a good idea of how submitting a form works. We do not have any pages created in the `/register` route and submitting a form by redirecting it to a separate page is no longer a good user experience (we are in the era of **Single-Page Applications (SPAs)**). Taking this into account, I have created a small Node.js server app, which can receive form requests. We are going to disable the default form submit action and will be submitting the form with JavaScript as an AJAX request.

Reading form data in JavaScript

Time to code! Keep Webpack dev server running with the `npm run watch` command (the `NODE_ENV` variable should be `dev`). Open the project folder in VSCode and open the `home.js` file from the `src/js/` directory. I have already added a reference to `dist/home.js` in the `index.html` file. I would have also added code to import the `general.js` file in `home.js`. Now, add the following code below the import statement:

```
class Home {
  constructor() {

  }

}

window.addEventListener("load", () => {
 new Home();
});
```

This will create a new class `Home` and will create a new instance of it when the page has completed loading. We need not assign the instance object to any variables because we are not going to use it inside the HTML file like we did in the ToDo list app. Everything will be handled from JavaScript itself.

Our first step is to create a reference to all the input fields in the form and the form itself. This includes the form itself and the loading indicator that is currently hidden in the page using the `.hidden` Bootstrap class. Add the following code to the class's constructor:

```
this.$form = document.querySelector('#registrationForm');
this.$username = document.querySelector('#username');
this.$email = document.querySelector('#email');
this.$phone = document.querySelector('#phone');
this.$age = document.querySelector('#age');
this.$profession = document.querySelector('#profession');
this.$experience = document.querySelector('#experience');
this.$comment = document.querySelector('#comment');
this.$submit = document.querySelector('#submit');
this.$loadingIndicator = document.querySelector('#loadingIndicator');
```

As I mentioned while building the Meme Creator, it is best to store references to DOM elements in variables prefixed with the $ symbol. Now, we can easily identify variables having references to DOM elements from other variables. This is purely for development efficiency and is not a strict rule you need to follow. In the preceding code, for experience radio buttons, the reference of only the first radio button is stored. This is for resetting the radio buttons; to read the value of the selected radio buttons, a different method needs to be used.

We can now access all the DOM elements within our `Home` class. The one event that is going to trigger the entire form validation process is when the form is submitted. The form submit event happens when a DOM element with the attribute `type="submit"` inside the `<form>` element is clicked. In our case, the `<button>` element contains this attribute and is referenced as the `$submit` variable. Even though `$submit` triggers the submit event, the event belongs to the entire form, that is, `$form` variable. Hence, we need to add an event listener to `this.$form` in our class.

We are only going to have a single event listener. So, just add the following code to the constructor after the preceding variables are declared:

```
this.$form.addEventListener('submit', event => {
  this.onFormSubmit(event);
});
```

This will attach an event listener to the form and will call the `onFormSubmit()` method of the class when the form is submitted with the form submit event as its parameter. So, let's create the `onFormSubmit()` method inside our `Home` class:

```
onFormSubmit(event) {
  event.preventDefault();
}
```

`event.preventDefault()` will prevent the default event action from happening. In our case, it will prevent the submission of the form. Open the page in Chrome (`http://localhost:8080/`) and try clicking **Submit** now. If no action occurs, then great! Our JavaScript code is blocking the form from being submitted.

We can use this function for initiating form validation. The first step in form validation is to read the values of all the input elements in the form. Create a new method `getFormValues()` inside the `Home` class, which will return the values of form fields as a JSON object:

```
getFormValues() {
  return {
    username: this.$username.value,
    email: this.$email.value,
    phone: this.$phone.value,
    age: this.$age.value,
    profession: this.$profession.value,
    experience:
parseInt(document.querySelector('input[name="experience"]:checked').value),
    comment: this.$comment.value,
  };
}
```

See how I used `document.querySelector()` to read the value of the checked radio button? The function is self-explanatory itself. I have added `parseInt()`, since the value will be returned as a string and needs to be converted to Int for validation purposes. Create a variable inside the `onFormSubmit()` method to store the values of all the fields in the form. Your `onFormSubmit()` method will now look as follows:

```
onFormSubmit(event) {
  event.preventDefault();
  const formValues = this.getFormValues();
}
```

Try printing the `formValues` variable in the Chrome DevTools console using `console.log(formValues)`. You should see all the fields with their respective values in a JSON object. Now that we have the required values, our next step is to validate the data.

In our JS Meetup app, we only have a single form. But in larger applications, you might have more than one form in different parts of the application that do the same thing. However, due to design purposes, the forms will have different HTML classes and IDs but the form values will remain the same. In such cases, the validation logic can be reused across the app. This is a perfect opportunity to build your first reusable JavaScript module.

Form validation module

By using Webpack, we now have the ability to create separate modules and import them in JavaScript. However, we need some kind of approach to organizing our created modules. As the size of the application grows, you might have tens or even hundreds of modules. Organizing them in such a way that they can be easily identified will greatly help your team, as they will be able to easily find a module when needed instead of recreating a module with the same functionality.

In our application, let's create a new folder inside the `src/js/` directory called `services`. This directory will contain all the reusable modules. Now, inside the `services` directory, create another directory called `formValidation`, inside which we will create the `validateRegistrationForm.js` file. Your project `src/js/` directory will now look as follows:

```
.
├── about.js
├── general.js
├── home.js
├── services
│    └── formValidation
│         └── validateRegistrationForm.js
└── status.js
```

Now, imagine yourself as a different developer who is looking at this code for the first time. Inside the `js` directory, there is another directory called `services`. Inside that, `formValidation` is available as a service. You now know that there is a service for form validation. If you look inside this directory, it will have the `validateRegistrationForm.js` file, which informs you of the purpose of this module just by its filename.

If you want to create a validation module for a login form (just an imaginary scenario), simply create another file inside the `formValidation` directory with the name `validateLoginForm.js`. This way, your code will be easily maintainable and scalable by reusing all the modules to a maximum.

Don't worry about long filenames! Maintainable code is more important, but if the filename is long it makes it easy to understand the purpose of that file. But if you are working in a team, stick to the rules of the lint tools used by your team.

Time to build the module! In the `validateRegistrationForm.js` file you just created, add the following code:

```
export default function validateRegistrationForm(formValues) {
}
```

Having the same name for the module's file and its default exported item will make import statements look easier to understand. You will see that when you import this module into your `home.js` file. The preceding function will accept the `formValues` (which we read from the form in the previous section) JSON object as the parameter.

Before we write this function, we need to set up validation logic for each of the input fields as separate functions. These functions will return true when the input satisfies the validation criteria. Let's start with validating the username. Below `validateRegistrationForm()`, create a new function `validateUserName()`, as follows:

```
function validateUserName(name) {
  return name.length > 3 ? true: false;
}
```

We use this function to check whether the username is at least 3 characters long. We use the conditional operator to return `true` if the length is greater than 3 and `false` if it is smaller.

We have used conditional operator `()?:` once before in the ToDo list app. If you are still having problems understanding this operator, visit the following MDN page: `https://developer.mozilla.org/en/docs/Web/JavaScript/Reference/Operators/Conditional_Operator`.

We can make this function event shorter:

```
function validateUserName(name) {
  return name.length > 3;
}
```

This way, JavaScript will automatically evaluate whether the length is greater than three and assign true or false based on the result. Now, to validate the email address, we need to use regular expressions. We used a regular expression to change the mime type of the image in the Meme Creator app. This time, we'll look into how regular expressions work.

Working with regular expressions in JavaScript

Regular expressions (RegExp) are basically a definition of a pattern (such as a sequence of characters, numbers, and so on) that can be searched within other text. For example, say you need to find all the words in a paragraph that start with the letter *a*. Then, in JavaScript, you define the pattern as:

```
const pattern = /^a+/
```

Regular expressions are always defined inside / /. In the preceding code snippet, we have the following:

- ^ means in the beginning of
- + means having at least one

This regular expression will match strings that start with the letter *a*. You can test these statements in: https://jsfiddle.net/. To test a string with this regular expression, do the following:

```
pattern.test('alpha') // this will return true
pattern.test('beta') // this will return false
```

To validate the email address, use the following function, which contains a regular expression to validate an email address:

```
function validateEmail(email) {
  const emailRegex = /^(([^<>()\[\]\\.,;:\s@"]+(\.[^<>()\
[\]\\.,;:\s@"]+)*)|(".+"))@((\[[0-9]{1,3}\.[0-9]{1,3}\.[0-9]{1,3}\.[0-9]{1,
3}])|(([a-zA-Z\-0-9]+\.)+[a-zA-Z]{2,}))$/;
  return emailRegex.test(email);
}
```

Don't be overwhelmed by the RegExp, it is something commonly available on the internet. Whenever you need regular expressions for common formats, such as an email address or phone number, you can find them on the internet. To validate a mobile number, do the following:

```
function validatePhone(phone) {
  const phoneRegex = /^\(?([0-9]{3})\)?[-. ]?([0-9]{3})[-. ]?([0-9]{4})$/;
  return phoneRegex.test(phone);
}
```

This validates whether the phone number is in the format of XXX-XXX-XXXX (this format is given in the placeholder of the form).

You will have to write your own regular expressions if your requirement is very specific. At that time, refer to the following page: `https://developer.mozilla.org/en/docs/Web/JavaScript/Guide/Regular_Expressions`.

Email address is validated by default in the form, since the email input field's type attribute is set to email. However, it is necessary to validate it in JavaScript, as not all browsers might support this attribute and the HTML can be easily edited from the Chrome DevTools. The same applies to other fields.

To validate age, let's assume the user should be in the age group 10-25 years:

```
function validateAge(age) {
    return age >= 10 && age <= 25;
}
```

To validate profession, the accepted values for profession are `school`, `college`, `trainee`, and `employee`. They are the values of the `<option>` element of the profession selection field in your `index.html` file. To validate `profession`, do the following:

```
function validateProfession(profession) {
    const acceptedValues = ['school','college','trainee','employee'];
    return acceptedValues.indexOf(profession) > -1;
}
```

JavaScript arrays have a method called `indexOf()`. It accepts an array element as a parameter and returns the index of the element within the array. However, if the element is not present in the array, it returns -1. We can use this function to check whether the value of profession is one of the accepted values by finding its index within the array and checking whether the index is greater than -1.

Finally, to validate experience, the values of the experience radio buttons are 1, 2, and 3. So, experience should be a number between 0-4:

```
function validateExperience(experience) {
    return experience > 0 && experience < 4;
}
```

Since the comments field is optional, we do not need to have validation logic for this field. Now, inside the `validateRegistrationForm()` function which we created initially, add the following code:

```
export default function validateRegistrationForm(formValues) {

    const result = {
        username: validateUserName(formValues.username),
```

```
      email: validateEmail(formValues.email),
      phone: validatePhone(formValues.phone),
      age: validateAge(formValues.age),
      profession: validateProfession(formValues.profession),
      experience: validateExperience(formValues.experience),
   };

}
```

The result object now contains the validation status (true/false) of each of the form inputs. Check whether the form is valid overall. The form is valid only if all the properties of the result object is true. To check whether all the properties of the result object are true, we need to use a for/in loop.

The for/in loop iterates over the properties of the object. Since all the properties of the result object need to be true, create a variable isValid with the initial value true. Now, iterate over all the properties of the result object and simply AND (&&) the values with the isValid variable:

```
let field, isValid = true;
for(field in result) {
   isValid = isValid && result[field];
}
```

Generally, you access the property of an object using the dot notation (.). However, since we are using the for/in loop, the property name is stored in the variable field. In this case, we need to access the property using the bracket notation result[field] if field contains the value age; this is equivalent to result.age in dot notation.

The isValid variable will be only true when all the properties of the result object are true. This way, we have both the form's validation status and the individual field's status. The validateRegistrationForm() function will return both the isValid variable and the result object as properties of another object:

```
export default function validateRegistrationForm(formValues) {
   ...
   ...
   return { isValid, result };
}
```

We are using the ES6 feature object literal property value shorthand here. Our form validation module is ready! We can import this module into our home.js file and use it with the Event Registration app.

In your `home.js` file, before the class `Home`, add the following line:

```
import validateRegistrationForm from
'./services/formValidation/validateRegistrationForm';
```

Then, inside the class `Home` in the `onFormSubmit()` method, add the following code:

```
onFormSubmit(event) {
  event.preventDefault();

  const formValues = this.getFormValues();
  const formStatus = validateRegistrationForm(formValues);

  if(formStatus.isValid) {
    this.clearErrors();
    this.submitForm(formValues);
  } else {
    this.clearErrors();
    this.highlightErrors(formStatus.result);
  }
}
```

The preceding code does the following:

- It calls the `validateRegistrationForm()` module we created before with `formValues` as its parameter and stores the returned value in the `formStatus` object.
- First, it checks whether the entire form is valid using the value of `formStatus.isValid`.
- If it is `true`, it calls a method `clearErrors()` to clear all the error highlights in the UI (our HTML form) and then calls another method `submitForm()` to submit the form.
- If it is `false` (the form is not valid), it calls the `clearErrors()` method to clear the form and then calls the `highlightErrors()` method with `formStatus.result`, which contains validation details of individual fields as a parameter to highlight the fields that have errors.

We need to create the methods that are being called in the preceding code inside the `Home` class, since they are methods of the `Home` class. The working of the `clearErrors()` and `highlightErrors()` methods are straightforward. `clearErrors` simply removes the `.has-error` class from the parent `<div>` of the input field. While `highlightError` adds the `.has-error` class to the parent `<div>` if the input field fails validation (if the result of the field is `false`).

The code for the `clearErrors()` method is as follows:

```
clearErrors() {
  this.$username.parentElement.classList.remove('has-error');
  this.$phone.parentElement.classList.remove('has-error');
  this.$email.parentElement.classList.remove('has-error');
  this.$age.parentElement.classList.remove('has-error');
  this.$profession.parentElement.classList.remove('has-error');
  this.$experience.parentElement.classList.remove('has-error');
}
```

The code for the `highlightErrors()` method is as follows:

```
highlightErrors(result) {
  if(!result.username) {
    this.$username.parentElement.classList.add('has-error');
  }
  if(!result.phone) {
    this.$phone.parentElement.classList.add('has-error');
  }
  if(!result.email) {
    this.$email.parentElement.classList.add('has-error');
  }
  if(!result.age) {
    this.$age.parentElement.classList.add('has-error');
  }
  if(!result.profession) {
    this.$profession.parentElement.classList.add('has-error');
  }
  if(!result.experience) {
    this.$experience.parentElement.classList.add('has-error');
  }
}
```

For now, leave the `submitForm()` method empty:

```
submitForm(formValues) {
}
```

Open the form on your browser (hopefully you left the Webpack dev server running). Try entering some values in the input fields and click **Submit**. If you entered valid input values, it shouldn't perform any action. If you entered invalid input entries (as per our validation logic), the input field will be highlighted with a red border, since we added the `.has-error` Bootstrap class to the field's parent element. If you correct the field with a valid value and click **submit** again, the error should disappear, since we used the `clearErrors()` method to clear all the old error highlighting.

Submitting the form using AJAX

We are now in the second half of the form section, submitting the form. We have disabled the default submit behavior of our form and we now need to implement an AJAX form to submit logic.

AJAX is the abbreviation for **Asynchronous JavaScript And XML (AJAX)**. It is not a programming tool, but it is a concept by which you make a network request, get data from the server, and update certain parts of your website without having to reload the entire page.

 The name Asynchronous JavaScript And XML might sound confusing but, initially, XML was widely used to exchange data with the server. We can also use JSON/normal text to exchange data with the server.

For submitting the form to the server, I have created a small Node.js server (built using express framework) that pretends to save your form details and returns a success message. The server is available in `Chapter03` folder of the code files. To start the server, simply run `npm install` inside the server's directory, followed by the `npm start` command. This will start the server in the `http://localhost:3000/` URL. If you open this URL in the browser, you will see a blank page with the message **Cannot GET /**; this means the server is running properly.

The server has two API endpoints, one of which we need to communicate with to send the details of the user. This is how the registration API endpoint works:

```
Route: /registration,
Method: POST,
Body: the form data in JSON format
{
  "username":"Test User",
  "email":"mail@test.com",
  "phone":"123-456-7890",
  "age":"16",
  "profession":"school",
  "experience":"1",
  "comment":"Some comment from user"
}
If registration is success:
status code: 200
response: { "message": "Test User is Registered Successfully" }
```

In a real-world JavaScript application, you will have to work with a lot of network requests like this. Most of your user actions will trigger an API call which needs to be processed by the server. In our scenario, we need to call the preceding API to register the user.

Let's strategize how the API call should work:

- As the name suggests, this event is going to be asynchronous. We need to use a new concept of ES6, called Promises, to handle this API call.
- We are going to have another API call in the next section. It's better to create the API call as a module-like form validation module.
- We must validate whether the registration is successful in the server using the server's response.
- Since the whole API call will take some time, we should also show a loading indicator to the user during the process.
- Finally, if the registration is successful, we should immediately notify the user and clear the form.

Making network requests in JavaScript

JavaScript has XMLHttpRequest for making AJAX network requests. A new specification called fetch is introduced in ES6, which makes working with network requests more modern and efficient with Promises support. Other than these two methods, jQuery has the $.ajax() method, which is widely used for making network requests. Axios.js is another npm package that is also widely used for making network requests.

We will use fetch in our application for making network requests.

 Fetch does not work with Internet Explorer and requires polyfills. Check out: https://caniuse.com/ for the browser compatibility of any new HTML/CSS/Javascript components you'd like to use.

What is a Promise?

You'll probably be wondering by now what it is that I'm calling a Promise? Well, a Promise, as it sounds, is a Promise made by JavaScript that the asynchronous function will complete execution at some point.

In the previous chapter, we came across an asynchronous event: reading the contents of a file using `FileReader`. This is how `FileReader` worked:

- It starts reading the file. Since reading is an asynchronous event, other JavaScript code will continue execution while reading is still happening.

You might be wondering, *what if I need to execute some code only after the event is complete?* This is how `FileReader` handles it:

- Once the reading is complete, `FileReader` fires a `load` event
- It also has an `onload()` method that listens for the `load` event and, when the `load` event is triggered, the `onload()` method will start executing
- So, we need to put our required code inside the `onload()` method and it will execute only after `FileReader` has completed reading the file contents

This might look like an easier way to handle asynchronous events, but imagine if there are multiple asynchronous events that need to happen one after another! How many events would you have to fire and how many event listeners would you need to keep track of? This will result in code that is very difficult to understand. Also, event listeners in JavaScript are expensive resources (they consume a lot of memory) and they must be minimized as much as possible.

Callback functions are used a lot to handle asynchronous events. But if you have a lot of asynchronous functions happening one after another, your code will look something like this:

```
asyncOne('one', () => {
  ...
  asyncTwo('two', () => {
    ...
    asyncThree('three', () => {
      ...
      asyncFour('four', () => {
      });
    });
  });
});
```

After writing lot of callbacks, your closing brackets will be arranged like a pyramid. This is called callback hell. Callback hell is messy and should be avoided when building applications. So, callbacks are not useful here.

Enter Promises, a new way to deal with asynchronous events. This is how a JavaScript `Promise` works:

```
new Promise((resolve, reject) => {
  // Some asynchronous logic
  resolve(5);
});
```

A `Promise` constructor creates a function with two parameters, resolve and reject, which are functions. Then, `Promise` will return the value only when resolve or reject is called. Resolve is called when the asynchronous code is executed successfully, and reject is called when an error occurs. Here, `Promise` returns a value, 5, when the asynchronous logic is executed.

Say you have a function called `theAsyncCode()`, which does some asynchronous stuff. You also have another function `onlyAfterAsync()` that needs to run strictly only after `theAsyncCode()` and uses the value returned by `theAsyncCode()`.

Here's how you deal with these two functions with Promises:

```
function theAsyncCode() {
  return new Promise((resolve, reject) => {
    console.log('The Async Code executed!');
    resolve(5);
  });
}
```

First, `theAsyncCode()` should return a `Promise` instead of a value. Your asynchronous code should be written inside that `Promise`. Then, you write the `onlyAfterAsync()` function:

```
function onlyAfterAsync(result) {
  console.log('Now onlyAfterAsync is executing...');
  console.log(`Final result of execution - ${result}`);
}
```

To execute the preceding functions one after another, we need to chain them using the `Promise.then().catch()` statements. Here, `Promise` is returned by the `theAsyncCode()` function. Hence, the code should be:

```
theAsyncCode()
.then(result => onlyAfterAsync(result))
.catch(error => console.error(error))
```

When `theAsyncCode()` executes `resolve(5)`, the `then` method is automatically called with the resolved value as its parameter. We can now execute the `onlyAfterAsync()` method inside the `then` method. If `theAsyncCode()` executes `reject('an error')` instead of `resolve(5)`, it will trigger the `catch` method instead of `then`.

If you have another function, `theAsyncCode2()`, which uses the data returned by `theAsyncCode()`, it should be executed before the `onlyAfterAsync()` function:

```
function theAsyncCode2(data) {
  return new Promise((resolve, reject) => {
    console.log('The Async Code 2 executed');
    resolve(data);
  });
}
```

You just need to update your `.then().catch()` chain, such that:

```
theAsyncCode()
.then(data => theAsyncCode2(data))
.then(result => onlyAfterAsync(result))
.catch(error => console.error(error));
```

This way, all three functions will be executed one after another. If either `theAsyncCode()` or `theAsyncCode2()` returns with `reject()`, then the `catch` statement will be called.

If we only need to call a function with the resolved value of the previous function in the chain as the parameter, we can further simplify the chain as:

```
theAsyncCode()
.then(theAsyncCode2)
.then(onlyAfterAsync)
.catch(console.error);
```

This will give the same result. I have set up a small JS fiddle at: `https://jsfiddle.net/jjq60Ly6/4/`, where you can experience the working of Promises in action. Visit the JS fiddle, open the Chrome DevTools console, and click **Run** at the top-left of the JS fiddle page. You should see the `console.log` statements printed from the three functions in order. Feel free to edit the fiddle and experiment with the Promises.

Shortly after finishing this chapter, ES8 was announced, which confirmed the `async` functions to be part of the JavaScript language. ES8's `async` and `await` keywords provide an even simpler way to resolve Promises instead of the `.then().catch()` chain we used in ES6. To learn using the `async` functions, go to the following MDN page: `https://developer.mozilla.org/en-US/docs/Web/JavaScript/Reference/Statements/async_function`.

Creating the API call module

We will use a POST API call to register our users. However, in the status section of the app, we need to use a GET request to show the statistic data of the people interested in the event. So, we are going to build a generic API call module.

To create the API call module, inside the `services` directory, create another directory called `api` and, inside it, create `apiCall.js`. The structure of your `services` directory should be as follows:

```
.
├── api
│   └── apiCall.js
└── formValidation
    └── validateRegistrationForm.js
```

Inside `apiCall.js file`, create the following function:

```
export default function apiCall(route, body = {}, method='GET') {
}
```

In the preceding function, route is a required parameter, while body and method have their default values defined. This means they are optional. If you call the function with only one argument, the other two parameters will use their default values:

```
apiCall('/registration) // values of body = {} and method = 'GET'
```

If you call the function with all three parameters, it will work like a normal function:

```
apiCall('/registration', {'a': 5}, 'POST'); // values of body = {'a': 5}
and method = 'POST'
```

Default parameters are also introduced only in ES6. We are using default parameters because a GET request does not require a body attribute. It only sends the data as query parameters in the URL.

We have already seen the workings of GET and POST requests in action in the default form's **Submit** section. Let's construct an apiCall function that can do both GET and POST requests:

Inside the apiCall function, create a new Promise object with the name request:

```
export default function apiCall(route, body = {}, method='GET') {

  const request = new Promise((resolve, reject) => {
    // Code for fetch will be written here
  });

}
```

The fetch API accepts two parameters as input and returns Promise, which resolves when the network request is complete. The first parameter is the request URL and the second parameter contains an object with information regarding the request, such as headers, cors, method, body, and so on.

Constructing the request details

Write the following code inside the request Promise. First, since we are working with JSON data, we need to create a header with the content type application/json. We can use the Headers constructor for this purpose:

```
const headers = new Headers({
  'Content-Type': 'application/json',
});
```

Now, using the headers created earlier and the method variable from the parameter, we create the requestDetails object:

```
const requestDetails = {
  method,
  mode: 'cors',
  headers,
};
```

Note that I have included mode: 'cors' in requestDetails. **Cross-Origin Resource Sharing (CORS)** allows servers to do cross-domain data transfers securely. Imagine you have a website running in www.mysite.org. You need to make an API call (network request) to another server running in www.anothersite.org.

Then, it is a cross-origin request. To make a cross-origin request, the server in www.anothersite.org must have the Access-Control-Allow-Origin headers set to allow www.mysite.org. Otherwise, browsers will block the cross-origin request to prevent unauthorized access to another server. The request from www.mysite.org should also include mode: 'cors' in its request details.

In our Event Registration app, the Webpack dev server is running in http://localhost:8080/, while the Node.js server is running in http://localhost:3000/. Hence, it is a cross-origin request. I have already enabled Access-Control-Allow-Origin and set Access-Control-Allow-Headers so that it won't cause any problems with the apiCall function.

 Detailed information on CORS requests can be found in the following MDN page: https://developer.mozilla.org/en/docs/Web/HTTP/Access_control_CORS.

Our requestDetails object should also include a body of the request. However, the body should only be included for the POST request. Hence, it can be written below the requestDetails object declaration, as follows:

```
if(method !== 'GET') requestDetails.body = JSON.stringify(body);
```

This will add the body property for the POST requests. To do the fetch request, we need to construct the request URL. We have already set the environment variable SERVER_URL=http://localhost:3000, which Webpack will transform into a global variable SERVER_URL accessible everywhere inside the JavaScript code. The route is passed in the apiCall() function's parameter. The fetch request can be constructed as follows:

```
function handleErrors(response) {
  if(response.ok) {
    return response.json();
  } else {
    throw Error(response.statusText);
  }
}

fetch(`${SERVER_URL}/${route}`, requestDetails)
  .then(response => handleErrors(response))
  .then(data => resolve(data))
  .catch(err => reject(err));
```

Here's what the `handleErrors` function does. It will check whether the response returned by the server is successful (`response.ok`). If so, it will decode the response and return it (`response.json()`). Otherwise, it will throw an error.

We can further simplify the Promise chain using the method we discussed earlier:

```
fetch(`${SERVER_URL}/${route}`, requestDetails)
  .then(handleErrors)
  .then(resolve)
  .catch(reject);
```

Fetch has a small problem. It cannot handle timeouts by itself. Imagine the server facing a problem and being unable to return a request. In that scenario, the fetch will never resolve. To avoid this, we need to do a workaround. Below the `request` Promise, create another `Promise` called `timeout`:

```
const request = new Promise((resolve, reject) => {
....
});

const timeout = new Promise((request, reject) => {
  setTimeout(reject, timeoutDuration, `Request timed out!`);
});
```

Create a constant `timeoutDuration` on top of the `apiCall.js` file outside the `apicall()` function, as follows:

```
const timeoutDuration = 5000;
```

This constant is placed on top of the file so that we can easily change the timeout duration in future (easier code maintainability). `timeout` is a simple Promise that automatically rejects after a time of 5 seconds (from the `timeoutDuration` constant). I have created the server in a way that it responds after 3 seconds.

Now, JavaScript has a cool way to resolve multiple Promises, the `Promise.race()` method. As the name suggests, this will make two Promises run simultaneously and accept the value of the one that is resolved/rejected first. This way, if the server doesn't respond within 3 seconds, a timeout will happen in 5 seconds and `apiCall` will be rejected with a timeout! To do this, add the following code within the `apiCall()` function after the `request` and `timeout` Promises:

```
return new Promise((resolve, reject) => {
  Promise.race([request, timeout])
    .then(resolve)
    .catch(reject);
```

```
});
```

The `apiCall()` function as a whole returns a Promise which is the resolved value of either the `request` or `timeout` Promise (depends on which one of them is executed faster). That's it! Our `apiCall` module is now ready to be used within our Event Registration app.

 If you find the `apiCall` function difficult to understand and follow, read it again with the `apiCall.js` file from the `Chapter03` completed code files as reference. It will make the explanation much simpler.

 To learn Promises in detail with more examples, read the following Google Developers page: `https://developers.google.com/web/fundamentals/getting-started/primers/promises` and MDN page: `https://developer.mozilla.org/en/docs/Web/JavaScript/Reference/Global_Objects/Promise`.

Other network request methods

Follow these links to learn about other plugins/APIs to make network requests in JavaScript:

- jQuery, the `$.ajax()` method: `http://api.jquery.com/jquery.ajax/`
- `XMLHttpRequest`: `https://developer.mozilla.org/en/docs/Web/API/XMLHttpRequest`
- `Axios.js`: `https://github.com/mzabriskie/axios`

To make fetch work with Internet Explorer, read the following page on how to add `polyfill` for fetch: `https://github.com/github/fetch/`.

Back to the form

The first step to start submitting is to hide the submit button and replace it with a loading indicator. This way, the user can't accidentally click **Submit** twice. Also, the loading indicator serves as an indication that a process is happening in the background. In the `home.js` file, inside the `submitForm()` method, add the following code:

```
submitForm(formValues) {
  this.$submit.classList.add('hidden');
  this.$loadingIndicator.classList.remove('hidden');
}
```

This will hide the submit button and display the loading indicator. To make `apiCall`, we need to import the `apiCall` function and notify the user that the request has been completed. I have added a package called `toastr` in the `package.json` file. It should have been installed already when you ran the `npm install` command.

At the top of the `home.js` file, add the following import statements:

```
import apiCall from './services/api/apiCall';
import toastr from 'toastr';
import '../../node_modules/toastr/toastr.less';
```

This will import `toastr` and its styles file (`toastr.less`), along with the recently created `apiCall` module. Now, inside the `submitForm()` method, add the following code:

```
apiCall('registration', formValues, 'POST')
  .then(response => {
    this.$submit.classList.remove('hidden');
    this.$loadingIndicator.classList.add('hidden');
    toastr.success(response.message);
    this.resetForm(); // For clearing the form
  })
  .catch(() => {
    this.$submit.classList.remove('hidden');
    this.$loadingIndicator.classList.add('hidden');
    toastr.error('Error!');
  });
```

Since `apiCall()` returns a Promise, we are using a `Promise.then().catch()` chain here. When the registration is a success, `toastr` will show a success toast in the top-right corner of the page with the message sent by the server. If a problem occurs, it will simply show an error toast. Also, we need to clear the form using the `this.resetForm()` method. Add the `resetForm()` method inside the `Home` class with the following code:

```
resetForm() {
  this.$username.value = '';
  this.$email.value = '';
  this.$phone.value = '';
  this.$age.value = '';
  this.$profession.value = 'school';
  this.$experience.checked = true;
  this.$comment.value = '';
}
```

Go back to the Event Registration page in Chrome and try submitting the form. If all the values are valid, it should successfully submit the form with a success toast message and the form values will be reset to their initial values. In real-world applications, the server will send a confirmation mail to the user. However, server-side coding is beyond the scope of this book. But I would like to explain this a little in the next chapter.

Try turning off the Node.js server and submitting the form. It should throw an error. You have successfully completed building your Event Registration form while learning some advanced concepts in JavaScript. Now, let's move on to the second page of our application-- the status page, where we need to show a chart for registered user statistics.

Adding charts to the website using Chart.js

We just created a nice little registration form for our users. It's now time to work with the second section of our Event Registration app. The status page shows a chart for the number of people interested in the event based on experience, profession, and age. If you open the status page now, it should show a **data loading...** message with the loading indicator image. But I have built all the necessary components needed for this page in the status.html file. They are all currently hidden using Bootstrap's .hidden class.

Let's see what's present in the status.html file. Try removing the .hidden class from each of the following sections to see how they look in the web application.

First is the loading indicator section which is currently being displayed on the page:

```
<div id="loadingIndicator">
  <p>Data loading...</p>
  <image src="./src/assets/images/loading.gif" class="loading-
indicator"></image>
</div>
```

It is followed by a section containing an error message to be showed when the API call fails:

```
<div id="loadingError" class="hidden">
  <h3>Unable to load data...Try refreshing the page.</h3>
</div>
```

After the preceding sections, we have a tabs section which will provide the user with an option to switch between different charts. The code will look as follows:

```
<ul class="nav nav-tabs hidden" id="tabArea">
  <li role="presentation" class="active"><a href=""
id="experienceTab">Experience</a></li>
  <li role="presentation"><a href="" id="professionTab">Profession</a></li>
  <li role="presentation"><a href="" id="ageTab">Age</a></li>
</ul>
```

The tabs are nothing but an unordered list with the classes .nav and .nav-tabs, which are styled by Bootstrap into tabs. The tab sections are list items with the class .active to highlight a selected tab section (role="presentation" is used for accessibility options). Inside the list items, there are anchor tags with an empty href attribute.

Finally, we have our chart area with three canvas elements to display charts for the three different categories mentioned in the preceding tabs:

```
<div class="chart-area hidden" id="chartArea">
  <canvas id="experienceChart"></canvas>
  <canvas id="professionChart"></canvas>
  <canvas id="ageChart"></canvas>
</div>
```

As we saw in the previous chapter, canvas elements are best for displaying graphics on a web page, since editing the DOM elements is an expensive operation. Chart.js uses the canvas element to display the given data as a chart. Let's strategize how the status page should work:

- The loading indicator should be shown while the API call is made to fetch statistic data from the server
- If the data is retrieved successfully, the loading indicator should be hidden and the tabs section and chart area should become visible
- Only the canvas corresponding to the selected tab should be visible; other canvas elements should be hidden
- A pie chart should be added to the canvas using the Chart.js plugin
- If data retrieval fails, all the sections should be hidden and the error section should be shown

Alright! Let's get to work. Open the `status.js` file which I already added as a reference in `status.html`. Create a class `Status` with a reference to all the required DOM elements in its constructor, as follows:

```
class Status {
  constructor() {
    this.$experienceTab = document.querySelector('#experienceTab');
    this.$professionTab = document.querySelector('#professionTab');
    this.$ageTab = document.querySelector('#ageTab');

    this.$ageCanvas = document.querySelector('#ageChart');
    this.$professionCanvas = document.querySelector('#professionChart');
    this.$experienceCanvas = document.querySelector('#experienceChart');

    this.$loadingIndicator = document.querySelector('#loadingIndicator');
    this.$tabArea = document.querySelector('#tabArea');
    this.$chartArea = document.querySelector('#chartArea');

    this.$errorMessage = document.querySelector('#loadingError');

    this.statisticData; // variable to store data from the server
  }

}
```

I have also created a class variable `statisticData` which can be used for storing the data that will be retrieved from the API call. Also, add the code to create an instance for the class when the page loads:

```
window.addEventListener("load", () => {
  new Status();
});
```

The first step to our status page is to make a network request to the get required data from the server. I have created the following API endpoint in the Node.js server:

Route: /statistics,
Method: GET,
Server Response on Success:
status code: 200
response:
{"experience":[35,40,25],"profession":[30,40,20,10],"age":[30,60,10]}

The server will return the data containing the number of people who are interested based on their experience, profession, and age in a format suitable for use with Chart.js. Let's use the apiCall module we built before to make this network request. In your status.js file, first add the following import statement above the Status class:

```
import apiCall from './services/api/apiCall';
```

After that, add the following method inside the Status class:

```
loadData() {
  apiCall('statistics')
    .then(response => {
      this.statisticData = response;

      this.$loadingIndicator.classList.add('hidden');
      this.$tabArea.classList.remove('hidden');
      this.$chartArea.classList.remove('hidden');
    })
    .catch(() => {
      this.$loadingIndicator.classList.add('hidden');
      this.$errorMessage.classList.remove('hidden');
    });
}
```

This time, we can use the apiCall() function with only a single parameter, because we are making a GET request and we have already defined the default parameters of the apiCall() function as body = {} and method = 'GET'. This way, we don't have to specify the body and method parameters while making a GET request. Inside your constructor, add the this.loadData() method so that it will make the network request automatically when the page loads:

```
constructor() {
  ...
  this.loadData();
}
```

Now, look at the web page in Chrome. After three seconds, it should show the tabs. At the moment, clicking the tabs will only reload the page. We'll handle this after creating the charts.

Adding charts to the canvas elements

We have the required data in our class variable `statisticData`, with which the charts should be rendered. I have already added Chart.js to the project dependencies in the `package.json` file and it should have been installed when you executed the `npm install` command. Let's import Chart.js into our project by adding the following code at the top of the `status.js` file:

```
import Chart from 'chart.js';
```

 It is not compulsory to add the `import` statements only on top of the file. However, adding the `import` statements on top gives us a clear view of all the dependencies of the module in the current file.

Chart.js provides a constructor with which we can create a new chart. The `Chart` constructor has the following syntax:

```
new Chart($canvas, {type: 'pie', data});
```

The first parameter of the `Chart` constructor should be a reference to the canvas element and the second parameter is the JSON object with two properties:

- The `type` property should contain the type of graph that we need to use in our project. We need to use a pie chart in our project.
- The `data` property should contain the datasets needed to create the graph as an object in a format based on the type of graph. In our case, for the pie chart, the required format is specified in the Chart.js documentation on the following page: `http://www.chartjs.org/docs/latest/charts/doughnut.html`.

The data object will have the following format:

```
{
  datasets: [{
    data: [],
    backgroundColor: [],
    borderColor: [],
  }],
  labels: []
}
```

The data object has the following properties:

- A `datasets` property with an array of another object having the `data`, `backgroundColor`, and `borderColor` as arrays
- A `labels` property with an array of labels in the same order as that of the array of data

The created charts will automatically occupy the entire space provided by their parent element. Create the following functions inside the `Status` class to load `Chart` into the status page:

You can create a chart based on experience, as follows:

```
loadExperience() {
  const data = {
    datasets: [{
      data: this.statisticData.experience,
      backgroundColor:[
        'rgba(255, 99, 132, 0.6)',
        'rgba(54, 162, 235, 0.6)',
        'rgba(255, 206, 86, 0.6)',
      ],
      borderColor: [
        'white',
        'white',
        'white',
      ]
    }],
    labels: [
      'Beginner',
      'Intermediate',
      'Advanced'
    ]
  };
  new Chart(this.$experienceCanvas,{
    type: 'pie',
    data,
  });
}
```

You can create a chart based on profession, as follows:

```
loadProfession() {
  const data = {
    datasets: [{
      data: this.statisticData.profession,
      backgroundColor:[
```

```
        'rgba(255, 99, 132, 0.6)',
        'rgba(54, 162, 235, 0.6)',
        'rgba(255, 206, 86, 0.6)',
        'rgba(75, 192, 192, 0.6)',
      ],
      borderColor: [
        'white',
        'white',
        'white',
        'white',
      ]
    }],
    labels: [
      'School Students',
      'College Students',
      'Trainees',
      'Employees'
    ]
  };
  new Chart(this.$professionCanvas,{
    type: 'pie',
    data,
  });
}
```

You can create a chart based on age, as follows:

```
loadAge() {
  const data = {
    datasets: [{
      data: this.statisticData.age,
      backgroundColor:[
        'rgba(255, 99, 132, 0.6)',
        'rgba(54, 162, 235, 0.6)',
        'rgba(255, 206, 86, 0.6)',
      ],
      borderColor: [
        'white',
        'white',
        'white',
      ]
    }],
    labels: [
      '10-15 years',
      '15-20 years',
      '20-25 years'
    ]
  };
```

```
   new Chart(this.$ageCanvas,{
      type: 'pie',
      data,
   });
}
```

These functions should be called when the data is loaded into the `statisticData` variable. So, the best place to call them is after the API call has been a success. In the `loadData()` method, add the following code, as shown:

```
loadData() {
   apiCall('statistics')
      .then(response => {
         ...
         this.loadAge();
         this.loadExperience();
         this.loadProfession();
      })
   ...
}
```

Now, open the status page in Chrome. You should see three charts rendered on the page. The charts have occupied the entire width of their parent element. To reduce their size, add the following style to your `styles.css` file:

```
.chart-area {
   margin: 25px;
   max-width: 600px;
}
```

This should reduce the size of the charts. The best part about Chart.js is that it is responsive by default. Try resizing the page in Chrome's responsive design mode. You should see the charts being resized when the height and width of the page are changed. We have now added three charts on our status page.

For our final step, we need the tabs to toggle the appearance of the chart so that only one chart is visible at a time.

Setting up tab sections

The tabs should work such that only one of the charts is visible at a given time. Also, the selected tab should be marked active using the .active class. A simple solution to this problem is hiding all the charts, removing .active from all the tab items, and then adding .active only to the clicked tab item and displaying the required chart. This way, we can easily get the required tab functionality.

First, create a method inside the Status class to clear the selected tabs and hide all the charts:

```
hideCharts() {
    this.$experienceTab.parentElement.classList.remove('active');
    this.$professionTab.parentElement.classList.remove('active');
    this.$ageTab.parentElement.classList.remove('active');
    this.$ageCanvas.classList.add('hidden');
    this.$professionCanvas.classList.add('hidden');
    this.$experienceCanvas.classList.add('hidden');
}
```

Create a method to add event listeners to the clicked tab items:

```
addEventListeners() {
    this.$experienceTab.addEventListener('click',
this.loadExperience.bind(this));
    this.$professionTab.addEventListener('click',
this.loadProfession.bind(this));
    this.$ageTab.addEventListener('click', this.loadAge.bind(this));
}
```

Also, call the preceding method inside constructor using this.addEventListeners(); so that the event listeners are attached when the page loads.

Whenever we click one of the tab items, it will call the respective load chart function. Say we clicked the **Experience** tab. This would call the loadExperience() method with event as a parameter. But we might want to call this function after the API call to load the chart without the event parameter. To make loadExperience() work in both scenarios, modify the method as follows:

```
loadExperience(event = null) {
    if(event) event.preventDefault();
    this.hideCharts();
    this.$experienceCanvas.classList.remove('hidden');
    this.$experienceTab.parentElement.classList.add('active');
```

```
    const data = {...}
    ...
}
```

In the preceding function:

- The event parameter is defined with a default value of `null`. If `loadExperience()` is called with the event parameter (when the user clicks on the tab), the `if(event)` condition will pass and `event.preventDefault()` will stop the default click action of the anchor tag. This will prevent the page from reloading.
- If `this.loadExperience()` is called from within the `apiCall` promise chain, it will not have the `event` parameter and the value of the event defaults to `null`. The `if(event)` condition will fail (since `null` is a falsy value) and `event.preventDefault()` won't be executed. This will prevent an exception, since `event` is not defined in this scenario.
- After that, `this.hideCharts()` is called, which will hide all the charts and remove `.active` from all the tabs.
- The next two lines will remove `.hidden` from the experience chart's canvas and add the `.active` class to the **Experience** Tab.

In the `apiCall` function's `then` chain, remove `this.loadAge()` and `this.loadProfession()` so that only the experience chart will be loaded first (since it is the first tab).

If you open Google Chrome and click on the **Experience** tab, it should re-render the graph without refreshing the page. This is because we added `event.preventDefault()` to stop the default action in the `loadExperience()` method and used Chart.js to render the graph when the tab was clicked.

By using the same logic in `loadAge()` and `loadProfession()`, we can now easily make the tabs work as expected. In your `loadAge()` method add the event handling code as follows:

```
loadAge(event = null) {
  if(event) event.preventDefault();
  this.hideCharts();
  this.$ageCanvas.classList.remove('hidden');
  this.$ageTab.parentElement.classList.add('active');

  const data = {...}
  ...
}
```

Similarly, In the `loadProfession()` method add the following code:

```
loadProfession(event = null) {
  if(event) event.preventDefault();
  this.hideCharts();
  this.$professionCanvas.classList.remove('hidden');
  this.$professionTab.parentElement.classList.add('active');
  const data = {...}
  ...
}
```

Open Chrome. Click on the tabs to check whether all of them are working properly. If so, you have successfully completed the status page! Chart.js is responsive by default; hence, if you resize the page, it will resize the pie chart automatically. Now, one last page remains, in which you need to add Google Maps to display the event location. In normal JavaScript, adding Google Maps is straightforward. But, in our case, since we are using Webpack to bundle our JavaScript code, we need to add one small step to the normal process (Google Maps need to access a JavaScript variable inside HTML!).

 Chart.js has eight types of charts. Do try each of them at: `http://www.chartjs.org/`, and if you are looking for a more advanced Charting and Graphics library, check out `D3.js` (**Data-Driven Documents**) at: `https://d3js.org/`.

Adding Google Maps to the web page

Open the `about.html` file in VSCode or your text editor. It will have two paragraph `<p>` tags, in which you can add some information regarding your event. After that, there will be a `<div>` element with the ID `#map`, which is supposed to show the location of your event in a map.

I have asked you to generate an API key to use Google Maps before. If you haven't generated it, please get one from: `https://developers.google.com/maps/documentation/javascript/get-api-key` and add it to your `.env` file's `GMAP_KEY` variable. According to the Google Maps documentation, to add a Map with a marker to your web page, you must include the following script on the page:

```
<script async defer
src="https://maps.googleapis.com/maps/api/js?key=API_KEY&callback=initMap">
```

Here, the `async` and `defer` attributes of the `<script>` tag will load the script asynchronously and make sure it is executed only after the document is loaded.

To know more about the workings of `async` and `defer`, refer to the following w3schools pages. For Async: `https://www.w3schools.com/tags/att_script_async.asp` and for Defer: `https://www.w3schools.com/tags/att_script_defer.asp`.

Let's look into the `src` attribute. Here, there is a URL, followed by two query parameters, key and callback. Key is where you need to include your Google Maps API key, and callback should be a function that needs to be executed once the script has completed loaded (the script is loading asynchronously). The challenge lies in that the script needs to be included in the HTML where our JavaScript variables are not accessible (we are Webpack users now!).

But, as I have explained before, in the `webpack.config.js` file, I have added the `output.library` property, which will expose the objects, functions, or variables that are marked with the keyword `export` in the entry files of Webpack to the HTML by making their scope global (changing their scope from `const` or `let` to `var`). However, they are not directly accessible by their names. The value of `output.library` I have given is `bundle`. So, the things that are marked with the `export` keyword will be available as a property of the `bundle` object.

Open the Event Registration app in Chrome and open your Chrome DevTools console. If you type `bundle` into your console, you can see that it prints out an empty object. This is because we haven't made any exports from the *Webpack's entry files* (we did some exports in `apiCall.js` and `registrationForm.js` but those files are not in the `webpack.config.js` entry property). Hence, we only have an empty bundle object at the moment.

Let's think of a way to successfully include the Google Maps script in our web app:

- The API key is currently available as a global variable `GMAP_KEY` in our JavaScript code. So, it would be better to create the script element from the JavaScript and append it to the HTML when the page has loaded. This way, we don't have to export the API key.
- For the callback function, we will create a JavaScript function and export it.

Open the `about.js` file in VSCode and add the following code:

```
export function initMap() {
}

window.addEventListener("load", () => {
  const $script = document.createElement('script');
  $script.src =
```

```
`https://maps.googleapis.com/maps/api/js?key=${GMAP_KEY}&callback=bundle.in
itMap`;
    document.querySelector('body').appendChild($script);
});
```

The preceding code does the following:

- When the page has finished loading, it will create a new script element `document.createElement('script')` and store it in `$script` constant object.
- Now, we add the `src` attribute to the `$script` object with the value as the required script URL. Note that I have included the GMAP_KEY variable in the key and `bundle.initMap` as the callback function (since we are exporting `initMap` in `about.js`).
- Finally, it will append the script to the body element as a child. This will make the Google Maps script work as expected.
- We didn't need `async` or `defer` here, since load the script only after the page has loaded.

In your Chrome DevTools console, while you are on the about page, try typing `bundle` again. This time, you should see an object printed with `initMap` as one of its properties.

 In our ToDo List app, we created HTML elements by writing the HTML code directly in template strings. It is very efficient for constructing a large number of HTML elements. However, for smaller elements, it is better to use the `document.createElement()` method, since it makes the code more readable and easy to understand when there are a lot of attributes to that element that need dynamic values.

Adding Google Maps with a marker

We have successfully included the Google Maps script on the page. When the Google Maps script finishes loading, it will call the `initMap` function we declared in the `about.js` file. Now, we will use that function to create the map with a marker pointing to the location of the JS Meetup Event.

The process of adding Google Maps with a marker and more functionalities is well explained in the Google Maps documentation, available at: https://developers.google. com/maps/documentation/javascript/adding-a-google-map.

The Google Maps script we included earlier provides us with a few constructors that can create `map`, `Marker`, and `infowindow`. To add a simple Google Maps with `marker`, add the following code inside the `initMap()` function:

```
export function initMap() {
  const map = new google.maps.Map(document.getElementById('map'), {
    zoom: 13,
    center: {lat: 59.325, lng: 18.070}
  });

  const marker = new google.maps.Marker({
    map,
    draggable: true,
    animation: google.maps.Animation.DROP,
    position: {lat: 59.325, lng: 18.070}
  });

  marker.addListener('click', () => {
    infowindow.open(map,marker);
  });

  const infowindow = new google.maps.InfoWindow({
    content: `<h3>Event Location</h3><p>Event Address with all the contact
details</p>`
  });

  infowindow.open(map,marker);
}
```

Replace the `lat` and `lng` values in the preceding code with the latitude and longitude of your event location and change the content of the `infowindow` object with the address and contact details for the event location. Now, open the `about.html` page on Google Chrome; you should see the map with a marker at your event's location. The information window will be open by default.

Congratulations! You have successfully built your Event Registration app! But, before we start inviting people to the event, there is one more thing you need to do in your application.

Generating a production build

You might have noticed something about both the Meme Creator and the Event Registration apps. The apps load plain HTML first; after that, styles are loaded. This makes the applications look plain for a moment. This problem does not exist in the ToDo List app because we load CSS first in the ToDo List app. In the Meme Creator app, there was an optional section called *Optimizing Webpack builds for different environments*. This might be a good time to read it. If you haven't read it yet, go back, give that section a read, and come back to generate the production build.

So far, our app has been working in a development environment. Remember? In the .env file, I told you to set NODE_ENV=dev. This is because, when you set NODE_ENV=production as per the webpack.config.js file I created, Webpack will go into production mode. The npm run watch command is used to run the Webpack dev server to create a development server for our use. In your package.json file, there should be another command called webpack. This command is used to generate production builds.

The webpack.config.js file included in this project has a lot of plugins that are used to optimize the code and make the app loading times faster for the end user. npm run watch will not work properly, only when NODE_ENV is production, since there are a lot of plugins included to do production optimizations. To generate a production build for your Event Registration app, follow these steps:

1. Change the value of the NODE_ENV variable in your .env file to production.
2. Run the following command npm run webpack from your project root folder in the terminal.

It will take a while for the command to finish execution, but once it's done, you should see a number of files in your project /dist folder. There will be JS files, CSS files, and .map files that contain source map information for the generated CSS and JS files. JS files will be compressed and well minified so that loading and execution times are very fast. There will also be a fonts directory containing the fonts used by Bootstrap.

So far, we have only included the JS file in the HTML, since it contains the CSS code too. However, it is the reason why the page shows blank HTML without CSS when it starts loading. The CSS file should be included before the <body> element so that it will load first and the page style will be uniform when it is loading (see how we included CSS files in Chapter 1, *Building a ToDo List App*). For the production build, we need to remove references to old JS files and include the newly generated CSS and JS files.

In your `dist/` directory, there will be a `manifest.json` file that contains the list of files generated for every entry in Webpack. `manifest.json` should look something like this:

```json
{
  "status": [
    "16f9901e75ba0ce6ed9c.status.js",
    "16f9901e75ba0ce6ed9c.status.css",
    "16f9901e75ba0ce6ed9c.status.js.map",
    "16f9901e75ba0ce6ed9c.status.css.map"
  ],
  "home": [
    "756fc66292dc44426e28.home.js",
    "756fc66292dc44426e28.home.css",
    "756fc66292dc44426e28.home.js.map",
    "756fc66292dc44426e28.home.css.map"
  ],
  "about": [
    "1b4af260a87818dfb51f.about.js",
    "1b4af260a87818dfb51f.about.css",
    "1b4af260a87818dfb51f.about.js.map",
    "1b4af260a87818dfb51f.about.css.map"
  ]
}
```

The prefix numbers are just hash values and they might be different for you; don't worry about that. Now, include the CSS and JS files for each HTML file. For example, take the `status.html` file and add the CSS and JS files in the status property of the preceding `manifest.json` file, such that:

```html
...
<head>
  ...
  <link rel="stylesheet" href="dist/16f9901e75ba0ce6ed9c.status.css">
</head>
<body>
  ...
  <script src="dist/16f9901e75ba0ce6ed9c.status.js"></script>
</body>
...
```

Repeat the same process for other HTML files and then your production build will be ready! You cannot use Webpack dev server now, so you could use the `http-server` tool to open the web page or directly open the HTML file with Chrome (I'd recommend using `http-server`). This time, while the page is loading, you won't see the HTML page without styles, since CSS is loaded before the body elements.

Shipping the code

Now that you have learned how to generate production builds, what if you want to send this code to someone else? Say the DevOps team or the server administrator. In this case, if you are using version control, add the `dist/` directory, the `node_modules/` directory, and the `.env` files to your ignore list. Send the code without these two directories and the `.env` file. The other person should be able to figure out which environment variables to use using the `.env.example` file, creating the `.env` file, and also using the `npm install` and `npm run webpack` commands to generate the `node_modules/` and `dist/` directories.

For all the other steps, neatly document the procedure in a `README.md` file in your project root folder and send it along with the other files.

 The main reason why sharing the `.env` file should be avoided is because the environment variables might contain sensitive information and should not be transported or stored in version control as plain text.

You have now learned about generating production builds for your applications built with Webpack. Now, the Meme Creator app does not have a production build yet! I'll let you use the `webpack.config.js` file used in this chapter as a reference. So, go ahead and create a production build for your Meme Creator.

Summary

Well done! You just built a really useful Event Registration app. Along the way, you have learned some really advanced concepts of JavaScript, such as building ES6 Modules for reusable code, making asynchronous AJAX calls with fetch, and handling asynchronous code using Promises. You also used the Chart.js library to build charts to visually display the data and, finally, created a production-ready build with Webpack.

Having learned all these concepts, you are no longer a beginner in JavaScript; you can proudly call yourself a pro! But, apart from these concepts, there's still a lot going on with modern JavaScript. As I told you before, JavaScript is no longer a scripting language used only for form validation on browsers. In the next chapter, we are going to build a peer-to-peer video calling application using JavaScript.

4

Real-Time Video Call App with WebRTC

Hey! Just to let you know, the JS Meetup was a great success after getting a backend developer to complete the serverside of the application. But you did great completing the entire frontend of the application. You created a complete Event Registration website, which lets users sign up the events, while learning some really important concepts, such as building reusable ES6 modules, making AJAX requests while handling asynchronous code using Promises, creating beautiful charts out of data, and of course, the classic form validation with a validation service.

The backend code was also written with JavaScript (Node.js), so you might really be interested in writing serverside code. But sadly, as I mentioned earlier, Node.js is beyond the scope of this book. Actually, you can do some really cool things with plain JavaScript, although many people think, "*It needs a lot of server-side code!*" Since you will have already read the chapter title - yup! We are going to build a real Video Call app in this chapter with *almost zero* server-side code. The best part is, just like our other applications, this one is also going to be responsive and will work with most mobile browsers.

Let's first take a look at the list of concepts we are about to learn in this chapter:

- Introduction to WebRTC
- WebRTC APIs in JavaScript
- Working with a SimpleWebRTC framework
- Building a Video Call app

Apart from these main concepts, there is a lot more to learn in this chapter. So, before we start, make sure you have the following hardware:

- A PC or laptop with webcam and microphone (you might want to use another computer to experience a video call in action)
- An Android or iPhone device (optional)
- A LAN connection so that all your devices are on the same local network to test the application in development (can be either Wi-Fi or wired Ethernet)

 One of the dependencies used in this project requires you to have Python 2.7.x installed in your system. Linux and Mac users have Python pre-installed. Windows users can download Python 2.7.x version from `https://www.python.org/downloads/`

Introduction to WebRTC

Before we start building the application, it's best to know a few things about WebRTC so that you get a good idea about the workings of the app.

History of WebRTC

Real-time communication capabilities have become a common feature of many of the applications we use nowadays. Say you want to chat with your friend or watch a live soccer game. Real-time communication is a must for these applications. However, having live video calls on a browser in the past was quite a difficult task for users, because they had to install plugins into their system for different applications to use video calling on the web browser, and with plugins came vulnerabilities, hence, regular updates.

To overcome this problem, Google released an open source project in May 2011 for browser-based real-time communication standards, called WebRTC. The concept of WebRTC is simple. It defines a set of standards that should be used across all applications so that applications can communicate directly with each other (peer-to-peer communication). By implementing WebRTC, there will not be any need for plugins anymore, since the communication platform is standardized.

Currently, WebRTC is being standardized by the **World Wide Web Consortium (W3C)** and the **Internet Engineering Task Force (IETF)**. WebRTC is actively being implemented by most browser vendors and it will also work with native Android and iOS applications. If you want to know whether your browser is ready to support WebRTC, you can visit: `http://iswebrtcreadyyet.com/`.

At the time of writing this book, the browser support status is:

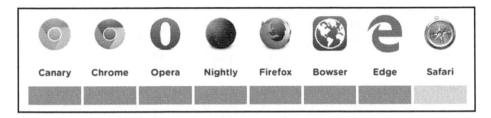

Even though most commonly used browsers support WebRTC, except Safari, there are still a lot of issues and bugs with the implementation, hence, it is recommended to use a shim such as `adapter.js` (`https://github.com/webrtc/adapter`) so that the application will not suffer any problems during changes to spec or vendor prefixes. We'll see more about this when we look into the JavaScript APIs for WebRTC.

WebRTC is also supported in the mobile versions of Chrome and Firefox; hence, you can use video calls even in mobile browsers with no plugins.

For iPhone users

Neither Safari mobile browser or Chrome support WebRTC on the iPhone yet. So, you either have to install Firefox or the Bowser app from the app store. Link for Bowser: `https://itunes.apple.com/app/bowser/id560478358?mt=8`.

JavaScript WebAPIs

So far, we have used a few WebAPIs such as `FileReader`, document (used in the `document.querySelector()` methods), `HTMLImageElement` (the `new Image()` constructor we used in Meme Creator), and so on. They are not part of the JavaScript language, but they are part of the WebAPIs. When running JavaScript in browsers, it will be provided with a `window` object that contains all the methods of the WebAPIs. The scope of the `window` object is global and the properties and methods of the `window` object are also global. This means, if you want to use navigator WebAPI, you can either do the following:

```
window.navigator.getUserMedia()
```

Or, you can simply do as follows:

```
navigator.getUserMedia();
```

Both will work just fine and implement the same methods. However, do note that WebAPI (`window` object) is available for JavaScript only when you run JavaScript on a browser. If you are using JavaScript on other platforms, such as Node.js or React Native, you will not have WebAPIs for use.

WebAPIs are growing more powerful nowadays and provide JavaScript with the ability to do more functions, such as recording video and audio directly from the browser. Progressive web applications are one such example, powered by the `ServiceWorker` WebAPI.

 We are going to use a lot of WebAPIs in this chapter and the upcoming chapters. For a full list of the WebAPIs available for JavaScript, visit the following MDN page: `https://developer.mozilla.org/en-US/docs/Web/API`.

JavaScript WebRTC API

Since browsers support WebRTC natively, JavaScript WebAPIs have been created by browser vendors so that developers can easily build applications. Currently, WebRTC implements the following three APIs that are used by JavaScript:

- MediaStream
- RTCPeerConnection
- RTCDataChannel

MediaStream

MediaStream API is used for getting access to the video and audio devices of the user. Generally, browsers will prompt the user as to whether he/she wants to allow the website to access the camera and microphone of his/her device. Even though the underlying concept for MediaStream API is the same, different browser vendors have implemented the API differently.

 While using the `getUserMedia()` method with `{audio: true}` to access your own microphone, *either mute the speakers or mute the HTML video element*. Otherwise, *it might cause feedback that can damage your speakers*.

For example, in Chrome, to use MediaStream API, you need to use the `navigator.getUserMedia()` method. Also, Chrome allows MediaStream to work only in localhost or HTTPS URLs.

`navigator.getUserMedia()` accepts three parameters. The first one is the configuration object that tells the browser what the website needs access to. The other two are callback functions for success or failure response.

Create a simple HTML file, say `chrome.html`, inside an empty directory. Inside the HTML file, add the following code:

```
<video></video>
<script>
const $video = document.querySelector('video');
if (navigator.getUserMedia) {
  navigator.getUserMedia(
    {audio: true, video: true},
    stream => {
      $video.srcObject = stream;
      $video.muted = true; // Video muted to avoid feedback
      $video.onloadedmetadata = () => {
        $video.play();
      };
    },
    error => console.error(error)
  );
}
</script>
```

This code does the following:

- It will create a reference to the `<video>` element in the `$video` object.
- It then checks whether `navigator.getUserMedia` is available. This is done to avoid errors when a browser that is not compatible with WebRTC is used.
- Then, it calls the `navigator.getUserMedia()` method with the following three parameters:
  - The first parameter specifies what is needed by the website to the browser. In our case, both audio and video. Hence, we should pass `{audio: true, video: true}`.

- The second parameter is the success callback function. The received video and audio stream from the user is available in the `stream` object that is passed as the parameter to this function. It adds the `srcObject` attribute to the `<video>` element with the value as the `stream` object of the received video and audio from the user's input device. `$video.onloadedmetadata` will be called when the stream is loaded and it will start playing the video, since we added `$video.play()` to its callback function.
- The third parameter is called when the user denies permission to the website to access the camera or microphone, or some other error occurs and the media stream cannot be retrieved. This function has an `error` object as its parameter, which contains the error details.

Now, open the file with Chrome in localhost using `http-server`. First, Chrome will prompt you to allow access to the device's camera and microphone. It should look as follows:

If you click **Allow**, you should see your video streamed through your front camera. I have set up a JS fiddle at: `https://jsfiddle.net/1odpck45/`, with which you can play around with the video stream.

Once you click **Allow** or **Block**, Chrome will remember this preference for the website. To change the website's permission, you have to click the lock or information icon on the left-hand side of the address bar and it will show a menu, as follows, from which you can change the permissions again:

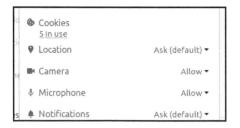

Since we use http-server or the Webpack dev server for developments that are running on localhost, we can develop WebRTC apps in Chrome. However, if you want to deploy the app in production, you need to deploy them with an HTTPS URL. Otherwise, the application won't work on Chrome.

The video we created works great on Chrome, but if you try to run this code on a different browser, Firefox, it won't work. This is because Firefox has a different implementation of the MediaStream API.

In Firefox, you need to use the `navigator.mediaDevices.getUserMedia()` method that returns a Promise. The `stream` object can be used using a `.then().catch()` chain.

The code for Firefox is as follows:

```
<video></video>
<script>
const $video = document.querySelector('video');
navigator.mediaDevices.getUserMedia({audio: true, video: true})
.then(stream => {
  $video.srcObject = stream;
  $video.muted = true;
  $video.onloadedmetadata = function(e) {
    $video.play();
  };
})
.catch(console.error);
</script>
```

You can run this code in Firefox either by creating a `firefox.html` file in the same directory you created the `chrome.html` file or by opening the following JS fiddle in your Firefox browser: `https://jsfiddle.net/hc39mL5g/`.

Setting up the HTTPS server for production is beyond the scope of this book. But, depending on the type of server you want to use, it is fairly simple to find the instructions on the internet.

Using Adapter.js library

Since the WebRTC implementation varies between browsers, it is recommended to use a shim, such as the `adapter.js` library (`https://github.com/webrtc/adapter`), which insulates the code from differences in browser implementations. By including `adapter.js` library, you can run the WebRTC code written for Chrome in your Firefox browser. Try running the following JS fiddle in Firefox, which has the WebRTC code that works on Chrome but has `adapter.js` included: `https://jsfiddle.net/1ydwr4tt/`.

If you are wondering about the `<video>` element, it was introduced in HTML5. To know more about using the video element, visit the w3schools page: `https://www.w3schools.com/html/html5_video.asp` or the MDN page: `https://developer.mozilla.org/en/docs/Web/HTML/Element/video`.

RTCPeerConnection and RTCDataChannel

While the MediaStream API is used to retrieve the video and audio stream from the user's device, the RTCPeerConnection and RTCDataChannel APIs are used for establishing a peer-to-peer connection and transferring data between them. In our Video Call app, we are going to use the SimpleWebRTC framework, which will abstract these APIs and provide us with a simpler object to establish a connection with other devices. Hence, we are not going to look into these two APIs.

However, there is one important thing to know while working with WebRTC. Even though WebRTC was created to make devices connect with each other directly without any servers, it is currently impossible to achieve this, because to connect with a device, you need to know where the device is located on the internet, that is, the device's IP address on the internet. But, generally, devices will only know their local IP address (192.168.1.x type). The public IP address is managed by firewall or router. To overcome this issue and send the exact IP address to the other device, we need signalling servers, such as **STUN** or **TURN**.

The device will send the request to the STUN server to retrieve its public IP Address and send that information to the other devices. This is widely used and is applicable for most scenarios. But if the router or the firewall's NAT service assigns a different port number to each of the device's connection's or the device's local address keeps changing, the data received from the STUN server might not be enough, hence, the TURN server must be used. A TURN server acts as a relay between the two devices, that is, the device sends data to the TURN server, which will relay the data to the other devices. However, the TURN server is not as efficient as the STUN server, since it consumes a lot of server-side resources.

Usually, an **ICE** implementation is used, which determines whether a STUN or TURN server is needed between two devices (it will mostly go with STUN while using TURN as the last resort), hence, keeping the connectivity more efficient and stable.

 Real-time communication with WebRTC is quite a large topic to be covered in a chapter, but if you are interested in learning more about WebRTC, you can go to WebRTC's official website `https://webrtc.org/` to look into some of the various resources available to get started with WebRTC.

Building the Video Call application

The app we are going to build in this chapter is a simple video conferencing app with which you create a room and then share the room URL to others. Whoever clicks on the URL will be able to join the call. For the UI part, we can arrange the video of participants in small boxes and, when you click on a participant, we can enlarge the video. This type of Video Call app is widely used nowadays. Here's how the app will look on a desktop browser:

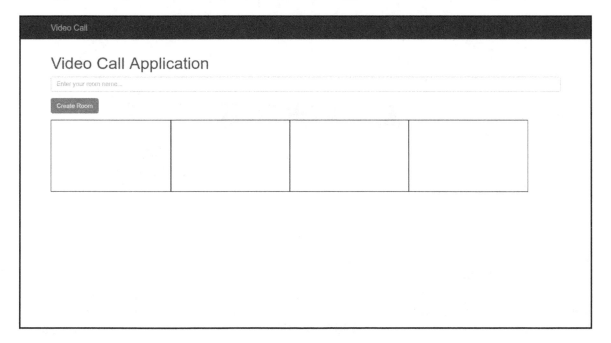

The blue box will display your video, while the other boxes are supposed to display the videos of the other participants. The row will automatically wrap to a new row when the number of participants increases (flex-wrap). In mobile devices, we can show the videos in columns instead of rows, since it will be more effective for smaller screens. So, for mobiles, the application should look as follows:

The boxes are just placeholders. For real videos, we can use margin/padding to give spacing between each video. Also, for sharing the link, we can use a click to **Copy** button, which will be really user-friendly. Now that you have a good understanding of what we are going to build, let's get started!

Initial project setup

The initial setup isn't much different from what we did in the previous Event Registration app. Open up the starter files from Chapter04 folder in VSCode and create a .env file. From the .env.example file, you should know that, for this application, we only need a single environment variable, NODE_ENV, whose value will be production only for the production environment. For development, we can simply assign it some other value, such as dev.

Once you have created your `.env` file, open the terminal in VSCode or your native terminal (navigate to project root folder) and run `npm install` to install all the dependencies for the project. After that, run `npm run webpack` in the terminal, which should start the Webpack dev server.

Adding styles to the page

You know how to work with the Webpack dev server. So, let's move on to adding styles to our page. First, go through the `index.html` file to understand the basic structure of the page.

The body of the page is divided into two sections:

- Navbar
- Container

The container is further divided into three sections:

1. First, `create-room-area`, which contains the input fields needed to create a new room with a room name.
2. Second, `info-area`, which contains the information regarding the room (room name and room URL). It also has two buttons that are going to be used to copy the room URL (currently hidden using the `.hidden` Bootstrap style class).
3. Finally, `video-area`, which is used to display the videos of all the participants.

First, add the following code in `src/css/styles.css` file to prevent the container section from overlapping with the navigation bar:

```
body {
  padding-top: 65px;
}
```

With Webpack hot reloading enabled, you should see the CSS changes instantly. The `create-room-area` looks just fine with the default Bootstrap styles. So, let's move on to the second section, info-area. To work on `info-area`, temporarily remove the `.hidden` class from the HTML. Also, remove `.hidden` from the two buttons and add some text in the paragraph element, which will contain the room URL. It'd be great if the room URL and the buttons are aligned in a single row. To align them, add the following CSS in the `styles.css` file:

```
.room-text {
```

```
    display: flex;
    flex-direction: row;
    padding: 10px;
    justify-content: flex-start;
    align-items: center;
    align-content: center;
}
.room-url {
    padding: 10px;
}
.copy {
    margin-left: 10px;
}
.copied {
    margin-left: 10px;
}
```

For `video-area`, the videos need to be arranged in a column for mobile devices, while they should be arranged in a row for desktops. Hence, we can use a media query to assign different styles to it. Also, for the size of the video element (`.video-player`), we can set `max-width` and `max-height` to 25 viewport width so that its dimensions will be responsive for all devices. In your `styles.css` file, add the following styles:

```
@media only screen and (max-width: 736px) {
    .video-area {
        display: flex;
        flex-direction: column;
        align-items: center;
        justify-content: center;
    }
}
@media only screen and (min-width: 736px) {
    .video-area {
        display: flex;
        flex-direction: row;
        flex-wrap: wrap;
    }
}
.video-player {
    max-height: 25vh;
    max-width: 25vh;
    margin: 20px;
}
```

That's all for the styles needed right now. So, let's start writing the JavaScript for the application.

Building the Video Call app

Everything's in place, so let's start coding. As usual, as we did in the previous apps, open your `home.js` file and create your `Home` class with a constructor:

```
class Home {
  constructor() {

  }
}
```

After that, create an instance of the `Home` class and assign it to an object, `home`, as follows:

```
const home = new Home();
```

We are going to have a use for the home object later. We now add the `SimpleWebRTC` package to our project by running the following command in the terminal from our project root folder:

npm install -S simplewebrtc

And add the following import statement to the top of your `home.js` file:

```
import SimpleWebRTC from 'simplewebrtc';
```

As per the `SimpleWebRTC` documentation, we need to create an instance of the `SimpleWebRTC` class with some configuration to use it in our application. In your `home.js` file, before the `Home` class, add the following code:

```
const webrtc = new SimpleWebRTC({
  localVideoEl: 'localVideo',
  remoteVideosEl: '',
  autoRequestMedia: true,
  debug: false,
});
```

Your application should now ask for permissions to access camera and microphone. This is because, behind the scenes, `SimpleWebRTC` has started working on setting up everything needed to initiate a video call. If you click **Allow**, you should see your video appear in a small rectangular box. This is what the configurations in the object you added in the previous code do:

- `localVideoEl`: Contains the ID of the element that should contain your local video. Here, the `video#localVideo` element from our `index.html` file is going to display our own video, hence, it is chosen as its value.

- `remoteVideosEl`: Contains the ID of the container in which the remote videos need to be added. We haven't created that element yet and it's better to add videos later, so just leave it as an empty string.
- `autoRequestMedia`: Used to prompt the user to give permission to access the camera and microphone and needs to be set to `true`.
- `debug`: If true, it will print all the `webrtc` events in the console. I have set it to `false`, but set it to true on your system to see the events happening.

By default, `SimpleWebRTC` uses the free STUN server provided by Google, which is `stun.l.google.com:19302`. This STUN server is enough in most cases, unless you are behind some corporate firewall with complex routing protocols. Otherwise, you can set up your own ICE configuration with both STUN and TURN servers. For that, you need to install signalmaster (`https://github.com/andyet/signalmaster`) and add the ICE configuration details to the earlier mentioned constructor. However, that is beyond the scope of this book. We'll simply carry on with the default configuration.

For our first step, we'll create the class variables and references to the DOM elements inside our constructor:

```
constructor() {
  this.roomName = '';

  this.$createRoomSection = document.querySelector('#createRoomSection');
  this.$createRoomButton = document.querySelector('#createRoom');
  this.$roomNameInput = document.querySelector('#roomNameInput');

  this.$infoSection = document.querySelector('#infoSection');
  this.$roomName = document.querySelector('#roomNameText');
  this.$roomUrl = document.querySelector('#roomUrl');
  this.$buttonArea = document.querySelector('.room-text');
  this.$copy = document.querySelector('.copy');
  this.$copied = document.querySelector('.copied');

  this.$remotes = document.querySelector('.video-area');
  this.$localVideo = document.querySelector('#localVideo');
}
```

That's a lot, but they are all needed for different steps of our application. The only variable we created here is `roomName`, which as the name suggests, contains the room's name. The others are all references to DOM elements.

Creating a room

The first step of this app is to create a room so that other members can join a call in the room. As per the current UI design, we need to create the room when the user clicks the **Create Room** button. So, let's register a click event handler on that button.

So far, we have been using different methods to handle events:

- In our ToDo list app, we added the `onclick` attribute to the HTML to call JavaScript functions `onclick` event.
- In the Meme Creator, we attached event listeners to each element, where we wanted to listen for a specific event to happen (keyup, change, and click events). The same goes for the Event Registration form, where we added an event listener to listen for the form submit action.
- There is also another method in which you add a callback function to the event property of the reference to the DOM element. In our case, we need to detect a click event on the **Create Room** button. We can handle it as follows:

```
this.$createRoomButton.onclick = () => {
}
```

So, whenever the **Create Room** button is clicked, it will execute the code written inside the preceding function. It is entirely up to you and your requirements to decide which event handler to use. Usually, the first method is avoided because it will expose your JavaScript code inside HTML and it's difficult to keep track of all the JavaScript functions called inside HTML in large projects.

If you have a large number of elements, say about 100 rows in a table, attaching 100 event listeners to each row is inefficient. You can either use the third method by attaching a function to the `onclick` method of the reference of each row's DOM element or you can attach a single event listener to the row's parent element and use that event listener to listen to the events of its children elements.

 For a list of all the DOM events, visit the W3Schools page: `https://www.w3schools.com/jsref/dom_obj_event.asp`.

In our application, we need to handle a lot of click events. So, let's create a method inside the `Home` class to register all the click events:

```
registerClicks() {
}
```

And call this method inside the constructor:

```
constructor() {
  ...
  this.registerClicks();
}
```

Inside the `registerClicks()` method, add the following code:

```
this.$createRoomButton.onclick = () => {
}
```

There are few things that need to happen when the user clicks the **Create Room** button. They are as follows:

- Get the room name. But the room name cannot contain any special characters that cause problems with the URL
- Create a room using `SimpleWebRTC`
- Redirect the user to a URL created for the room (a URL with the room name as query string)
- Show the URL that he/she can share with others who need to participate in the call

You should write the following code inside the `onclick` method you created in the preceding code:

```
this.roomName = this.$roomNameInput.value.toLowerCase().replace(/\s/g, '-').replace(/[^A-Za-z0-9_\-]/g, '');
```

This will get the room name that is typed in the input field and convert it into URL-friendly characters using regular expressions. If the room name is not empty, we can proceed to the creation of the room in `SimpleWebRTC`:

```
if(this.roomName) {
  webrtc.createRoom(this.roomName, (err, name) => {
    if(!err) {
      // room created
    } else {
      // unable to create room
      console.error(err);
    }
  });
}
```

The preceding code does the following:

- The `if` condition will check whether the room name is not empty (an empty string is falsy).
- `webrtc.createRoom()` will create the room. It accepts two parameters: the first one is the room name string and the second one is a callback function that executes when the room is created.
- The callback function has the parameters `err` and `name`. Usually, we should check whether the process is a success. So, `if(!err) {}` will contain the code to execute when the process is a success. `name` is the room name created by `SimpleWebRTC`.

Inside the `if(!err)` condition, add the following code:

```
const newUrl = location.pathname + '?' + name;
history.replaceState({}, '', newUrl);
this.roomName = name;
this.roomCreated();
```

The `location` object contains information regarding the current URL. `location.pathname` is used to set or get the current URL of the web page. So, we can construct a URL by appending the room name to it. So, if your current URL is `http://localhost:8080/` then, after creating the room, your URL should become `http://localhost:8080/?roomName`.

To replace the URL without affecting the current page, we can use the `history` object provided by the History Web API. The `history` object is used to manipulate the browser's history. If you want to perform the back action that happens when the user clicks the browser's back button, you can do as follows:

```
history.back();
```

Likewise, for going forward, you can do as follows:

```
history.forward();
```

But what we need in our application is to change the current URL without affecting the browser history. That is, we need to change the URL from `http://localhost:8080/` to `http://localhost:8080/?roomName` without affecting the back or forward buttons of your browser.

For such complex actions, you can use the `pushState()` and `replaceState()` methods introduced in HTML5 for the history object. `pushState()` creates a new history entry on the browser and changes the URL of the page without affecting the current page. `replaceState()` does the same, but instead of creating a new history entry, it replaces the current entry, making it ideal for our purpose.

Both the `pushState()` and `replaceState()` methods accept three parameters. The first one is `state` (a JSON object), the second one is `title` (string), and the third one is the new URL. This is how both `pushState()` and `replaceState()` works:

- Every time `pushState()` or `replaceState()` is called, it triggers a `popstate` event in the `window` object. The first parameter, state object, is used by the callback function of that event. We have no use for it now, so we set it to an empty object.
- Currently, most browsers just ignore the second parameter, so we just set it to an empty string.
- The third parameter URL is what we really need. It changes the browser URL to the provided URL string.

Since the room has been created and the URL has been changed, we need to hide the `.create-room-area` div and display the `.info-area` div instead. That's why I added the `this.roomCreated()` method. In the `Home` class, create the new method:

```
roomCreated() {
  this.$infoSection.classList.remove('hidden');
  this.$createRoomSection.classList.add('hidden');
  this.$roomName.textContent = `Room Name: ${this.roomName}`;
  this.$roomUrl.textContent = window.location.href;
}
```

This method will show the information section while hiding the create room section. Also, it will change the room name and URL using the `textContent()` method, which changes the text that is present in the respective DOM element.

More information on location objects can be found on the w3schools page: `https://www.w3schools.com/jsref/obj_location.asp`.

More information on the history object can be found on the MDN page: `https://developer.mozilla.org/en-US/docs/Web/API/History`. Also, if you want to learn to manipulate the browser history, visit `https://developer.mozilla.org/en-US/docs/Web/API/History_API`.

Adding participants to your room

You have an active room and the room URL with which you need to invite others. But wouldn't it be easier if you had a click to copy feature to copy the URL? That is actually a really nice feature to have. So, before we add participants to the room, let's build a click to copy feature.

Click to copy text

Currently, this is how the info area looks:

For the click to copy feature, if you hover the mouse over the room URL, it should show a **Copy** button:

If you click the **Copy** button, it should copy the text and turn into the **Copied** button:

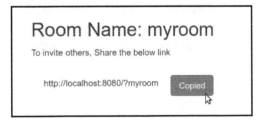

For this functionality, we need to add some event listeners. So, inside your home class, create a new method addEventListeners() and call it inside the constructor:

```
class Home {
  constructor() {
    ...
    this.addEventListeners();
  }
  addEventListeners() {
  }
}
```

The reference to the div containing the copy buttons is stored in the this.$buttonArea variable. Whenever the mouse enters a div, it will fire a mouseenter event. When this event happens in $buttonArea, we need to remove the .hidden class from the copy button.

Inside your addEventListeners() method, add the following code:

```
this.$buttonArea.addEventListener('mouseenter', () => {
  this.$copy.classList.remove('hidden');
});
```

The page will reload and you will have to create a room again. If you hover the mouse pointer over the room URL now, it should make the **Copy** button visible. We also need the button to be hidden when the pointer leaves div. Similar to mouseenter, div will fire a mouseout event when the pointer leaves it. So, once again, add the following code next to the preceding code:

```
this.$buttonArea.addEventListener('mouseout', event => {
  this.$copy.classList.add('hidden');
  this.$copied.classList.add('hidden');
});
```

Now, once again, try hovering your pointer over the room URL. Surprisingly, it doesn't work as expected. It should have done, but it didn't. It is because of the mouseout event, which also fires when your pointer enters the child elements of $buttonArea. It considers the child elements as outside the div. To fix this, we need to filter the event object that is passed in the callback function so that no action happens if the pointer moves outside by entering the child elements.

This one is tricky, but if you print the event object in the console, you will see that there are a lot of properties and methods containing all the details of the event. The `toElement` property or the `relatedTarget` property will contain the element to which the pointer moved to depending on the browser. So, we need to check whether the parent of that element is `$buttonArea`. If so, we should prevent any actions from happening. To do this, change the preceding code to the following:

```
this.$buttonArea.addEventListener('mouseout', event => {
  const e = event.toElement || event.relatedTarget;
  if(e) {
    if (e.parentNode == this.$buttonArea || e == this.$buttonArea) {
      return;
    }
  }
  this.$copy.classList.add('hidden');
  this.$copied.classList.add('hidden');
});
```

Note the line:

```
const e = event.toElement || event.relatedTarget;
```

This is a short-circuit evaluation. What it does is, if the first value is truthy, it will assign it to the constant e. If it is falsy, the OR operator will evaluate the second one and assign its value to e. You can have any number of values declared like this. Say:

```
const fun = false || '' || true || 'test';
```

Here, the value of fun will be the first truthy statement on the list, hence, its value will be true. `'test'` is also a truthy value but it won't get evaluated, since there is a truthy value before it. This type of assignment is commonly used and is handy for certain tasks.

Now, the e object contains the target element. So, we just need to check whether e exists (to prevent exceptions) and, if so, whether its parent element or the element itself is `$buttonArea`. If it is true, we simply return. This way, the callback function stops executing without hiding the copy and copied buttons. We hide the copied button too because we are going to make it visible when the user clicks the **Copy** button.

Try hovering over the room URL again in your application and it should work as expected. The last step is to copy the URL when the user clicks on the copy button. So, let's register a click in the `registerClicks()` method we created earlier in our `Home` class. Inside the `registerClicks()` method, add the code to handle the clicks on the **Copy** and **Copied** buttons and create a new method `copyUrl()` inside the `Home` class to do the copy action:

```
registerClicks() {
  ...
  this.$copy.onclick = () => {
    this.copyUrl();
  };
  this.$copied.onclick = () => {
    this.copyUrl();
  };
}

copyUrl() {

}
```

In the preceding code, inside the `registerClicks()` method, clicking on both the **Copy** button and the **Copied** button will call the `copyUrl()` method of the class. We need to add the code to copy text inside the `copyUrl()` method.

To copy text, first, we need to get a range of nodes (the DOM elements) from which we need to copy text. To do so, create a range object and select the `this.$roomUrl` node, which contains the text of the room URL. Inside the `copyUrl()` method, add the following code:

```
const range = document.createRange();
range.selectNode(this.$roomUrl);
```

Now, the range object contains the element `$roomUrl` as the selected node. Then, we need to select the text in the node just as a user usually selects text with his/her cursor. The `window` object has the `getSelection()` method, which we can use for this purpose. We must remove all the ranges to clear the previous selections and then select a new range (which is the range object we created previously). Add the following code to the preceding code:

```
window.getSelection().removeAllRanges();
window.getSelection().addRange(range);
```

Finally, we don't know whether the user's browser supports executing the copy command, so we do the copying inside a `try{} catch(err){}` statement so that, if any error occurs, it can be handled in the catch statement. The `document.execCommand('copy')` method will copy the text in the selected range and return it as a string. Also, we need to hide the copy button and display the copied button when, as copy is successful. The code to do copying is as follows:

```
try {
  const successful = document.execCommand('copy');
  const msg = successful ? 'successful' : 'unsuccessful';
  console.log('Copying text command was ' + msg);
  this.$copy.classList.add('hidden');
  this.$copied.classList.remove('hidden');
} catch(err) {
  console.error(err);
}
```

After adding the preceding code, create a room in the application and try clicking **Copy** again. It should turn into the **Copied** button and the room URL text will be highlighted, because we selected the text just like how we select it, using the cursor with JavaScript. But it would be nice to clear the selection once copying is done. So, add this line at the end of the `copyUrl()` method:

```
window.getSelection().removeAllRanges();
```

This will clear the selection, so next time you click copy, the room URL text will not be highlighted. You can then simply paste the selected URL wherever you like to share it with others.

Joining a room

Now that you have a link, we need to make a user join the room using that link. The process is simple: when the user opens the link, he joins the room and video of all the participants is displayed to him. To make a user join a room, `SimpleWebRTC` has the `joinRoom('roomName')` method, where the room name string is passed as a parameter. Once a user is in a room, it will look for the videos of other users connected in the room and will fire a `videoAdded` event for each video it finds, along with a callback function, which has the video object and the peer object of that user.

Let's strategize on how the process should work:

- First, we need to check whether the URL the user entered contains the room name in its query string. That is, if it ends with '?roomName'.
- If the room name exists, then we should make the user join the room while hiding the .create-room-area div and displaying the .info-area div with the room details.
- Then, we need to listen for the videoAdded events and, if an event is triggered, we add the video to .video-area div.

SimpleWebRTC fires a readyToCall event when it has finished loading. It also has the on() method to listen for the events fired. We can use the readyToCall event to check for the room name in the URL. This code should be outside the Home class. So, after the line where you called the Home class constructor, add the following code:

```
webrtc.on('readyToCall', () => {
  if(location.search) {
    const locationArray = location.search.split('?');
    const room = locationArray[1];
  }
});
```

We are using the location object to get the URL. First, we need to check whether the URL contains the query string using location.search. So, we used it in an if condition and, if it contains the query string, we can continue the process.

The split() method splits the string into an array of substrings divided by the value passed to it as the parameter. The URL will be something like as follows:

```
http://localhost:8080/?myRoom
```

location.search will return the query string part of the URL:

```
'?myRoom'
```

So, location.search.split('?') will convert the string into an array as follows:

```
[ '', 'myRoom']
```

We have the room name at the index 1 of the array. Writing like this works, but here we can use a short-circuit evaluation. We used an evaluation with the OR operator before, where it will take the first truthy value. In this case, we can use the AND operator that takes the first falsy value, or the last truthy value if there are no falsy values. The preceding code will be simplified into the following:

```
webrtc.on('readyToCall', () => {
  const room = location.search && location.search.split('?')[1];
});
```

If the URL does not contain the query string, `location.search` will be an empty string (`""`), which is a falsy value. Hence, the value of room will be an empty string.

If the URL does contain the query string with the room name, then `location.search` will return `'?roomName'`, which is a truthy value, so the next statement `location.search.split('?')[1]` gets evaluated, which does the split and returns the first index in the array (room name). Since it is the last truthy value, the room constant will now contain the room name string! We just simplified three lines of code into a single line using short-circuit evaluation.

> Detailed information on short-circuit evaluation can be found at: `https://developer.mozilla.org/en-US/docs/Web/JavaScript/Reference/Operators/Logical_Operators#Short-circuit_evaluation`.

Setters and getters

We just need to add one more line to make the user join the room:

```
webrtc.joinRoom(room);
```

This will add the user to the room, however, once the user is inside the room, we need to hide the `.create-room-area` div and display the `.info-area` div. These are available in the `roomCreated()` method of the `Home` class. But that method depends on the `this.roomName` class variable, which should contain the room name. So, we need to update a class variable and call the `class` method from outside the class.

Even though we can do it by using the `home` object we created earlier, it would make more sense if we could just update the class's room property and it will perform the actions automatically. For that, we can use setters. Setters are special methods that are used for assigning a new value to the object's property. We have used getters and setters several times before. Remember how we get the value of the input field?

```
const inputValue = this.$roomNameInput.value
```

Here, the value property is a getter. It returns a value from the `$roomNameInput` object. However, if we do the following:

```
$roomNameInput.value = 'New Room Name'
```

Then, it will change the value of the input field to `'New Room Name'`. This is because the value now acts as a setter and updates a property inside the `$roomNameInput` object.

We will create a setter for our `Home` class to join a room. Creating a setter is simple; we simply create a method prefixed with the `set` keyword and the method should have *exactly one parameter*. Inside your `Home` class, add the following code:

```
set room(room) {
  webrtc.joinRoom(room);
  this.roomName = room;
  this.roomCreated();
}
```

Now, use the setter (only if the room is not an empty string) in your `readyToCall` event handler:

```
const home = new Home();

webrtc.on('readyToCall', () => {
  const room = location.search && location.search.split('?')[1];
  if(room) home.room = room;
});
```

Once you have added the code, create a room in your Video Call app and then copy the URL and paste it in a new tab. It should automatically get the room name from the URL and join the room. If you can see the room information, then you are good to go. We are nearing the final stage of the application--adding and removing videos.

 If and else conditions do not require `{}` curly braces if there is only one statement after them. That is, `if (true) console.log('true');` `else console.log('false');` will work just fine! But it should be avoided, since it is always better to use `if else` conditions with `{}` curly braces.

To create a getter, you simply prefix the method with `get` instead of `set`, but the method should contain *no parameters* and it should *return a value*. Say, in your `Home` class, you need to know the room name using getter. Then, you can add the following method:

```
get room() {
  return this.roomName;
}
```

If you try `console.log(home.room)` outside the class, you should get the value stored in the `roomName` class variable.

Adding and removing videos

Similar to the `readyToCall` event, `SimpleWebRTC` will fire a `videoAdded` event for every video it finds in the room with a callback function having the video object and the peer object containing the ID (the unique ID of that user).

To test multiple videos, we are going to open two tabs on the same browser in the same system. This might cause feedback to damage your audio devices, so keep your volume muted!

Create a new method inside the `Home` class `addRemoteVideo($video, peer)`, as follows:

```
class Home {
  ...
  addRemoteVideo($video, peer) {
  }
}
```

Let's add another event handler for the `videoAdded` event, just as we did for the `readToCall` event:

```
webrtc.on('videoAdded', ($video, peer) => home.addRemoteVideo($video, peer));
```

Whenever a video gets added, it will call the `addRemoteVideo` method of the `Home` class with the video object and the peer object. We have a div `.video-area`, which is supposed to contain all the videos. So, we need to construct a new div element similar to the one used for the local video, such as:

```
<div class="video-container" id="container_peerid">
  <video class="video-player"></video>
</div>
```

And we should append this element to the `.video-area` div, which is currently referenced by `this.$remotes` variable. This is quite simple, just as we added the `script` element in the previous chapter. Inside your `addRemoteVideo()` method, add the following code:

```
addRemoteVideo($video, peer) {
  const $container = document.createElement('div');
  $container.className = 'video-container';
  $container.id = 'container_' + webrtc.getDomId(peer);

  $video.className = 'video-player';

  $container.appendChild($video);

  this.$remotes.appendChild($container);
}
```

The preceding code does the following:

- First, we create a `div` element using the `document.createElement('div')` method and assign it to the `$container` object.
- Then, we set the class name of `$container` to `'video-container'` and ID to `'container_peerid'`. We can get the peer ID from the peer object we received using the `webrtc.getDomId()` method.
- The `$video` object we received is an HTML element just like `$container`. So, we assign it the class name `'video-player'`.
- Then, for the last step, we append `$video` as a child inside `$container` and, finally, append `$container` as a child inside `this.$remotes`.

This will construct the HTMLs we need with the classes and IDs. When a user leaves the room, the `videoRemoved` event will be fired, which is similar to the `videoAdded` event. Whenever the user leaves the room, we need to use the peer ID to remove the div containing the ID `'container_peerid'`, where `peerid` is the ID of the user who left. To do so, add the following code:

```
class Home {
  ...
  removeRemoteVideo(peer) {
    const $removedVideo = document.getElementById(peer ? 'container_' +
webrtc.getDomId(peer) : 'no-video-found');
    if ($removedVideo) {
      this.$remotes.removeChild($removedVideo);
    }
  }
```

```
    }
    ...

webrtc.on('videoRemoved', ($video, peer) => home.removeRemoteVideo(peer));
```

The `removeRemoteVideo()` method will find the div containing the remote video using the peer ID and will remove it from this `this.$remotes` object using the `removeChild()` method.

Time to test our Video Call app. Open the application in Chrome and create the room. Copy the room URL and paste it in a new tab (keep your volume muted!). It might take a few seconds, but unless STUN didn't work for you, you should see two videos in each of the tabs. You are streaming video between the tabs.

The first video is your video. If you close one of the tabs, you should see that the second video will be removed from the other tab. Before we test this app in other devices, there is one more feature that would really look great in this app. That is increasing the size of the selected video.

Selecting a video

Currently, all the videos are small in size. Hence, we need a feature to enlarge the videos, such as:

- In desktops, clicking on a video will increase the size of the video and bring it to the first spot among the list of videos
- In mobiles, tapping a video will only increase the size of the video

This sounds fine. To make this happen, let's add some styles to our `styles.css` file:

```css
@media only screen and (max-width: 736px) {
  .video-selected {
    max-height: 70vw;
    max-width: 70vw;
  }
}
@media only screen and (min-width: 736px) {
  .video-selected {
    max-height: 50vh;
    max-width: 50vh;
  }
  .container-selected {
    order: -1;
  }
}
```

```
}
```

We have added two sets of styles using media queries. One for mobile (`max-width:736px`) and another for desktops (`min-width: 736px`).

For every click made in a video, we should add the `.video-selected` class to that video and `.container-selected` to the parent div of that video:

- In mobiles, it will increase the size of the video up to 70% of the viewport width.
- In desktops, it will increase the size up to 50% of the viewport width and also assign `order: -1` to its parent div. This way, since the parent div is part of flex, it will become the first item of the flex elements (but other elements should not contain order in their styles).

In your `Home` class, add the following method:

```
clearSelected() {
  let $selectedVideo = document.querySelector('.video-selected');
  if($selectedVideo) {
    $selectedVideo.classList.remove('video-selected');
    $selectedVideo.parentElement.classList.remove('container-selected');
  }
}
```

This will find the video containing the `.video-selected` class and remove the `.video-selected` class from that video and the `.container-selected` class from that video's parent div. This is useful because we can call it to clear the selected ones before we select another video.

We can register a click event on the local video inside the `registerClicks()` method. Inside the `registerClicks()` method, add the following code:

```
this.$localVideo.onclick = () => {
  this.clearSelected();
  this.$localVideo.parentElement.classList.add('container-selected');
  this.$localVideo.classList.add('video-selected');
};
```

This will add the required classes to the video element and its parent div. For remote videos, we cannot register clicks here because we create those elements dynamically. So, we either have to create an event listener or register a click event when the remote video elements are created.

Creating an event listener for each video is not quite efficient here because the videos will be removed when the user leaves, so we will have unwanted event listeners running for each video. We will have to remove those event listeners using the `removeEventListener()` method or avoid this by creating an event listener to the parent div `.video-area` instead of the video elements. Still, this means that we need to filter through each of the clicks made inside `.video-area` div to check whether that click was made on a video.

Clearly, it's simpler to register a click using the `onclick()` method when the video element is created. This saves us the trouble of dealing with event listeners. Inside your `addRemoteVideo()` method, add this code after the existing code:

```
$video.onclick = () => {
  this.clearSelected();
  $container.classList.add('container-selected');
  $video.classList.add('video-selected');
};
```

Now try clicking on a video in Chrome. You should see that the video will increase its size and move to the first position on the list. Congratulations! You have successfully built your Video Call application! Time to test Video Call in action.

Video Call in action

You got the application ready, so let's test it locally. First, generate the production build for your app. You have already done this before in the Event Registration app. You need to set `NODE_ENV=production` in your `.env` file.

After that, in your project root folder, kill Webpack dev server and run the `npm run webpack` command. It should generate the production builds for your JS and CSS files. The filename will be available in the `dist/manifest.json` file. Include those CSS and JS files in your `index.html` page.

Now, run `http-server` in your project root folder. It should print two IP address. Open the one starting with 192 in your browser. This IP address is accessible to all the devices in your LAN, unless you have blocked the port using a firewall. However, Chrome will not display your video! This is because the `getUserMedia()` method will only work in localhost and HTTPS URLs. Since our local address is using HTTP only, the video will not work.

We can add HTTPS by deploying our WebRTC application on a public server with an SSL certificate from a certificate authority. However, for our local development environment, we can use a self-signed certificate. An SSL certificate from a certificate authority will be trusted by all browsers, but a self-signed certificate will not be trusted, hence, a warning will be shown, in which we should manually select the option to trust the website on our browser. For this reason, self-signed certificates are not suitable for production and should only be used for development purposes.

Creating a self-signed certificate is a big process but, luckily, there is an npm package that can do this in a single line. We need to install this package globally, since it is a command-line tool like `http-server`. In your terminal, run the following command:

```
npm install -g local-ssl-proxy
```

Linux users might have to add `sudo` to their command to install packages globally. By default, `http-server` will serve your files from port number 8080. Say, if your current URL is as follows:

```
http://192.168.1.8:8080
```

Then, open another terminal and run the following command:

```
local-ssl-proxy --source 8081 --target 8080
```

Here, source is the new port number and target is the port number in which http-server is running. You should then open the same IP address with the new port number and `https://` prefix in Chrome, as shown in the following code block:

```
https://192.168.1.8:8081
```

If you open this page in Chrome, you should receive a warning similar to the following screenshot. In that case, select **Advanced** as shown in the following image:

Once you click Advanced, you will see a page similar to the following image where you should click proceed link:

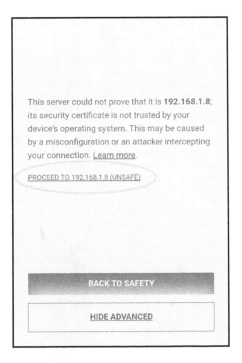

You can now use this HTTPS URL to open the app in any device that is connected to your LAN. Make sure there is enough distance between the devices so that it doesn't cause feedback.

Summary

Hopefully, you had a great time building the Video Call application. In this chapter, we did some new things with JavaScript and learned some new concepts, such as JavaScript WebRTC APIs and the SimpleWebRTC framework. Along the way, we did lot of cool things, such as manipulating browser history, selecting text using JavaScript, and working with URLs. Also, we shortened some of our code with short-circuit evaluation and learned about setters and getters for manipulating class variables in JavaScript.

`SimpleWebRTC` comes with many other events and actions which allow you to do more in the app, such as mute your microphone, mute audio from others, and so on. If you are interested, you can check out the SimpleWebRTC home page for more examples.

We know how to create reusable JavaScript modules, which we did in the previous chapter. In the next chapter, we are going to take it a step further and build our own reusable HTML elements using web components.

5
Developing a Weather Widget

Hey! Good work with the Video Call app. Hope you made some calls to your friends. In the previous chapter, we built a Video Call app using the SimpleWebRTC framework. Isn't it great to know that you can build all these cool applications with JavaScript? You have the power to access the user's device hardware straight from the browser.

So far, you have been building entire applications by yourself, so you had complete knowledge of the app's structure, such as the classes and IDs used in HTML and CSS and the classes, functions, and services used in JavaScript. But in the real world, you seldom work alone. If anything, you work in teams of sizes ranging from a few members to hundreds of developers working across the globe. In this case, you will not have knowledge about the entire web application. For this chapter, you are part of a huge web application project. You are in your first week of work and then your manager walks in and hands you your task for the week.

Can you build a Weather Widget?

So, your project has around 40 developers working in different parts of the web application and a new requirement just popped up. They need to show a Weather Widget in some areas of the website. The Weather Widget needs to be responsive so that it can squeeze into any available space in any section of the web application.

We can surely build a Weather Widget but there is a problem. We have no idea about the rest of the web application! For example, what are the class and ID used in its HTML, since the styles created by CSS are always global? If we were to accidentally use a class that is already being used in some other part of the HTML in the web application, our widget will inherit the style of that DOM element, which we really need to avoid!

Another problem is will be that we would have created `<div>`. For example:

```
<div class="weather-container">
  <div class="temperature-area">
  ....
  </div>
  <div>...</div>
  <div>...</div>
  <!-- 10 more divs -->
</div>
```

Along with a CSS file and some JS files, we have all the logic needed to make our widget work. But how are we going to deliver it to the rest of the team (given we didn't hopefully reuse any other used class names or IDs from the web app in the widget)?

If it were a simple JavaScript module, we simply build an ES6 module, which the team can import and use, since the scope of variables in the ES6 modules do not leak out (you should only use `let` and `const`; you really don't want to accidentally create a global variable with `var`). But it's a different story for HTML and CSS. Their scope is always global and they always need to be handled with care (you don't want some one else in the team to accidentally tamper with your widget)!

So, let's get started! We are going to think of some really random (and cool!) class names and IDs for the DOM elements, which no one else in your team can think of and then write a 10 page `readme` file to document the working of the Weather Widget with all the dos and don'ts and then later spend our time working on carefully updating the `readme` file whenever we do some enhancements and bug fixes to the widget. Also, be sure to memorize all the class names and the IDs!

About the last paragraph, Nope! We are definitely not going to do that! I'm already getting goosebumps thinking about it! Instead, we are going to learn about web components and we are going to write a simple ES6 module, which should be imported by the rest of your team members and then they should simply add the following DOM element in their HTML file:

```
<x-weather></x-weather>
```

That's it! You need to build a DOM element (such as the `<input>`, `<p>`, and `<div>` elements), which will show a Weather Widget. `x-weather` is a new HTML5 *custom element*, which we are going to build in this chapter. It is going to overcome all the problems we might face in the previous approach.

Introduction to web components

Web components are a set of four different technologies that can be used together or separately to build reusable user interface widgets. Just as we can create reusable modules using JavaScript, we can create reusable DOM elements with web component technologies. The four technologies that form the web components are:

- Custom elements
- HTML templates
- Shadow DOM
- HTML imports

The web components were created to provide developers simple APIs to build highly reusable DOM elements. There are many JavaScript libraries and frameworks that focus on providing reusability by organizing the entire web application into simpler components, such as React, Angular, Vue, Polymer, and so on. In the next chapter, we are going to build an entire web application by putting together multiple independent React components. However, despite all the frameworks and libraries available, web components hold a big advantage, since they are supported natively by the browser, which means no additional libraries to increase the size of your widget.

For our widget, we are going to use custom elements and shadow DOM. Before we start building our widget, let's take a quick look into the other two, which we will not use in this chapter.

 Web components are a new standard and they are actively being implemented by all the browser vendors. However, at the time of writing this book, *only Chrome supports all the features of the web components*. If you want to check whether your browser supports web components, visit: `http://jonrimmer.github.io/are-we-componentized-yet/`.

You should only use Chrome for the project in this chapter, since other browsers do not yet have proper support for web components. At the end of this chapter, we'll discuss how to add polyfills to make web components work in all the browsers.

HTML templates

An HTML template is a simple `<template>` tag, which we can add in our DOM. However, even if we add it in our HTML, the contents of the `<template>` element will not get rendered. If it contains any external resources, such as images, CSS, and JS files, they will also not get loaded into our application.

Hence, the template element only holds some HTML content, which can be used later by JavaScript. For example, say you have the following template element:

```
<template id="image-template">
  <div>
    <h2>Javascript</h2>
    <img
src="https://s3-us-west-2.amazonaws.com/s.cdpn.io/4621/javascript.png"
alt="js-logo" style="height: 50px; width: 50px;">
  </div>
</template>
```

This element holds `div` that will not be rendered by the browser. However, we can create a reference of that `div` using JavaScript, as follows:

```
const $template = document.querySelector('#image-template');
```

Now, we can make any changes to this reference and add it to our DOM. Even better, we can make a deep copy of this element so that we can use it in multiple places. A deep copy is a copy of the object in which changes to the copy will not be reflected in the original. By default, JavaScript always makes a shallow copy of the object when we do an assignment using the = operator. `$template` is a shallow copy of the DOM element, which we call as a reference to the DOM element. Hence, any change to `$template` is reflected in the DOM. But if we make a deep copy of `$template`, then the changes to that deep copy will not be reflected in the DOM, since it won't affect `$template`.

To make a deep clone of a DOM element, we can use the `document.importNode()` method. It accepts two parameters: the first one is the DOM element it needs to clone and the second one is a boolean for whether it needs to be a deep copy. If the second argument is true, it will make a deep copy of the element. See the following code:

```
const $javascript = document.importNode($template.content, true);
$body.appendChild($javascript);
```

Here, I made a deep copy of the contents of the template element (`$template.content`) in the `$javascript` object and added `$javascript` to the DOM element. Any modifications to `$javascript` will not affect `$template`.

For a more detailed example, I have set up a JSFiddle at: `https://jsfiddle.net/tgf5LcOv/`. Do check it out to see the working of the template elements in action.

HTML imports

HTML imports are simple. They let you import an HTML document inside another HTML document in the same way as you include CSS and JS files. The import statement looks as follows:

```
<link rel="import" href="file.html">
```

HTML imports have a lot of benefits when we work in an environment that *does not* use a build tool such as Webpack; for example delivering the web components for use across the web application.

 For more information regarding using the HTML imports feature, refer to the html5rocks tutorial at: `https://www.html5rocks.com/en/tutorials/webcomponents/imports/`.

The main reason why we are not going to use HTML templates and HTML imports in our Weather Widget is that they are more focused on usage with HTML files. Our build system that we are going to use in this chapter (Webpack) works better with JavaScript files. So, we'll continue with the rest of the chapter, learning about custom elements and shadow DOM.

Building the Weather Widget

For this chapter, we need a server to fetch weather information for a given location. In the browser, we can use navigator object to retrieve the exact geolocation (`latitude` and `longitude`) of the user. Then, using these coordinates, we need to find the name of the region and its weather information. For this purpose, we need to use third-party weather providers and the Google Maps API, which we used in `Chapter 3`, *Event Registration App*. The weather provider we are going to use in this project is **Dark Sky**.

Let's set up the server for the Weather Widget. Open up the `Chapter05\Server` directory in the book code. Inside the server directory, first run `npm install` to install all the dependencies. You need to get the API keys for both Dark Sky and Google Maps. You might already have the Google Map API key, since we used it recently. To generate your API keys for both the services, do the following:

- **Dark Sky**: Sign up for a free account at: `https://darksky.net/dev/`, and then you will get a secret key.
- **Google Maps**: Follow the steps provided at: `https://developers.google.com/maps/documentation/javascript/get-api-key`.

Once you get both the keys, create a `.env` file inside the `Server` root directory and add the keys inside it in the following format:

```
DARK_SKY_KEY=DarkSkySecretKey
GMAP_KEY=GoogleMapAPIKey
```

Once you have added the keys, run `npm start` in the terminal from the `Server` root directory to start the server. The server will be running at the `http://localhost:3000/` URL.

We have the server ready. Let's set up the starter files for the project. Open up the `Chapter05\Starter` files and then run `npm install` inside that directory to install all the dependencies. Create a `.env` file in the project root directory and add the following lines inside it:

```
NODE_ENV=dev
SERVER_URL=http://localhost:3000
```

Just as we did in the previous chapter, we should set `NODE_ENV=production` for generating production builds. `SERVER_URL` will contain the URL of the project's server that we just set up. Both `NODE_ENV` and `SERVER_URL` will be available as global variables for the JavaScript code in our app (I have used the Webpack defined plugin in `webpack.config.js`).

Finally, execute `npm run watch` in the Terminal to start the Webpack dev server. You will have your project running in `http://localhost:8080/` (the project URL will be printed in the Terminal). Currently, the web app will display three texts: large, medium, and small. It has three containers of different sizes, which will hold the Weather Widget. At the end of the project, the Weather Widget will look as follows:

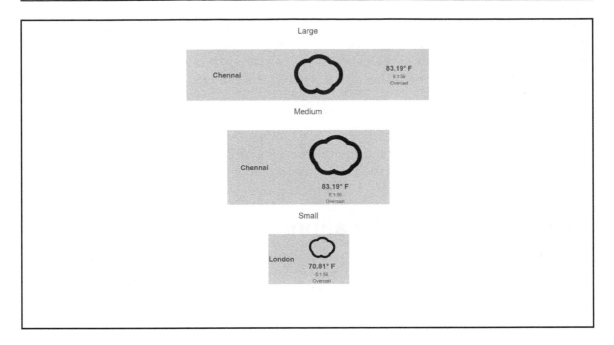

Working of the Weather Widget

Let's strategize the working of our Weather Widget. Since our Weather Widget is an HTML custom element, it should work just like other native HTML elements. For example, consider the `<input>` element:

```
<input type="text" name="username">
```

This will render a normal text input. However, we can use the same `<input>` element with a different attribute, as follows:

```
<input type="password" name="password">
```

It will render a password field instead of the text field with all the input text content hidden. Likewise, for our Weather Widget, we need to display the current weather condition for a given location. The best way to pinpoint the user's location is to use the HTML5 geolocation, which will get the user's current latitude and longitude information directly from the browser.

However, we should make our widget customizable for the rest of the developers. They might want to manually set a location for our Weather Widget. So, we'll leave the logic to retrieve the location to other developers. Instead, we can manually accept `latitude` and `longitude` as attributes for our Weather Widget. Our weather element will look as follows:

```
<x-weather latitude="40.7128" longitude="74.0059" />
```

Now, we can read `latitude` and `longitude` from the respective attributes and set the weather information in our widget, and other developers can easily customize the location by simply changing the values of the `latitude` and `longitude` attributes.

Retrieving the geolocation

Before we start building the widget, let's take a look at the steps to retrieve the user's geolocation. In your `src/js/home.js` file, you should see an import statement, which will import the CSS into the web application. Below that import statement, add the following code:

```
window.addEventListener('load', () => {
  getLocation();
});

function getLocation() {
}
```

This will call the `getLocation()` function when the page completes loading. Inside this function, we must first check whether the `navigator.geolocation` method is available in the browser. If it is available, we can use the `navigator.geolocation.getCurrentPosition()` method to retrieve the user's geolocation. This method accepts two functions as parameters. The first function will be called when the location is retrieved successfully and the second function is called if the location cannot be retrieved.

In your `home.js` file, add the following functions:

```
function getLocation() {
  if (navigator.geolocation) {
    navigator.geolocation.getCurrentPosition(showPosition, errorPosition);
  } else {
    console.error("Geolocation is not supported by this browser.");
  }
}

function showPosition(position) {
```

```
    const latitude = position.coords.latitude;
    const longitude = position.coords.longitude;

    console.log(latitude);
    console.log(longitude);
}

function errorPosition(error) {
    console.error(error);
}
```

Open the app in Chrome. The page should ask you for permission to access your location, just as it did for accessing the camera and microphone in the previous chapter. If you click **Allow**, you should see your current latitude and longitude printed in Chrome's console.

The preceding code does the following:

- First, the getLocation() function will use the navigator.getlocation.getCurrentPosition(showPosition, errorPosition) method to get the location of the user.
  - If you click **Allow** when the page asks for permission, then it will call the showPosition function with the position object as a parameter.
  - If you click **Block**, then it will call the errorPosition function with the error object as a parameter.
- The position object contains the latitude and longitude of the user in the position.coords property. This function will print the latitude and longitude in the console.

 For more information regarding the usage of the geolocation, refer to the MDN page: https://developer.mozilla.org/en-US/docs/Web/API/Geolocation/Using_geolocation.

Creating the weather custom element

We have the geolocation. So, let's start creating the custom element. Currently, your folder structure will be as follows:

```
.
├── index.html
├── package.json
├── src
│   ├── css
│   │   └── styles.css
│   └── js
│       └── home.js
└── webpack.config.js
```

We want to keep our custom element to be independent of other JavaScript modules. Inside the src/js directory, create a file under the path CustomElements/Weather/Weather.js. Do note that I have used capital letters for the first letters in the folder and filenames (PascalCase). You can use PascalCase for files and folders, which will export an entire class. This is only for easily identifying classes in your project folder and need not be a strictly followed rule.

Now, your folder structure will become:

```
.
├── index.html
├── package.json
├── src
│   ├── css
│   │   └── styles.css
│   └── js
│       ├── CustomElements
│       │   └── Weather
│       │       └── Weather.js
│       └── home.js
└── webpack.config.js
```

Open the Weather.js file in VSCode. All the native HTML elements are implemented using the HTMLElement class (interface) either directly or through an interface that inherits it. For our custom weather element, we need to create a class that extends HTMLElement. By extending a class, we can inherit the properties and methods of the parent class. In your Weather.js file, write the following code:

```
class Weather extends HTMLElement {

}
```

As per the custom elements v1 spec, a custom element should be extended from HTMLElement directly only using a class. However, we are using babel-loader with the env preset, which converts all the classes into functions. This will cause a problem with the custom elements, which need to be classes. But there is a plugin that can be used to overcome this issue: *transform-custom-element-classes*. I have already added this plugin in your webpack.config.js file so that you wouldn't face any problems in this chapter. You can find it in the .js rules section of your Webpack configuration file.

Let's declare the initial class variables in our Weather class's constructor:

```
Class Weather extends HTMLElement {

  constructor() {
    super();

    this.latitude = this.getAttribute('latitude');
    this.longitude = this.getAttribute('longitude');
  }

}
```

Note that in the constructor's first line, I have made a call to the super() method. This will call the constructor of the parent class HTMLElement. Whenever your class extends another class, always add super() inside your class's constructor. This way, the parent class will also get initialized before your class methods start working.

The two class variables (properties), this.latitude and this.longitude, will get the value of the attributes lat and long from the custom weather element using the this.getAttribute() method.

We also need to add HTML to our custom element. Since the Weather class is similar to the reference of a DOM element we used before, this.innerHTML can be used to add HTML for the weather element. Inside the constructor, add the following line:

```
this.innerHTML = ` `;
```

Now, this.innerHTML is an empty template string. I have already created the HTML and CSS needed for the custom element. You can find it in the Chapter 05\WeatherTemplate directory of the book code. Copy the contents of the weather-template.html file and paste it inside the template string.

Testing the custom element

Our custom element now contains the HTML needed for displaying the contents. Let's test it. At the end of your `Weather.js` file, add the following line:

```
export default Weather;
```

This will export the entire `Weather` class and make it available to be used inside other modules. We need to import this into our `home.js` file. Inside your `home.js` file, add the following code at the top:

```
import Weather from './CustomElements/Weather/Weather';
```

Next, we need to define the custom element, that is, associate the custom element with a tag name. Ideally, we would like to call our element `<weather>`. It would be nice! But according to the custom element spec, we should name the element so that it has a dash – in its name. So, for simplicity, we call our element `<x-weather>`. This way, whenever we see an element prefixed with `x-`, we will immediately know it is a custom element.

The `customElements.define()` method is used for defining custom elements. `customElements` is available on the global `window` object. It accepts two parameters:

- The first parameter is a string that should contain the custom element name
- The second parameter should contain the class that implements the custom element

Add `customElements.define('x-weather', Weather)` to your callback function of the window load event listener, which we previously added in `home.js` to get the geolocation. `window.addEventListener` will now look as follows:

```
window.addEventListener('load', () => {
  customElements.define('x-weather', Weather);
  getLocation();
});
```

Let's add the custom element to our `index.html` file. In your `index.html` file, add the following line inside the `div.large-container` element:

```
<x-weather />
```

Since it is a change in the HTML file, you have to manually reload the page in Chrome. Now, you should get a Weather Widget showing a loading message, as follows:

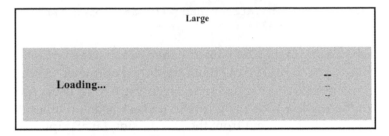

If you inspect the element using Chrome DevTools, it should be structured as follows:

```
▼ <x-weather> == $0
  ▶ <style>…</style>
  ▼ <div class="weather-container">
    ▼ <div class="title">
        <h2 id="city">Loading...</h2>
      </div>
    ▼ <div class="details">
        <canvas id="dayIcon" class="day-icon">
        ▶ <div class="text">…</div>
      </div>
    </div>
  </x-weather>
```

As you can see, your HTML is now attached inside the custom element along with the styles. However, we are facing one serious problem here. The scopes of styles are always *global*. This means that, if anyone were to add style for the `.title` class, say `color: red;` in the page's CSS, it will affect our Weather Widget too! Or, if we add styles to any class that is used in the page, say `.large-container`, inside our widget, it will affect the entire page! We really don't want this to happen. To overcome this problem, let's learn the last remaining topic of the web components.

Attaching a shadow DOM

A shadow DOM provides encapsulation between DOM and CSS. A shadow DOM can be attached to any element and the element to which the shadow DOM is attached is called the shadow root. A shadow DOM is considered separate from the rest of the DOM tree; hence, the styles from outside the shadow root will not affect the shadow DOM and vice versa.

To attach a shadow DOM to an element, we simply need to use the `attachShadow()` method on that element. Take a look at the following example:

```
const $shadowDom = $element.attachShadow({mode: 'open'});
$shadowDom.innerHTML = `<h2>A shadow Element</h2>`;
```

Here, firstly, I attached a shadow DOM named `$shadowDom` to `$element`. After this, I added some HTML to `$shadowDom`. Note that I used the parameter `{mode: 'open'}` to the `attachShadow()` method. If `{mode: 'closed'}` were to be used, access to the shadow DOM from the shadow root using JavaScript is closed and other developers will not be able to manipulate our element from the DOM using JavaScript.

We need the developers to manipulate our element using JavaScript so that they can set the geolocation for the Weather Widget. Generally, the open mode is widely used. The closed mode is used only when you want to completely prevent others from making changes to your element.

To add the shadow DOM to our custom weather element, perform the following steps:

1. Attach a shadow DOM to our custom element. This can be done by adding the following line to the constructor:

```
this.$shadowRoot = this.attachShadow({mode: 'open'});
```

2. Replace `this.innerHTML` with `this.$shadowRoot.innerHTML` and your code should now look as follows:

```
this.$shadowRoot.innerHTML = ` <!--Weather template> `;
```

3. Open the page in Chrome. You should see the same Weather Widget; however, if you inspect the element using Chrome DevTools, your DOM tree will be structured as follows:

You can see that the contents of the `<x-weather>` element will be separated from the rest of the DOM by specifying `x-weather` as a shadow root. Also, the styles defined inside the weather element will not leak out to the rest of the DOM and the styles outside the shadow DOM will not affect our weather element.

Generally, to access the shadow DOM of an element, you can use the `shadowRoot` property of that element. For example:

```
const $weather = document.querySelector('x-weather');
console.log($weather.shadowRoot);
```

This will print the entire shadow DOM attached to a shadow root in the console. However, if your shadow root is *closed*, then it will simply print `null`.

Working with the custom element

We now have the UI ready for our Weather Widget. Our next step is to retrieve the data from the server and display it in the Weather Widget. Generally, widgets, such as our Weather Widget, will not be present in the HTML directly. Like with the tasks in our Chapter 1, *Building a ToDo List*, developers often create the element from JavaScript, attach attributes, and append it to the DOM. Also, if they need to make any changes, such as changing the geolocation, they will use a reference to the element in JavaScript to modify its attributes.

This is very common and we have been modifying a lot of DOM elements this way in all our projects. Now, the same will be expected from our custom weather element. The `HTMLElement` interface from which we extended our `Weather` class provides special methods called lifecycle callbacks to our `Weather` class. Lifecycle callbacks are methods that get called when a certain event happens.

For a custom element, four lifecycle callback methods are available:

- `connectedCallback()`: This is called when the element is inserted into a DOM or a shadow DOM.
- `attributeChangedCallback(attributeName, oldValue, newValue, namespace)`: This is called when an observed attribute of the element is modified.
- `disconnectedCallback()`: This is called when the element is removed from the DOM or shadow DOM.
- `adoptedCallback(oldDocument, newDocument)`: This is called when an element is adopted into a new DOM.

For our custom element, we are going to use the first three callback methods. *Remove* the `<x-weather />` element inside your `index.html` file. We are going to add it from our JavaScript code.

In your `home.js` file, inside the `showPosition()` function, create a new function name: `createWeatherElement()`. This function should accept a class name (the HTML class attribute) as a parameter and create a weather element with that class name. We already have the geolocation in the `latitude` and `longitude` constants. The code for the `showPosition()` function is as follows:

```
function showPosition() {
  ...
  function createWeatherElement(className) {
    const $weather = document.createElement('x-weather');
    $weather.setAttribute('latitude', latitude);
    $weather.setAttribute('longitude', longitude);
    $weather.setAttribute('class', className);
    return $weather;
  };
}
```

This function will return a weather element with three attributes, which will look like the following snippet in the DOM:

```
<x-weather latitude="13.0827" longitude="80.2707" class="small-widget"></x-
weather>
```

To add the Weather Widget inside all the large, medium, and small containers, add the following code after the preceding function:

```
const $largeContainer = document.querySelector('.large-container');
const $mediumContainer = document.querySelector('.medium-container');
const $smallContainer = document.querySelector('.small-container');

$largeContainer.appendChild(createWeatherElement('large'));
$mediumContainer.appendChild(createWeatherElement('medium'));
$smallContainer.appendChild(createWeatherElement('small'));
```

You should see Weather Widgets attached to all the three different sized containers. Our final widget should look as follows:

The Weather Widget contains the following details:

- City name
- Weather icon
- Temperature
- Time (*hours:minutes:seconds*)
- Summary of the weather status (*Overcast*)

Adding dependency modules

Our Weather Widget needs to make an HTTP request to the server. For this, we can reuse the APICall module we built previously in Chapter 3, *Event Registration App*. Also, since we will be using the Dark Sky service for displaying weather information, we can use their icon library, Skycons, for displaying the weather icon. Currently, Skycons is not available in npm. You can get both the files from the book code Chapter05\weatherdependencies directory or from the completed code files.

Currently, your JS folder will be structured as follows:

```
.
├── CustomElements
│   └── Weather
│       └── Weather.js
└── home.js
```

You should add the `apiCall.js` file under the `CustomElements/Weather/services/api/apiCall.js` path and the `skycons.js` file under the `CustomElements/Weather/lib/skycons.js` path. Your JS folder should now look as follows:

```
.
├──── CustomElements
│     └──── Weather
│           ├──── lib
│           │     └──── skycons.js
│           ├──── services
│           │     └──── api
│           │           └──── apiCall.js
│           └──── Weather.js
└──── home.js
```

Retrieving and displaying weather information

In your `weather.js` file, add the following import statements at the top:

```
import apiCall from './services/api/apiCall';
import './lib/skycons';
```

The Skycons library will add a global variable, `Skycons`, to the window object. It is used to show an animated **Scalable Vector Graphics** (**SVG**) icon in the canvas element. Currently, all the class variables, such as `latitude` and `longitude`, are created in the constructor. But instead, it is better to create them only when the Weather Widget is added to the DOM. Let's move the variables to the `connectedCallback()` method so that the variables are created only when the widget is added to the DOM. Your `Weather` class will now look as follows:

```
class Weather extends HTMLElement {
  constructor() {
    this.$shadowRoot = this.attachShadow({mode: 'open'});
    this.$shadowRoot.innerHTML = ` <!-- Weather widget HTML --> `;
  }

  connectedCallback() {
    this.latitude = this.getAttribute('latitude');
    this.longitude = this.getAttribute('longitude');
  }
}
```

Also, just as we created the reference for elements in the DOM in the previous chapters, let's create references to the elements in the shadow DOM of the Weather Widget. Inside the `connectedCallback()` method, add the following code:

```
this.$icon = this.$shadowRoot.querySelector('#dayIcon');
this.$city = this.$shadowRoot.querySelector('#city');
this.$temperature = this.$shadowRoot.querySelector('#temperature');
this.$summary = this.$shadowRoot.querySelector('#summary');
```

Start the server included with this chapter and let it run in the `http://localhost:3000/` URL. For retrieving the weather information, the API endpoint is as follows:

```
http://localhost:3000/getWeather/:lat,long
```

Here, `lat` and `long` are latitude and longitude values. If your (`lat`, `long`) values are (`13.1358854`, `80.286841`), then your request URL will be as follows:

```
http://localhost:3000/getWeather/13.1358854,80.286841
```

The response format of the API endpoint is as follows:

```
{
  "latitude": 13.1358854,
  "longitude": 80.286841,
  "timezone": "Asia/Kolkata",
  "offset": 5.5,
  "currently": {
    "summary": "Overcast",
    "icon": "cloudy",
    "temperature": 88.97,
    // More information about current weather
    ...
  },
  "city": "Chennai"
}
```

To set the weather information in the Weather Widget, create a new method inside the `Weather` class `setWeather()` and add the following code:

```
setWeather() {
  if(this.latitude && this.longitude) {
    apiCall(`getWeather/${this.latitude},${this.longitude}`, {}, 'GET')
      .then(response => {
        this.$city.textContent = response.city;
        this.$temperature.textContent = `${response.currently.temperature}°
F`;
        this.$summary.textContent = response.currently.summary;
        const skycons = new Skycons({"color": "black"});
```

```
        skycons.add(this.$icon,
Skycons[response.currently.icon.toUpperCase().replace(/-/g,"_")]);
        skycons.play();
    })
    .catch(console.error);
    }
}
```

Also, call the preceding method by adding `this.setWeather()` at the end of the `connectedCallback()` method. Open the page in Chrome and you should see the Weather Widget working as expected! You will be able to see the city name, weather information, and the weather icon. The working of the `setWeather()` method is straightforward, as follows:

- First, it will check whether both the latitude and longitude are available. Otherwise, it will be impossible to make the HTTP request.
- Using the `apiCall` module, a GET request is made and the `response` is available in the `Promise.then()` chain.
- From the `response` of the HTTP request, the required data, such as city name, temperature, and summary, are included in the respective DOM elements.
- For the weather icon, the global `Skycons` variable is a constructor that creates an object with all the icons in a specific color. In our case, black. The instance of the constructor is stored in the `skycons` object.
- For adding the animated icon, we use the `add` method with the canvas element (`this.$icon`) as the first parameter and the icon name as the second parameter in the required format. For example, if the value of the icon from the API is `cloudy-day`, the equivalent icon is `Skycons['CLOUDY_DAY']`. For this purpose, we first convert the entire string to uppercase and replace - with _ by using a replace method with regular expression `.replace(/-/g, "_")`.

Adding the current time to the widget

We are still missing time in our widget. Unlike other values, time does not depend on the HTTP request but it needs to be updated every second automatically. In your weather class, add the following method:

```
displayTime() {
  const date = new Date();
  const displayTime =
`${date.getHours()}:${date.getMinutes()}:${date.getSeconds()}`;
  const $time = this.$shadowRoot.querySelector('#time');
```

```
    $time.textContent = displayTime;
}
```

The `displayTime()` method does the following:

- A date object is created using the `new Date()` constructor. The `new Date()` constructor creates a `date` object with all the details regarding the date and time passed as parameters. If no parameters are passed, it will create an object containing all the information regarding the current date and time (up to milliseconds). In our case, since we didn't pass any parameters, it contains all the details of the date and time in the moment it was initialized.
- We get the hours, minutes, and seconds from the date object. By using template strings, we simply constructed the time in the required format easily and stored it in the `displayTime` constant.
- Finally, it sets the time as the text content of the *p#time* (`$time`) element in the shadow DOM.

 the date object is an important concept and is part of everyday software development in JavaScript. To learn more about date objects, refer to the w3schools page at: `https://www.w3schools.com/js/js_dates.asp`.

This method is used to set the time once but we need to execute this method every second so that users can see the exact time in the widget. JavaScript has a method called `setInterval()`. It is used to execute a function repeatedly in a specific time interval. The `setInterval()` method accepts two parameters:

- The first one is the function that needs to be executed in a specific time interval
- The second one is the time interval in milliseconds

However, `setInterval()` executes the function repeatedly even if the DOM element is removed from the DOM for some reason. To overcome this, you should store `setInterval()` in a variable and then use the `disconnectedCallback()` method to execute `clearInterval(intervalVariable)`, which clears the interval function.

To implement this, use the following code:

```
connectedCallback() {
  ...
  this.ticker = setInterval(this.displayTime.bind(this), 1000);
}

disconnectedCallback() {
  clearInterval(this.ticker);
}
```

Open up the Weather Widget in Chrome and you should see the current time in the widget updated for every second, which looks normal to the user.

Responding to changes in element attributes

We have a full working Weather Widget but the weather information gets loaded only when the widget gets added to the DOM for the first time. If you try to change the value of the attributes latitude and longitude either from Chrome DevTools or from JavaScript, the value changes but the Weather Widget will not get updated. To make the weather element respond to the changes in latitude and longitude, we need to declare them as observed attributes. To do so, inside your Weather class, add the following line:

```
static get observedAttributes() { return ['latitude', 'longitude']; }
```

This will create a static getter observedAttributes() that will return an array of all the attribute names, for which the Weather Widget should listen for changes. Static methods are special methods of Class that can be accessed without creating a class instance object. For all the other methods, we need to create a new instance (object) of the class; otherwise, we won't be able to access them. Since static methods do not need an instance, the this object will be *undefined* inside these methods.

 Static methods are used to hold common (class variables and methods independent) functions associated with the class that can be used in other places outside the class.

Since we marked latitude and longitude as observed attributes, whenever they get modified using any method, it will trigger attributeChangedCallback() with the modified attribute's name, and the old value of that attribute and the new value of that attribute as parameters. So, let's add attributeChangedCallback() inside our Weather class:

```
attributeChangedCallback(attr, oldValue, newValue) {
```

```
      if (attr === 'latitude' && oldValue !== newValue) {
        this.latitude = newValue;
        this.setWeather();
      }
      if(attr === 'longitude' && oldValue !== newValue) {
        this.longitude = newValue;
        this.setWeather();
      }
    }
```

This method is simple. Whenever the value of the `latitude` or `longitude` attribute changes, it updates the respective class variable and calls `this.setWeather()` to update the weather to the new geolocation. You can test this by editing the attribute of the Weather Widget directly in the DOM tree of Chrome DevTools.

Using setters and getters

We use `setters` and `getters` all the time when we create a reference to the DOM element. If we have a reference to the weather custom element, we would simply want to set or get `latitude` or `longitude` as follows:

```
currentLatitude = $weather.lat;
$weather.lat = newLatitude;
```

In this case, we need the widget to update if we set a new `latitude` or `longitude`. To do that, add the following setters and getters to your `Weather` class:

```
get long() {
  return this.longitude;
}

set long(long) {
  this.longitude = long;
  this.setWeather();
}

get lat() {
  return this.latitude;
}

set lat(lat) {
  this.latitude = lat;
  this.setWeather();
}
```

To test if the setters and getters are working properly, let's remove (or comment) the line where the Weather Widget gets appended to $smallContainer. Instead of that, add the following code:

```
const $small = createWeatherElement('small');
$smallContainer.appendChild($small);
setTimeout(() => {
  console.log($small.lat, $small.long);
  $small.lat = 51.5074;
  $small.long = 0.1278;
  console.log($small.lat, $small.long);
}, 10000);
```

You should see that after 10 seconds, the weather in the small container automatically changes to London. The old and new geolocation will also get printed in the Chrome DevTools console.

You have successfully completed the Weather Widget! Before you use it in your project, you need to add polyfills, because at the time of writing this book, only Chrome supports all the features of the web components.

Fixing browser compatibility

To improve the browser compatibility of our Weather Widget, we need the set of polyfills provided by the webcomponents.js library in the: https://github.com/webcomponents/webcomponentsjs repository. These polyfills make our widget work with most of all the modern browsers. To add these polyfills to our project, first run the following command in the Terminal from the project root folder:

```
npm install -S webcomponents.js
```

This will install and add webcomponents.js to our project dependency. After that, import it in your home.js file:

```
import 'webcomponents.js';
```

Currently, we are initializing the project after listening to the window load event. Webcomponents.js loads the polyfills asynchronously and, once it is ready, it will fire a 'WebComponentsReady' event. So, instead of the load event, we should now listen for this new event:

```
window.addEventListener('WebComponentsReady', () => {
  customElements.define('x-weather', Weather);
  getLocation();
```

```
});
```

Now, for the last part, you need to document how to use the weather custom element and the web components polyfill in a readme file so that the rest of the team will know how to add it to the project. But this time, the readme document will be less than a single page and should be simple to maintain! I'll leave the readme part to you. Bet you are celebrating the completion of the fifth chapter already.

Essential things to know

These are a few things to know that will come in handy when working with custom elements. Just as we extended the general HTMLElement interface, we can also extend inbuilt elements, such as the paragraph element <p>, the button element <button>, and so on. This way, we can inherit all the properties and methods available in the parent element. For example, to extend the button element, do as follows:

```
class PlasticButton extends HTMLButtonElement {
  constructor() {
    super();

    this.addEventListener("click", () => {
      // Draw some fancy animation effects!
    });
  }
}
```

Here, we are extending the HTMLButtonElement interface instead of the HTMLElement interface. Also, just as inbuilt elements can be extended, custom elements can also be extended, which means we can create another type of widget by extending our Weather Widget class.

Even though JavaScript now supports classes and extend classes, it does not yet support private or protected class variables and methods like other object-oriented languages. Currently, all the class variables and methods are public. Some developers add the underscore '_' prefix to variables and methods that need to be private so that they don't accidentally use them in the extended class.

If you are interested in working more with web components, you should probably check out the following libraries, which are created to improve the usability and workflow of using web components along with inbuilt polyfills:

- Polymer: https://www.polymer-project.org/
- X-Tag: https://x-tag.github.io/

To learn more about extending native inbuilt HTML elements, refer to the following tutorial on the Google Developers page: `https://developers.google.com/web/fundamentals/getting-started/primers/customelements`.

Summary

In this chapter, you built a Weather Widget for your team while learning about the web components. You created a reusable HTML custom element, which uses shadow DOM to abstract CSS from the rest of the document, making the widget easily pluggable into the rest of the project. You also learned about some methods, such as geolocation and set intervals. But the most important thing you learned in this chapter is the advantage of creating independent components in a team environment. By creating a reusable weather component, you made the work easier for yourself and for the rest of the team.

So far, we have been working on pure JavaScript. However, there are a lot of modern frameworks and libraries today, which makes programming with JavaScript more easier, efficient, and scalable to a large extent. Most of the frameworks concentrate on organizing your entire application into smaller, independent, and reusable components, which we experienced with the web components in this chapter. In the next chapter, we are going to build an entire application using the awesome UI library created by Facebook-**React.js**.

6
Building a Blog with React

Hey! Good work making it to the last section of the book, where you are going to learn Facebook's React library. Before we start with this chapter, let's take a look at your journey through the book:

- You first built a simple ToDo list app using the JavaScript's ES6 syntax and then created a build script to compile it down to ES5 so that it will be compatible with older browsers.
- Then, you built a Meme Creator while setting up your own automated development environment, learning lots of new concepts and tools along the way.
- Next, you used the development environment and built an Event Registration app in which you built your first reusable JavaScript module for API calls and form validation.
- Then, you utilized the power of JavaScript WebAPIs to build a peer-to-peer video calling app with WebRTC.
- Lastly, you built your own HTML5 custom element that will display a weather widget and can be easily imported and used with other projects.

From a beginner level, you built some really awesome applications and now you are familiar with many important concepts of modern JavaScript. Now, it's time for you to employ these skills to learn a JavaScript framework, which will turbocharge your development process. This chapter will focus on helping you get started with React.

Why use a framework?

Modern application development is all about speed, maintainability, and scalability. Given the web is the major platform for many applications, the same will be expected for any web applications. JavaScript may be a great language but writing plain JavaScript can be a tedious process at times when you are dealing with a large application in a team environment.

In such applications, you will have to manipulate a lot of DOM elements. Whenever you make changes to the CSS of a DOM element, it is called a repaint. It will affect how an element appears on the browser. Whenever you remove, change, or add an element in the DOM, then it is called a reflow. A reflow of a parent element causes all its child elements to reflow too. Repaints and reflows are expensive operations because they are synchronous. It means when a repaint or reflow happens, JavaScript will not be able to run at that time. This will lead to lagging or slow execution of web applications (especially on smaller devices, such as low-end smartphones). So far, we have been building very small applications; therefore, we haven't noticed any performance issues but for applications, such as Facebook, this is crucial (there are literally 1,000s of DOM elements).

Also, writing lot of JavaScript code means increasing the file size of your code. For mobile users who rely on 3G or lower connections, it means your application will take a longer time to load. This causes a bad user experience.

Finally, frontend JavaScript code needs to deal with a lot of side effects (events such as click, scroll, hover, and network requests). When working in a team environment, every developer should know what kind of side effects your code deals with. When the web application grows, every side effect needs to be properly tracked. In plain JavaScript, writing maintainable code in such an environment is also difficult.

Luckily, the JavaScript community is well aware of all these scenarios and, hence, there are lots of open source JavaScript libraries and frameworks created and actively maintained to address the preceding issues and improve developer productivity.

Selecting a framework

Choosing a JavaScript framework in 2017 is more difficult than learning JavaScript itself (yeah, it's true!) due to the release of a new framework almost every week. But unless your requirement is very specific, you won't need to worry about most of them. Currently, there are a few frameworks that are really popular among the developers, such as React, Vue.js, Angular, Ember, and so on.

These frameworks are really popular because they get you up and running with your application in almost no time, followed by excellent support from the huge community of developers who use these frameworks. These frameworks also come with their own build tools, which will save you the trouble of setting up your own development environment.

React

In this chapter, we are going to learn the basics of building web applications with React. React is built and is widely used by Facebook. Many other famous applications, such as Instagram, Airbnb, Uber, Pinterest, Periscope, and so on, also use React in their web applications, which has helped to develop React into a mature and battle-tested JavaScript library. At the time of writing this book, React is the most popular frontend JavaScript framework in GitHub with an active community of over 70,000 developers.

Unlike most of the other JavaScript frameworks, React does not consider itself a framework but as a library for building user interfaces. It perfectly handles the view layer of your application by composing each section of your app into smaller functional components.

Functions are simple JavaScript code that perform a task. We have been using functions since the very beginning of this book. React uses the concept of functions to build each component of the web app. For example, look at the following element:

```
<h1 class="hello">Hello World!</h1>
```

Say you want to replace the word `world` with a dynamic variable, for example, someone's name. React achieves this by converting the element into a result of a function:

```
const hello = (name) => React.createElement("h1", { className: "hello"},
"Hello ", name, "!")
```

Now, the function `hello` contains the required elements as its result. If you try, `hello('Rahul')`, you will get the following:

```
<h1 class="hello">Hello Rahul!</h1>
```

But wait! What is that `React.createElement()` method? Forgot to tell you. That is how React creates HTML elements. But applying that to building applications is impossible for us! Imagine how many of those you will have to type in order to create an application with lots of DOM elements.

For this purpose, React introduced **JavaScript inside XML (JSX)**. It is the process of writing an XML-styled markup inside JavaScript, which gets compiled to the `React.createElement()` method by React to cut a long story short, you can also write the `hello` function as follows:

```
const hello = (name) => <h1 className="hello">Hello {name}!</h1>
```

This will make more sense because we are simply writing HTML inside the return statement of JavaScript. What's cool about this is the content of the element depends directly on the parameter of the function. You need to note a few things while working with JSX:

- The attributes of JSX elements cannot contain JavaScript keywords. See that the class attribute is replaced with `className` because a class is a reserved keyword in JavaScript. Similarly, for attribute, it becomes `htmlFor`.
- To include variables or expressions inside JSX, you should wrap them inside curly braces `{}`. It is similar to `${}` we use in template strings.
- JSX requires the Babel React preset to get compiled to JavaScript.
- All the HTML elements in JSX should only use small case letters.
  - For example: `<p></p>`, `<div></div>`, and `<a></a>`.
- Having capital letters for HTML is invalid.
  - For example: `<Div></Div>` and `<Input></Input>` are all invalid.
- The custom components we created should start with capital letters.
  - For example: consider the `hello` function that we created before, which is a stateless React component. To include it in JSX, you should name it as `Hello` and include it as `<Hello></Hello>`.

The preceding function is a simple **stateless** React component. A stateless React component outputs elements directly depending on the variables supplied as parameters to the function. Its output does not depend on any other factors.

 Detailed information on JSX can be found at: `https://facebook.github.io/react/docs/jsx-in-depth.html`.

This representation is suitable for smaller elements but many DOM elements come with a variety of side effects, such as DOM events and AJAX calls that will cause modification of DOM elements from factors (or variables) outside the scope of the function. To address this, React came up with a concept of **stateful** components.

A stateful component has a special variable called `state`. The `state` variable contains a JavaScript object and it should be immutable. We'll look at immutability in a moment. For now, look at the following code:

```
class Counter extends React.Component {
  constructor() {
    super();
    this.state = {
      count: 0,
    }
  }

  render() {
    return ( <h1>{this.state.count}</h1> );
  }
}
```

This is a simple stateful React component. As you can see, we are extending a class from the `React.Component` interface similar to how we extended it from `HTMLElement` to create our custom elements in the previous chapter and, just like custom elements, React components also have life cycle methods.

The react lifecycle methods are called at different stages of a component being inserted into the DOM or when it gets updated. The following life cycle methods are called (in the exact order) when a component is being inserted into the DOM:

1. constructor()
2. componentWillMount()
3. render()
4. componentDidMount()

The following lifecycle methods are called when an update is caused due to change of state or props of the component.

1. componentWillReceiveProps()
2. shouldComponentUpdate()
3. componentWillUpdate()
4. render()
5. componentDidUpdate()

There is also a lifecycle method which is called when the component is being removed from the DOM:

- componentWillUnmount()

 For a detailed explanation of how each of the lifecycle method works in react, refer the following page in react documentation: `https://facebook.github.io/react/docs/react-component.html#the-component-lifecycle`

The `render` method in the preceding `Counter` class is one of the lifecycle methods of a React component. As the name suggests, a `render()` method is used to render the elements in the DOM. The `render` method is called whenever a component is mounted and updated.

An update in a React component happens whenever a `state` or `props` of the component get changed. We haven't looked at props yet. To detect the change of the state variable, React requires the state to be an immutable object.

Immutable state

An immutable object is an object that cannot be changed once it is set! Yup, that's right. Once you create that object, there is no going back. That gets you wondering *"What if I need to modify a property of that object?"* Well, it's simple; you simply create a new object from the old object but with the new property this time.

Now, that may seem like a lot of work, but trust me, it is actually better to create a new object. Because, most of the time, React simply needs to know if the object is changed to update the view. For example:

```
this.state = { a: 'Tree', b: 'Flower', c: 'Fruit' };
this.state.a = 'Plant';
```

This is a standard way of changing the property of a JavaScript object. Here, let's call it the mutable way. Great! You just modified the state. But how can React know that the state is modified and it should call its lifecycle methods to update the DOM elements? Now that's a problem.

To overcome this, the React component has a special method called `setState()`, which can update the state in an immutable way and call the required life cycle methods (including `render`, which will update the DOM element). Let's see how to update the state in an immutable way:

```
this.state = { a: 'Tree', b: 'Flower', c: 'Fruit' };
this.setState({ a: 'Plant' });
```

This will update your state by creating a new state object instead of the older one. Now, the old state and new state are two different objects:

```
oldState = { a: 'Tree', b: 'Flower', c: 'Fruit' }
newState = { a: 'Plant', b: 'Flower', c: 'Fruit' }
```

React can now easily check whether the state is changed by a simple comparison of two objects, `oldState !== newState`, which will return true if the state is changed; therefore, giving a fast update in the view. Comparing objects this way is much faster and efficient than iterating over the properties of each object and checking whether any property is changed.

> The goal of using `setState()` is to call the `render` method, which will update the view. Hence, `setState()` should not be used inside the `render` method, or else it will result in an infinite loop.

JavaScript data types are not immutable; however, working with immutable data types are very important and you'll learn more about them soon.

Props

Props are data passed to a react component from a parent component. Props are similar to states except that props are read-only. You should not change props of a component from within the component itself. For example, consider the following component:

```
class ParentComponent extends Component {
  render() {
    return (
      <ChildrenComponent name={'World'} />
    )
  }
}

class ChildrenComponent extends Component {
  render() {
```

```
    return (
      <h1>Hello {this.props.name}!</h1>
    )
  }
}
```

Here, the name attribute passed to `ChildrenComponent` element inside the render method of `ParentComponent` has become a prop for the `ChildrenComponent`. This prop should not be changed by the `ChildrenComponent`. However, if the value is changed from the `ParentComponent`, the `ChildrenComponent` will also get re-rendered with the new props.

 To learn more about components and props, visit the following page in react documentation: `https://facebook.github.io/react/docs/components-and-props.html`

Building the Counter

Take a look at the `Counter` class we created before. As the name suggests, it should render a counter that increases by 1 every second. For that, we need to use `setInterval` to increase the count property of the counter's state object. We can use either the `componentWillMount` or `componentDidMount` lifecycle methods to add `setInterval`. Since this process does not need any reference to DOM elements, we can use `componentWillMount`.

Inside the `Counter` class, we need to add the following lines of code:

```
increaseCount() {
  this.setState({ count: this.state.count+1 })
}
componentWillMount() {
  setInterval(this.increaseCount.bind(this), 1000);
}
```

This will automatically perform the increment every second and the `render` method will update the required DOM element. To see the counter in action, visit the following JSFiddle page: `https://jsfiddle.net/reb5ohgk/`.

Now, on the JSFiddle page, look at the **External Resources** section in the top left corner. You should see three resources included in it, as shown in the following screenshot:

Along with this, in the JavaScript code block, I have selected the language as **Babel+JSX**. If you click on the settings icon in the top right corner of the JavaScript section, you will be able to see a set of options as shown in the following screenshot:

Here's what the configurations are all about:

- The first JavaScript file I have included is the `react.js` library. The React library is the core that is responsible for creating the DOM elements as components. However, React renders the components in a *virtual DOM* instead of the real DOM.

- The second library I have included is `ReactDOM`. It is used to provide a wrapper for React components so that they can be rendered in the DOM. Consider the following line:

```
ReactDOM.render( <Counter />,  document.querySelector("app"));
```

- This will render the `Counter` component into the `<app></app>` element in the DOM using the `ReactDOM.render()` method.
- The third library is Bootstrap; I just added it for the styles. So, let's look into the next step of the configuration.
- In the JavaScript code block, I have selected the language as **Babel + JSX**. It is because the browsers only know JavaScript. They have no idea about JSX in the same way that older browsers didn't have any idea about ES6.
- So, I just instructed JSFiddle to use the in-browser Babel transformer to compile the ES6 and JSX code back to normal JavaScript so that it will work with all the browsers.
- In the real applications, we will use the Webpack and Babel loaders with the React preset to compile JSX just as we did for ES6.

By now, you should have a good idea of React So, let's get started with building your first React application-a ToDo list-in the next section.

The React crash course

In this section, we are going to spend 10 minutes building your first React application. For this section, you don't need any text editor because you will be building the app in JSFiddle!

Get started by visiting the JSFiddle page at: `https://jsfiddle.net/uhxvgcqe/`, where I have set up all the libraries and configurations needed for building a React application. You should write the code for the React crash course section in this page.

This page has React and `ReactDOM` available as the properties of a window object (global scope), since I have included these libraries in the external resources. We'll also create a component object from the React object. In ES6, there is a trick to obtain properties or methods of an object into standalone variables. Look at the following example:

```
const vehicles = { fourWheeler: 'Car', twoWheeler: 'Bike' };
const { fourWheeler, twoWheeler } = vehicles;
```

This will now create two new constants, fourWheeler and twoWheeler, from the vehicle object's respective properties. This is called a destructuring assignment and it works with both objects and arrays. Following the same principle, in the first line of your JSFiddle, add the following code:

```
const { Component } = React;
```

This will create the component object from the component property of the React object. Followed by that, I have included an <app></app> element in the HTML section, which is where we are going to render our React component. So, create a reference to the <app> element using the following line of code:

```
const $app = document.querySelector('app');
```

Let's create a stateful app component that will render our ToDo list. In the JSFiddle, type the following code:

```
class App extends Component {
  render() {
    return(
    <div className="container">
      <h1>To Do List</h1>
      <input type="text" name="newTask"/>
      <div className="container">
        <ul className="list-group">
          <li>Do Gardening</li>
          <li>Return books to library</li>
          <li>Go to the Dentist</li>
        </ul>
      </div>
    </div>
    );
  }
}
```

Outside the class, add the following code block that will render the React component in the DOM:

```
ReactDOM.render( <App/>,   $app);
```

Now, click **Run** in the top left corner of the JSFiddle page. Your app should now look like this: `https://jsfiddle.net/uhxvgcqe/1/`.

 For more information and usage details regarding destructuring assignments, visit the following MDN page: `https://developer.mozilla.org/en/docs/Web/JavaScript/Reference/Operators/Destructuring_assignment`.

Adding and managing states

The most important part of a stateful React component is its state, which provides the required data to render the DOM elements. For our application, we need two state variables: one containing the array of tasks while another containing the input value of the text field. Being a fully functional representation, we always need to maintain a state for every view change, including the value of input fields.

In your `App` class, add the following lines of code:

```
constructor() {
  super();
  this.state = {
    tasks: [],
    inputValue: "",
  }
}
```

This will add a constructor to the class, where we should make a call to `super()` first, since our class is an extended class. `super()` will call the constructor for the `Component` interface. In the next line, we have created the state variable's tasks and `inputValue`. `tasks` is an array, which will contain an array of strings with task names.

Managing the state for the input field

First, we'll attach the `inputValue` state with the input field. Inside your `render()` method, add the value attribute for the input JSX element, as shown in the following code:

```
<input type="text" name="newTask" value={this.state.inputValue} />
```

We have explicitly binded the value of the input field with the state variable. Now, try clicking **Run** and editing the input field. You should not be able to edit it.

This is because no matter what you type into this field, the render() method will simply render what we have specified in the return() statement, which is an input field with empty inputValue. So, how do we change the value of the input field? By adding an onChange attribute to the input field. Let me show you how.

Inside the App class, add the following lines of code in the position, as I have specified in the following code block:

```
class App extends Component {
  constructor() {
    ...
    this.handleChange = this.handleChange.bind(this);
  }
  handleChange(event) {
    this.setState({inputValue: event.target.value});
  }
  ...
}
```

This handleChange method will receive our typing event and will update the state based on the value of the event's target, which should be the input field. Note that, in the constructor, I have binded the this object with the handleChange method. This saves us the trouble of having to use this.handleChange.bind(this) inside the JSX elements.

Now, we need to add the handleChange method to the onChange attribute of the input element. In your JSX, add the onChange attribute to the input element, as follows:

```
<input type="text" name="newTask" value={this.state.inputValue}
onChange={this.handleChange} />
```

Click **Run** and you should be able to type in the input field again. But this time, your inputValue state gets updated every time you are editing the input field. Your JSFiddle should now look like this: https://jsfiddle.net/uhxvgcqe/2/.

This is the React's one-way data flow (or one-way data binding), where data only flows in one direction, from the state to the render method. Any events in the rendered components will have to trigger an update to the state to update the view. Also, the state should only be updated in an immutable way using the this.setState() method.

Managing the state for the tasks

The second state that we need to maintain in our app is the `tasks` array. Currently, we have an unordered list of sample tasks. Add those tasks as strings inside the `tasks` array. Your `state` object inside the constructor should now look as follows:

```
this.state = {
  tasks: [
    'Do Gardening',
    'Return books to library',
    'Go to the Dentist',
  ],
  inputValue: "",
};
```

Now, let's populate the tasks from the state. In your `render` method, inside the `<ul>` element, remove all the `<li>` elements and replace them with the following:

```
<ul className="list-group">
  {
    this.state.tasks.map((task, index) => <li key={index}>{ task }</li>)
  }
</ul>
```

The curly braces `{}` in JSX only accept expressions that return a direct value just like `${}` in template literals. Hence, we can use the array's map method that returns an array of JSX elements. Whenever we return JSX elements as arrays, we should add a `key` attribute with a unique value, which is used by React for identifying that element in the array.

So, in the preceding code, we need to perform the following steps:

1. We iterate over the `tasks` array of the `state` and return the list items as an array of the JSX elements using the `map()` method of the array.
2. For the unique value of the `key` attribute, we are using the `index` of each element in the array.

Click **Run** and your code should produce the same output as before, except that the tasks are now populated from the state. Your code should now look like this: `https://jsfiddle. net/uhxvgcqe/3/`.

Adding new tasks

Our final step in the app is to allow users to add a new task. Let's make it simple by adding a new task on hitting *Enter* or *return* on the keyboard. To detect the *Enter* button, we need to use an attribute on the input field similar to onChange, but it should happen before the onChange event. onKeyUp is one such attribute that gets called when the key is pressed and released by the user on the keyboard. It also happens before the onChange event. First create the method that will handle the keyup process:

```
class App extends Component {
  constructor() {
    ...
    this.handleKeyUp = this.handleKeyUp.bind(this);
  }

  handleKeyUp(event) {
    if(event.keyCode === 13) {
      if(this.state.inputValue) {
        const newTasks = [...this.state.tasks, this.state.inputValue];
        this.setState({tasks: newTasks, inputValue: ""});
      } else {
        alert('Please add a Task!');
      }
    }
  }
  ...
}
```

Here's how the handleKeyUp method will work:

1. First, it will check whether keyCode of the event is 13, which is keyCode for *Enter* (for Windows) and *return* (for Mac) keys. Then, it will check whether this.state.inputValue is available. Otherwise, it will throw an alert saying 'Please add a Task'.
2. The second and the most important part here is updating the array without mutating the state. Here, I have used the spread syntax to create a new tasks array and update the state.

In your render method, again modify the input JSX element into the following:

```
<input type="text" name="newTask" value={this.state.inputValue}
onChange={this.handleChange} onKeyUp={this.handleKeyUp}/>
```

Now, click **Run**, type a new task, and hit *Enter*. You should see that a new task gets added to the ToDo list. Your code should now look like `https://jsfiddle.net/uhxvgcqe/4/`, which is the completed code for the ToDo list. Before we discuss the advantages of using React here, let's take a look into the spread syntax we used for adding a task.

Preventing mutations using the spread syntax

In JavaScript, arrays and objects are passed by reference during an assignment. For example, open a new JSFiddle window and try the following code:

```
const a = [1,2,3,4];
const b = a;
b.push(5);
console.log('Value of a = ', a);
console.log('Value of b = ', b);
```

We are creating a new array b from array a. We then push a new value 5 into array b. If you look at the console, your output will be as follows:

Surprisingly, both arrays have been updated. This is what I meant by passing by a reference. Both a and b are holding the reference to the same array, which means updating either one of them will update both. This holds true for both arrays and objects. This means we will evidently *mutate the state* if we use a normal assignment.

However, ES6 comes with a *spread syntax* for arrays and objects. I have used this in the `handleKeyUp` method, where I am creating a `newTask` array from `this.state.tasks` array. In the JSFiddle window where you tried the preceding code, change the code into the following:

```
const a = [1,2,3,4];
const b = [...a, 5];
console.log('Value of a = ', a);
console.log('Value of b = ', b);
```

See how I have created a new array b this time. The three dots . . . (known as the spread operator) are used to expand all the elements in the array a. Along with it, a new element 5 is added, and a new array is created and is assigned to b. This syntax might be confusing at first but it is how we should update array values in React, since this will create a new array (in an immutable way).

Likewise, for objects, you should do the following:

```
const obj1 = { a: 'Tree', b: 'Flower', c: 'Fruit' };
const obj2 = { ...obj1, a: 'plant' };
const obj3 = { ...obj1, d: 'seed' };

console.log('Value of obj1 = ', obj1);
console.log('Value of obj2 = ', obj2);
console.log('Value of obj3 = ', obj3);
```

I have created a fiddle with the spread operators in `https://jsfiddle.net/bLo4wpx1/`. Feel free to play with it to understand the working of the spread syntax, which we will be using very often in this chapter and in the next.

 For more practical examples of using the spread syntax, visit the MDN page `https://developer.mozilla.org/en/docs/Web/JavaScript/Reference/Operators/Spread_operator`.

Advantages of using React

We have built a ToDo list app within 10 minutes using React. At the beginning of this chapter, we discussed why we need a JavaScript framework and the disadvantages of using plain JavaScript. In this section, let's look at how React overcomes those factors.

Performance

DOM updates are costly. Repaints and reflows are synchronous events and therefore, they need to be minimized as much as possible. React deals with this scenario by maintaining a virtual DOM, which makes React applications really fast.

Whenever we make a modification to the JSX element in the `render` method, React will update the virtual DOM instead of the real DOM. Updating the virtual DOM is fast, efficient, and much less expensive than updating the real DOM and only the elements that are changed in the virtual DOM will be modified in the actual DOM. React does this by using a smart diffing algorithm, which we mostly won't have to worry about.

To understand how React works in detail and its performance, you can read the following articles from the React documentation:

- `https://facebook.github.io/react/docs/reconciliation.html`
- `https://facebook.github.io/react/docs/optimizing-performance.html`

Maintainability

React shines great in this section, since it neatly organizes the application into states and corresponding JSX elements grouped as components. In the ToDo list app, we only used a single stateful component. But we can divide its JSX into smaller stateless child components too. This means any modification in the child components will not affect the parent. Therefore, the core functionality will not get affected even if we modify what the list looks like.

Check out the JSFiddle at: `https://jsfiddle.net/7s28bdLe/`, where I have organized the list items in a ToDo list as smaller child components.

This is really useful in a team environment, where everyone can create their own components and they can be easily reused by others, which will boost the developer's productivity.

Size

React is small. The entire React library is just around 23 KB when minified, while `react-dom` is around 130 KB. This means it does not cause any serious problems on page load times even on slow 2G/3G connections.

Building a blog with React

The objective of this section is to learn the basics of React and how it is being used in web applications by building a simple blog application. So far, we have been learning about React but now it's time to see how it is used in real web applications. React will work fine in our development environment, which we have been using in this book so far, except that we need to add an additional `react` preset to `babel-loader`.

But `react-community` has come up with a better solution, which is the `create-react-app` command-line tool. Basically, this tool creates your project with all the necessary development tools, Babel compilers, and plugins so that you need to focus only on writing code without worrying about Webpack configurations.

 `create-react-app` recommends using yarn instead of npm while working on React, but since we are very familiar with npm, we will not use yarn in this chapter. If you want to learn about yarn, visit: `https://yarnpkg.com/en/`.

To see how `create-react-app` works, first let's install the tool globally using npm. Open up your Terminal and type the following command (Since this is a global install it will work from any directory):

```
npm i -g create-react-app
```

Linux users might have to add the `sudo` prefix. Once it is installed, you can create a boilerplate for your React project by running a simple command:

```
create-react-app my-react-project
```

This command will take a while, since it has to create a `my-react-project` directory and install all the npm dependencies for your React development environment. Once the command is complete, you can run the application using the following commands in the Terminal:

```
cd my-react-project
npm start
```

This will start the React development server and will open the browser that will display a welcome page built with React, as shown in the following screenshot:

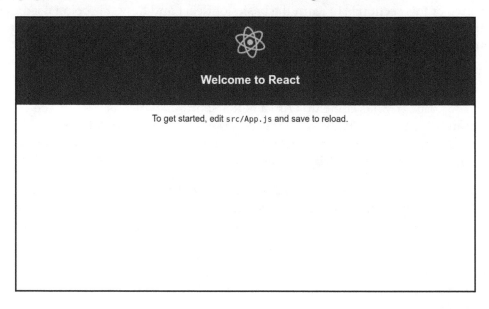

Let's see how the files are organized in the project. The project root folder will have files arranged in the following structure:

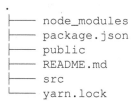

```
.
├── node_modules
├── package.json
├── public
├── README.md
├── src
└── yarn.lock
```

The public folder will contain the index.html file, which contains the div#root element to which our React component will get rendered to. Also, it contains the favicon and manifest.json file, which provides information to the Android devices when the web page is added to the home screen (commonly used in progressive web apps).

The src directory contains the source files of our React application. The file structure of the src directory will be as follows:

The index.js file is the entry point of the application, where it simply renders the App component from the App.js file in the index.html file present in the public directory. We write our primary App component in the App.js file. All the other components in the application will be children of the App component.

So far, we have been building multipage applications using JavaScript. But now, we are going to build a single page application using React. A **Single Page Application** (**SPA**) is one in which all the assets of the application get loaded initially and then it will work like a normal app on the user's browser. SPAs are the trend now, since they provide a great user experience across various devices for the users.

For building a SPA in React, we need a library to manage navigation between pages (components) in the app. react-router is one such library that will help us manage navigation between the pages (routing) in the app.

Just as in the other chapters, our blog will also be responsive on mobile devices. Let's take a look at the blog application we are about to build:

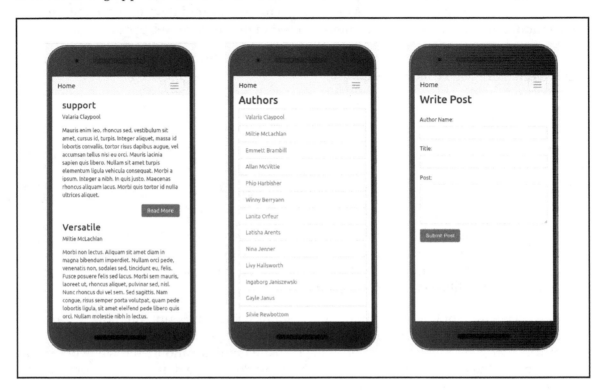

For this application, we are going to have to write a lot of code. Hence, I have already prepared the starter files for you to use. Instead of starting from the `create-react-app` tool, you should start from the starter files inside the `Chapter06` folder of the book codes.

Along with React and `react-dom`, the starter files contain the following libraries:

- React Router: `https://reacttraining.com/react-router/`
- Reactstrap: `https://reactstrap.github.io/`
- uuid: `https://www.npmjs.com/package/uuid`

The server that provides the API for the blog is available in the book code `Chapter06\Server` directory. You should keep this server running while building the application. I highly recommend you to see the completed application before starting to build the blog.

create-react-app supports reading environment variables from the
.env file straight out of the box; however, with the condition that all
environment variables should be prefixed with the REACT_APP_ keyword.
For more information, read: https://github.com/facebookincubator/
create-react-app/blob/master/packages/react-scripts/template/
README.md#adding-custom-environment-variables.

To run the completed application, perform the following steps:

1. Start the server first by running npm install, followed by npm start inside
   the server's directory.
2. It will print the URL that should be added to the .env file of Chapter
   6\completedCode files in the console.
3. Inside Chapter 6\CompletedCode files, create the .env file using the
   .env.example file and paste the URL printed in the first line of the console
   output as the value of REACT_APP_SERVER_URL.
4. Navigate inside the book code Chapter 6\CompletedCode files directory in
   your Terminal and run the same npm install and npm start commands.
5. It should open the blog on your browser. If it didn't open the blog, then manually
   open http://localhost:3000/ on your browser.

I have also created an API documentation using swagger for the server. To access the API
documentation, while your server is running, it will print the documentation URL in the
second line of console output. Simply open the URL in your browser. In the documentation
page, click on the default group and you should see a list of API endpoints, as shown in the
following screenshot:

You can see all the information regarding the API endpoints and even try them out by clicking on the API and then clicking **Try it out**:

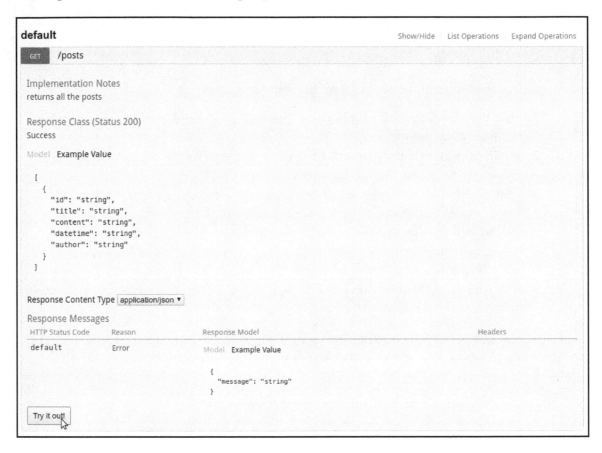

Take your time. Visit all the sections of the completed blog, try out all the APIs in the swagger document, and learn how it works. Once you are done with them, we'll move onto the next section, where we will start building the app.

Creating the navigation bar

Hope you tried the app. Currently, I have set the server to respond only after 3 seconds; therefore, you should see a loading indicator while trying to navigate between the pages.

The one thing common across all the pages in this application is the top navigation bar:

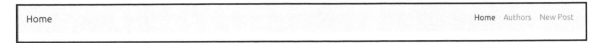

In the previous chapters, we created the navigation bar easily using Bootstrap. However, we can't use Bootstrap here because, in React, all the DOM elements are rendered dynamically through components. Bootstrap, however, requires jQuery, which only works on a normal DOM so that it can display animations while clicking the hamburger menu when the navbar is viewed on mobiles, as shown in the following screenshot:

However, several libraries are available which will let you use Bootstrap in React by providing the equivalent React components to each Bootstrap styled element. In this project, we are going to use one such library called the reactstrap. It requires Bootstrap 4 (alpha 6) to be installed with it; therefore, I have also installed Bootstrap 4 in the project's starter files.

Now, navigate to the book code `Chapter06\Starter files` directory and create the `.env` file in the project root directory. The `.env` file should have the same value as the completed code files for `REACT_APP_SERVER_URL`, which is the URL printed by the server in the console.

From the starter files directory in your Terminal, run `npm install`, followed by `npm start`. It should start the development server for the starter files. It will open the browser, which displays the message "**The app goes here...**". Open the folder in VSCode and see the `src/App.js` file. It should contain that message in the `render` method.

The starter files will be compiled with a lot of warnings saying **no-unused-vars**. It is because I have already included the import statements in all the files but none of them are yet used. Therefore, it is telling you that there are a lot of unused variables. Just ignore the warnings.

At the top of your `App.js` file, you should see that I have imported some modules from the reactstrap library. They are all React components:

```
import { Collapse, Navbar, NavbarToggler, Nav, NavItem } from 'reactstrap';
```

Explaining about each of the components here is not important, since this chapter focuses on learning React more than styling React components. Therefore, to learn about reactstrap, visit the project homepage at: `https://reactstrap.github.io/`.

In your `App` class, in the `App.js` file, replace the `return` statement of the `render` method with the following:

```
return (
  <div className="App">
    <Navbar color="faded" light toggleable>
      <NavbarToggler right onClick={() => {}} />
      <a className="navbar-brand" href="home">Blog</a>
      <Collapse isOpen={false} navbar>
        <Nav className="ml-auto" navbar>
          <NavItem>
            <a className="nav-link" href="home">Home</a>
          </NavItem>
          <NavItem>
            <a className="nav-link" href="authors">Authors</a>
          </NavItem>
          <NavItem>
            <a className="nav-link" href="new-post">New Post</a>
          </NavItem>
        </Nav>
      </Collapse>
    </Navbar>
  </div>
);
```

The preceding code will make use of the reactstrap components and will create a top navigation bar for the blog just like in the completed project. Check out the page in responsive design mode in Chrome to see how it looks on mobile devices. In the responsive design mode, the hamburger menu won't work.

This is because we haven't created any states and methods to manage expanding and collapsing the navigation bar. In your App class, add the following constructor and method:

```
constructor(props) {
    super(props);
    this.state = {
      isOpen: false,
    };
    this.toggle = this.toggle.bind(this);
}

toggle() {
    this.setState({
      isOpen: !this.state.isOpen
    });
}
```

This will add the state variable, isOpen, used for identifying the open/closed state of the hamburger menu, while the toggle method is used to expand or collapse the hamburger menu by changing the value of the isOpen state to true or false.

To bind these in your navigation bar, in the render method, perform the following steps:

1. Replace the false value of the isOpen attribue in the line with the <Collapse isOpen={false} navbar> component with this.state.isOpen. The line should now look as follows:

   ```
   <Collapse isOpen={this.state.isOpen} navbar>
   ```

2. Replace the empty function ()=>{} value of the onClick attribute in the line including <NavbarToggler right onClick={()=>{}} /> with this.toggle. The line should now look as follows:

   ```
   <NavbarToggler right onClick={this.toggle} />
   ```

Once you add these lines and save the file, the hamburger button in the navigation bar will work fine in your browser. However, clicking on the links in the navigation bar will only reload the page. We cannot do regular navigation using anchor tags in a single page application, since there is only a single page that the app is going to display. In the next section, we'll see how to implement navigation between pages using the React Router library.

Implementing routing and navigation using React Router

React Router implements routing by displaying the components based on the URL the user visits in your web application. React Router can be used in both React.js and React Native. However, since we are only focusing on React.js, we should use the specific React Router library, `react-router-dom`, that handles routing and navigation on the browser.

The first step to implement React Router is to wrap the entire `App` component inside a `<BrowserRouter>` component from `react-router-dom`. To wrap the entire application, open the `src/index.js` file in your project directory in VSCode.

At the top of the `index.js` file, add the following import statement:

```
import {BrowserRouter as Router} from 'react-router-dom';
```

This will import the `BrowserRouter` component with the name router. Once you have added the import statement, replace the `ReactDOM.render()` line with the following code:

```
ReactDOM.render(
  <Router>
    <App />
  </Router>
  ,
  document.getElementById('root')
);
```

This simply wraps the `<App />` component inside the `<Router>` component, which will allow us to use React Router in the rest of the `App` component's child components.

The routes file

In the starter files, I have included a `routes.js` file in the `src/routes.js` path. This file contains all the routes we are going to use on our blog in the form of JSON objects:

```
const routes = {
  home: '/home',
  authors: '/authors',
  author: '/author/:authorname',
  newPost: '/new-post',
  post: '/post/:id',
};

export default routes;
```

See the home page of the completed blog app. The URL will be pointing to the `'/home'` route. Likewise, each page has its respective route. However, some routes have dynamic values. For example, if you click **Read More** in a blog post, it will take you to the page with the URL:

```
http://localhost:3000/post/487929f5-47bc-47af-864a-f570d2523f3e
```

Here, the third part of the URL is the post's ID. To represent such URLs, I have used `'/post/:id'` in the routes file, where the ID means that React Router will understand that the ID will be a dynamic value.

You don't really have to manage all your routes in a single routes file. I have created a routes file so that it will be easier for you to add the routes while building the application.

Adding routes in the app component

What React Router does is pretty much simple; it simply renders a component based on the URL in the address bar. It uses history and location Web APIs for this purpose, but gives us simple, easy to use, component-based APIs, so that we can quickly set up our routing logic.

To add navigation between the components in the `App.js` file, add the following code in the `App.js` file's `render` method after the `<Navbar></Navbar>` component:

```
render() {
  return (
    <div className="App">
      <Navbar color="faded" light toggleable>
        ....
      </Navbar>

      <Route exact path={routes.home} component={Home} />
      <Route exact path={routes.post} component={Post} />
      <Route exact path={routes.authors} component={AuthorList} />
      <Route exact path={routes.author} component={AuthorPosts} />
      <Route exact path={routes.newPost} component={NewPost} />
    </div>
  );
}
```

Also, refer to the completed code files if you face any issues after adding the code files. I have already added all the import statements in the App.js file. Route component is imported from the react-router-dom package. Here's what the preceding route component does:

- The route component will check the URL of the current page and render the component that matches with the given path. Take a look at the following Route:

  ```
  <Route exact path={routes.home} component={Home} />
  ```

- React Router will render the Home component when your URL has the path '/home' (the value of routes.home from the routes file).
- Here's what each of its attributes means:
  - exact: Only when the path is matched exactly. This is optional if it is not present in '/home': It will hold true for '/home/otherpaths' too. We need the exact match; hence, I have included it.
  - path: The path that must be matched with the URL. In our case, it is '/home' from the routes.home variable from the routes file.
  - component: The component that must be rendered when the path matches with the URL.

Once you have added the route components, navigate back to the application in Chrome. If your application is running in http://localhost:3000/, you will only see a blank page. However, if you click on the menu items in the navigation bar, you should see the respective components being rendered on the page!

 By adding the navigation bar outside the route components, we can easily reuse the same navigation bar across the entire application.

However, we should have our application automatically navigate to the home page '/home' instead of displaying a blank page on the first load. To do that, we should programmatically replace the URL with the required '/home' path like we did in Chapter 4, *Real-Time Video Call App with WebRTC*, using the history object.

But we have a problem here. React Router maintains its own history object for navigation. This means we need to modify the history object of the React Router.

Managing history using withRouter

React Router has an `higher-order` component called `withRouter` with which we can pass in the React Router's history, location, and match objects to our React components as props. To use `withRouter`, you should wrap your `App` component inside `withRouter()` as a parameter. Currently, here's how we are exporting the `App` component at the last line of the `App.js` file:

```
export default App;
```

You should change this line to the following:

```
export default withRouter(App);
```

This will supply three props, `history`, `location`, and the `match` object to our `App` component. For our initial objective, displaying the home component by default, add the following `componentWillMount()` method to the `App` class:

```
componentWillMount() {
  if(this.props.location.pathname === '/') {
    this.props.history.replace(routes.home);
  }
}
```

Here's what the preceding code does:

1. Since it is written inside `componentWillMount`, it will get executed before the `App` component gets rendered.
2. It will check the path of the URL using the `location.pathname` property.
3. If the path is `'/'`, that is, the default `http://localhost:3000/`, it will automatically replace the history and URL with `http://localhost:3000/home`.
4. This way, the `home` component will be automatically rendered whenever the user navigates to the root URL of the web page.

Now, open `http://localhost:3000/` on your browser and it will display the homepage. Still, we have another problem here. Every time we click a link in the navigation bar, it is causing the page to reload. Since our blog is a single page app, reloading should be avoided, as all the assets and components are already downloaded. Reloading the application on every click during navigation will only lead to unnecessarily downloading the entire app multiple times.

Proptype validation

Whenever we are passing props to our React components, it is recommended to do proptype validation. A proptype validation is a simple type checking that happens in the development builds of React, which is used to check whether all the props are supplied properly to our React component. If not, it will display a warning message, which is very helpful for debugging.

All types of props that can be passed to our React component are defined in the 'prop-types' package, which gets installed along with create-react-app. You can see that I have included the following import statement at the top of the file:

```
import PropTypes from 'prop-types';
```

To do proptype validation for our App component, inside the App class, add the following static property before the constructor (having proptypes declared on top will make it easy to know what props the React component is dependent on):

```
static propTypes = {
  history: PropTypes.object.isRequired,
  location: PropTypes.object.isRequired,
  match: PropTypes.object.isRequired,
}
```

Refer the completed code files if you are confused about where to include the preceding code snippet. This is how the proptype validation works.

Consider the second line of the preceding code history: PropTypes.object.isRequired. This means that:

- history should be a prop to the App component
- The type of history should be the object
- The history prop is required (isRequired is optional and can be removed for props, that are optional)

For detailed information on proptype validation, refer to the React documentation page at https://facebook.github.io/react/docs/typechecking-with-proptypes.html.

Seamless navigation with NavLink

React Router has a perfect solution to fix the reloading problem during navigation. React Router provides `Link` and `NavLink` components, which you should use instead of the traditional anchor tags. `NavLink` has more features than the `link` component, such as specifying an active class name when the link is active. Therefore, we will use `NavLink` in our application.

For example, consider the following anchor tag we have used in the `App.js` file for navigating to the authors page:

```
<a className="nav-link" href="authors">Authors</a>
```

We can replace this with React Router's `NavLink` component as follows:

```
<NavLink className={'nav-link'} activeClassName={'active'}
to={routes.authors}>Authors</NavLink>
```

Here's what the attributes of the `NavLink` JSX components do:

- `className`: The class name given to the element when `NavLink` is rendered as an anchor tag in the DOM.
- `activeClassName`: The class name given to the element when the link is the currently active page.
- `to`: The path to which the link will navigate to.

Refer to the `App.js` file from the completed code files and replace all the anchor tags in the `App.js` file with `NavLink` components. Once you have done this change, whenever you click on the menu items in the navigation bar, your app will navigate seamlessly without any page reloads.

Also, since the `.active` class gets added to the active links, Bootstrap styles will highlight the menu item in the navigation bar with slightly darker black color when the respective navbar menu item is active.

We have successfully created the navigation bar for our application and implemented some basic routing. From our routes file, you can see that our blog has five pages. We'll build the home page in the next section.

Blog home page

You should already have an idea of how the blog's home page will look from exploring the app in the completed code files. Our blog has a simple home page that lists all the posts. You can click the **Read More** button in the posts to read the posts in detail. Since this blog is a project for learning purposes, this simple home page is enough for now.

Ideally, you should create each React component from scratch. However, to speed up the development process, I have already created all the stateless components and boilerplates for the stateful parent components. All the components are available in the src/Components directory. Since the React component names should start with capital letters, I have created all the component directory names with initial capital letters to indicate that they contain React components. This is the folder structure of the Components directory:

```
.
├──── Author
│     ├──── AuthorList.js
│     └──── AuthorPosts.js
├──── Common
│     ├──── ErrorMessage.js
│     ├──── LoadingIndicator.js
│     ├──── PostSummary.js
│     └──── SuccessMessage.js
├──── Home
│     └──── Home.js
├──── NewPost
│     ├──── Components
│     │     └──── PostInputField.js
│     └──── NewPost.js
└──── Post
      └──── Post.js
```

The home page of our blog is the Home component present in the src/Components/Home/Home.js file. Currently, the render method of the Home component only renders a Home text. We need to display the list of posts in the home page. Here's how we are going to achieve this:

1. The server has the /posts endpoint, which returns all the posts in a GET request as an array. Therefore, we can use this API to retrieve the post's data.

2. Since Home is a stateful component, we need to maintain states for every action in the Home component.

3. While the `Home` component is retrieving data from the server, we should have a state--loading, which should be a Boolean value to show the loading indicator.

4. If the network request is a success, we should store the posts in a state--posts, which can then be used to render all the blog posts.

5. If the network request fails, we should simply use another state--hasError, which should be a Boolean value to display the error message.

Let's get started! First, in your `Home` class, add the following constructor to define the state variables of the component:

```
constructor() {
  super();

  this.state = {
    posts: [],
    loading: false,
    hasError: false,
  };
}
```

Once you have defined the states, let's make the network request. Since the network request is asynchronous, we can have it in `componentWillMount`, but if you want to do a synchronous action, that will delay the render. It is better to add it in `componentDidMount`.

For making the network request, I have added the `apiCall` service, which we used in the previous chapters in the `src/services/api/apiCall.js` file, and included the import statement in the `Home.js` file. Here's the code for the `componentWillMount` method:

```
componentWillMount() {
  this.setState({loading: true});
  apiCall('posts', {}, 'GET')
  .then(posts => {
    this.setState({posts, loading: false});
  })
  .catch(error => {
    this.setState({hasError: true, loading: false});
    console.error(error);
  });
}
```

Here's what the preceding function does:

1. First, it will set the state variable loading to `true`.

2. The `apiCall` function is called to make the network request.

3. Since the network request is an asynchronous function, the `render` method will get executed and the component will get rendered.

4. After the rendering has happened, the network request will get completed in 3 seconds (I have set that much delay in the server).

5. If the `apiCall` is a success and the data is retrieved, it will update the post's state with the array of posts returned from the server and will set the loading state to `false`.

6. Otherwise, it will set the `hasError` state to `true` and will set the loading state to `false`.

To test the preceding code, let's add the JSX needed to render the posts. Since the JSX part requires a lot of code, I have already created the stateless components needed for use on this page in the `src/Components/Common` directory and included the import statement at the top of the `Home.js` file. Replace the `return` statement of the `render` method with the following code:

```
return (
  <div className={`posts-container container`}>
    {
      this.state.loading
      ?
        <LoadingIndicator />
      :
        null
    }
    {
      this.state.hasError
      ?
        <ErrorMessage title={'Error!'} message={'Unable to retrieve
posts!'} />
      :
        null
    }
    {
        this.state.posts.map(post => <PostSummary key={post.id}
post={post}>Post</PostSummary>)
    }
  </div>
);
```

Once you have added the preceding code snippet, keep your server running and visit the blog's home page. It should list all the posts, as shown in the following screenshot:

However, if you kill the server and reload the page, it will display the error message, as shown in the following screenshot:

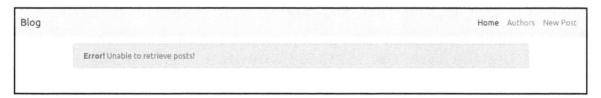

The implementation process is very simple once you get to know how the state and life cycle methods work with React. However, we still need to cover one important topic in this section, which is the child components that I have created previously for you to use.

Using child components

Let's take a look at the ErrorMessage component, which I have created to show an error message when we are unable to retrieve posts from the server. This is how the ErrorMessage component is included in the render method:

```
<ErrorMessage title={'Error!'} message={'Unable to retrieve posts!'} />
```

If the ErrorMessage is a stateful component created by extending the Component interface. The attributes of the ErrorMessage JSX element title and message will then become the props of the children ErrorMessage component. However, if you look at the implementation of the ErrorMessage element, you will see that it is a stateless functional component:

```
const ErrorMessage = ({title, message}) => (
  <div className="alert alert-danger">
    <strong>{title}</strong> {message}
  </div>
);
```

So, here's how the attributes work for functional components:

- Since functional components do not support state or props, the attributes become the parameters of the function call. Consider the following JSX element:

    ```
    <ErrorMessage title={'Error!'} message={'Unable to retrieve
    posts!'} />
    ```

- This will be equivalent to a function call with an object as its parameter:

```
ErrorMessage({
  title: 'Error!',
  message: 'Unable to retrieve posts!',
})
```

- By using the destructuring assignment you learned earlier, you can use the parameters in our function as follows:

    ```
    const ErrorMessage = ({title, message}) => {}; // title and message
    retrieved as normal variables
    ```

- We can use the propType validation for functional components too, but here, the propTypes are used to validate the function's arguments.

Whenever you are typing the JSX code in a functional component, make sure you have included the `import React from 'react'` statement in the file. Otherwise, the Babel compiler will not know how to compile the JSX back to JavaScript.

The `PostSummary` component comes with a **Read More** button with which you can see the entire post's details on a page. Currently, if you click this link, it will simply display the `'Post Details'` text. So, let's finish up our blog home page by creating the post details page.

Displaying post details

Each post in the blog has a unique ID associated with it. We need to use this ID to retrieve the post details from the server. When you click on the **Read More** button, I have created the `PostSummary` component in such a way that it will take you to the route `'/post/:id'`, where `:id` contains the ID of the post. This is how the post URL will look:

```
http://localhost:3000/post/487929f5-47bc-47af-864a-f570d2523f3e
```

Here, the third section is the post ID. Open the `Post.js` file from the `src/Components/Post/Post.js` path in VSCode. We need to access the ID that is present in the URL in our `Post` component. To access the URL parameter, we need to use the match object of the React Router. For this process, we will have to wrap our `Post` component inside `withRouter()` just as we did for the `App` component.

In your `Post.js` file, change the export statement into the following:

```
export default withRouter(Post);
```

Also, since this will provide the `history`, `location`, and `match` props to the `Post` component, we should also add the prototype validation to the `Post` class:

```
static propTypes = {
  history: PropTypes.object.isRequired,
  location: PropTypes.object.isRequired,
  match: PropTypes.object.isRequired,
}
```

We have to create the states for our `Post` component. The states are the same as that of the `Home` component; however, instead of the posts state (array), we will have the post state (object) here, since this page only requires a single post. In the `Post` class, add the following constructor:

```
constructor() {
  super();

  this.state = {
    post: {},
    loading: false,
    hasError: false,
  };
}
```

In the swagger document of the server, you should see an API endpoint, `GET /post/{id}`, which we are going to use in this chapter for retrieving `Post` from the server. The `componentWillMount` method we are going to use in this component will be extremely similar to that of the previous `Home` component, except that we will have to retrieve the `id` parameter from the URL. This can be done using the following line of code:

```
const postId = this.props.match.params.id;
```

Here, `this.props.match` is a prop provided to the `Post` component by the `withRouter()` component of React Router. So, your `componentWillMount` method should be as follows:

```
componentWillMount() {
  this.setState({loading: true});
  const postId = this.props.match.params.id;
  apiCall(`post/${postId}`, {}, 'GET')
  .then(post => {
    this.setState({post, loading: false});
  })
  .catch(error => {
    this.setState({hasError: true, loading: false});
    console.error(error);
  });
}
```

Finally, in the `render` method, add the following code:

```
return(
  <div className={`post-container container`}>
    {
      this.state.loading
```

```
              ?
                <LoadingIndicator />
              :
                null
          }
          {
            this.state.hasError
              ?
                <ErrorMessage title={'Error!'} message={`Unable to retrieve
post!`} />
              :
                null
          }
          <h2>{this.state.post.title}</h2>
          <p>{this.state.post.author}</p>
          <p>{this.state.post.content}</p>
        </div>
      );
```

This will create the post page. Now, you should be able to see the entire post by clicking the **Read More** button. This page will work in the same way the home page does. By using reusable components, you can see that we have minimized the code a lot.

Adding a new blog post

We have successfully built the home page for our blog. The next task is to build the author list page. However, I'll leave the construction of the author list to you. You can refer to the completed code files and build the author list page. This will be a good practice exercise for you.

So, that leaves us with the last page, which is the new post page. The API we are going to use for adding a new blog post is POST /post, which you can see in the swagger document. The body of the post request will be in the following form:

```
{
  "id": "string",
  "title": "string",
  "content": "string",
  "datetime": "string",
  "author": "string"
}
```

Here, `id` is the unique ID for the blog post and `datetime` is the epoch timestamp as a string. Usually, these two properties are generated by the server but since we are only using the mock server for our project, we need to generate them on the clientside.

Open the `NewPost.js` file from the `src/Components/NewPost/NewPost.js` path. This component requires three input fields:

- Author name
- Post title
- Post text

We need to maintain states for these three fields. The blog post will need `textarea`, which will dynamically increase its size (rows) as the blog post is typed. Thus, we need to maintain a state for the number of lines to manage the row count.

Along with this, we will also need the states we used in the previous component's loading and `hasError` for network requests. We will also need a state success for indicating to the user that the post has been submitted successfully.

In your `NewPost` class, create `constructor` with all the required state variables, as shown here:

```
constructor() {
  super();

  this.state = {
    author: '',
    title: '',
    content: '',
    noOfLines: 0,
    loading: false,
    success: false,
    hasError: false,
  };
}
```

Unlike the previous components, instead of just displaying the retrieved data from the server, we will have to send data from input fields to the server in this component. Whenever input fields are involved, it means we will need a lot of methods to edit the state of the input fields.

Replace the `render` method of your `NewPost.js` file with the `render` method from the `NewPost.js` file of the completed code files. Since both the author name and title use the same input fields, I have created a simple `PostInputField` component for them. Here's what the `PostInputField` component looks like for the author name input:

```
<PostInputField
  className={'author-name-input'}
  id={'author'}
  title={'Author Name:'}
  value={this.state.author}
  onChange={this.editAuthorName}
/>
```

Here's what the corresponding `PostInputField` function looks like:

```
const PostInputField = ({className, title, id, value, onChange}) => (
  <div className={`form-group ${className}`}>
    <label htmlFor={id}>{title}</label>
    <input type="text" className="form-control" id={id} value={value}
onChange={onChange}/>
  </div>
);
```

You can see that I basically made the `className`, `label`, `id`, `value`, and `onChange` properties dynamic in the returned JSX element. This will let me reuse the entire input field for multiple input elements in the same form. Since the final rendered DOM element will have different classes and IDs, but shares the same code, all you have to do is import and use it in your component. It will save many hours of long development work and, in many cases, it's more efficient than the custom elements you learned in the previous chapter.

Let's see how `textarea` works.

Inside the `render` method, you should see the following line where we are creating a `noOfLines` constant using the state variables:

```
const noOfLines = this.state.noOfLines < 5 ? 5 : this.state.noOfLines;
```

`this.state.noOfLines` will contain the number of lines present in the blog post. Using that, if the number of lines is less than 5, then we will set the value of row attribute to 5. Otherwise, we can increase the row attribute to the number of lines present in the blog post.

This is what the JSX for text input looks like:

```
<div className="form-group content-text-area">
  <label htmlFor="content">Post:</label>
  <textarea className="form-control" rows={noOfLines} id="content"
value={this.state.content} onChange={this.editContent}></textarea>
</div>
```

You can see that the value of the rows attribute is the noOfLines constant created in the render method. After the textarea field, we have the following sections:

- The loading section, where we can either show <LoadingIndicator /> or the **Submit** button based on the network request state (this.state.loading)
- The hasError and success sections where we can show the success or error message depending on the response from the server

Let's create the methods used by the input fields for updating their value. Inside your NewPost class, add the following methods:

```
editAuthorName(event) {
  this.setState({author: event.target.value});
}

editTitle(event) {
  this.setState({title: event.target.value});
}

editContent(event) {
  const linesArray = event.target.value.split('\n');
  this.setState({content: event.target.value, noOfLines:
linesArray.length});
}
```

Here, editContent is the method used by the text input field. You can see that I have used a split('\n') to divide the lines into an array based on the newline characters. We can then use the length of the array to count the number of lines present in the post. Also, remember to add the this binding to all the methods in the constructor. Otherwise, the methods called from JSX will not be able to use the this variable of the class:

```
constructor() {
  ...

  this.editAuthorName = this.editAuthorName.bind(this);
  this.editContent = this.editContent.bind(this);
  this.editTitle = this.editTitle.bind(this);
}
```

Submitting the post

The last part of the adding posts section is submitting the post. Here, we need to do two things: generate a UUID for the post and get the current date and time in the epoch timestamp format:

- For generating a UUID for using the ID of the post, I have included the uuid library. You just have to call uuidv4(), which will return the UUID for your use.
- For creating the date and time in the epoch timestamp format, you can use the following code:

```
const date = new Date();
const epoch = (date.getTime()/1000).toFixed(0).toString();
```

The **Submit** button in the JSX is already set to call the this.submit() method when it is clicked. So, let's create the submit method of the AddPost class with the following code:

```
submit() {
  if(this.state.author && this.state.content && this.state.title) {
    this.setState({loading: true});

    const date = new Date();
    const epoch = (date.getTime()/1000).toFixed(0).toString();
    const body = {
      id: uuidv4(),
      author: this.state.author,
      title: this.state.title,
      content: this.state.content,
      datetime: epoch,
    };

    apiCall(`post`, body)
    .then(() => {
      this.setState({
        author: '',
        title: '',
        content: '',
        noOfLines: 0,
        loading: false,
        success: true,
      });
    })
    .catch(error => {
      this.setState({hasError: true, loading: false});
      console.error(error);
    });
```

```
    } else {
      alert('Please Fill in all the fields');
    }
  }
```

Also, add the following code to your constructor for binding this with the **Submit** button:

```
this.submit = this.submit.bind(this)
```

This is what the preceding submit method does:

1. It constructs the body of the network request, which is the post we need to add, and then makes the request to the POST/post server endpoint.
2. If the request is a success, it will reset the input fields to an empty string using the state variables.
3. If the request fails, it will simply set the `hasError` state to true, which will show us an error message.

If it works as expected, then click on **Home** and you should see your new post added to the blog. Congratulations! You just successfully built your own blog application using React!

Do try to build the author list page yourself and get help by referring to the completed files if you face any problems while building it.

Generating production builds

The one thing that we have been doing in every chapter is to generate the production builds. We did this by setting the `NODE_ENV` variable in the `.env` file to `production` and then running `npm run webpack` in the Terminal. However, for this chapter, since we are using `create-react-app`, we don't have to worry about setting the environment variables. We just need to run the following command in the Terminal from the project root folder:

```
npm run build
```

Once you run this command, you will have your production build with all the optimizations done and ready for use in the build directory of the project. Generating builds with `create-react-app` is that simple!

Once the production build is generated, run `http-server` inside the build directory of your project and see how the application works by visiting the URL printed by `http-server` in the console on your browser.

 React has a browser extension, which will let you debug the component hierarchy, including the component's state and props. Since we are only working with a basic application in this chapter, we didn't use that tool. However, you can try it out yourself if you are building applications with React at `https://github.com/facebook/react-devtools`.

Summary

This book is designed to help you understand the basics of React. Since we only built a simple application in this chapter, we didn't get to explore many of React's cool features. In this chapter, you started off with a simple counter, then built a ToDo list in the React crash course, and finally, built a simple blog application using the `create-react-app` tool and some libraries, such as `react-router` and reactstrap.

Being a simple view layer of the app, React does need a few libraries used together to make it work like a full fledged framework. React isn't the only JavaScript framework out there but React definitely is a one of a kind library that is revolutionizing modern UI development.

Everything is really great about React and the blog application we just built, except that each of the pages in the blog takes an annoying 3 seconds to load. Well, we can work around this problem by storing the post details offline using the localStorage API of the browser and updating states using them. But then again, our application is making too many network requests to the server for retrieving data that has already been retrieved in the previous requests.

Before you start thinking about some complex ways to reuse the data while storing it offline, there is one more thing we need to learn in this book, which is the new library that is taking the modern frontend development by storm-**Redux**.

7
Redux

Hi! Good work with the blog in the preceding chapter, and welcome to the last chapter of the book, which is a sequel to the blog that we built in the preceding chapter. In this chapter, we will fix that annoying 3 second loading issue on the blog by learning about centralized state management with Redux.

Just as we covered only the basics of React in the preceding chapter, this chapter is simple and will cover the basic concepts of Redux, which will change building web applications forever. That leaves us with only one simple question: What is Redux?

What is Redux?

According to the Redux documentation at: `http://redux.js.org/`, Redux is "*a predictable state container for JavaScript apps*". To explain redux in detail, let's take a look at the story of **flux**, an application architecture built by Facebook.

Flux

React is all well and good for a small application such as the ToDo list or the blog we built in the preceding chapter, except for an application such as Facebook. Facebook has hundreds of stateful React components that work to render the web application. In our blog, each React component has its state, and each stateful component makes a network request to fill these states with data.

Once parent components get the data, it will get passed to child components as props. However, the child component can have its own states too. Likewise, there can be two or more parent components in the same level that require the same data for the states. React's one-way data flow has a severe problem here. If the data is passed to the child component as props, the child component cannot change the props, since it will lead to mutation of the data. Hence, the child component will have to call a method in the parent component, which also should have passed as a prop to make a simple change. Imagine that you have 10s and 100s of parent-child nested components, where the control always has to be passed back to the parent and the data flow has to be managed properly between the parent and children components.

Facebook needed a simple and maintainable solution for managing data across all these components. The ideal solution they came up with was to take the state out of the React component and manage it in a separate place called **stores**. The plan was simple--we take the state (data) out of the React component and keep it in separate stores. All React components will then depend on stores for their data. So, you have to pass the required data from stores to all the necessary components as props.

Any change in the stores will lead to a change of props in all the dependent components, and whenever props change, React will automatically re-render the DOM. They came up with special functions called **actions** and **dispatchers**, which are the only ones capable of updating stores. So, if any component needs to update a store, it will call these functions with the required data, and they will update the store. Since the store gets updated, all the components will receive new props, and they will get re-rendered with new data.

This explains the architecture of flux. The flux architecture was created not only for React, but also for general use by all the JavaScript frameworks. However, even though the concept of flux was simple, the implementation was quite complex, which was later overcome by a new state management library, that is, Redux. Since we focus on Redux in this chapter, we won't be discussing flux; however, if you are interested in knowing more about flux, you can visit its official page: `https://facebook.github.io/flux/`.

Introduction to Redux

The main problem faced by developers who are using flux is that the application state is not quite predictable. It's probably why Redux introduces itself as a predictable state container for JavaScript apps. Redux was created as a `stand-alone` library that can be used with any JavaScript applications. To use Redux with React, we will need another library called `react-redux`, which is provided by the React community, available at: `https://github.com/reactjs/react-redux`.

Redux has one of the best documentations for an open source library. It even comes with two free video courses by the creator of the library--*Dan Abramov*--which are available on the documentation's home page. Before we start adding Redux to our blog application, let's take a look at how Redux works and how it will help to improve our React application.

Consider the Blog app we created in the preceding chapter. We have an **App component** as the parent and all the other components are children of the **App component**. In our case, each component has its own state, as follows:

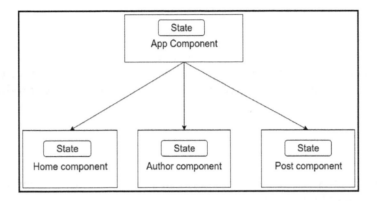

If we were to use flux, it would have multiple stores, and we could have the state of the **Post component** list and **Author component** list as two stores and let the entire application share those stores. However, if we use Redux, it will maintain a *single store*, which will hold the state for the entire application. You application structure will be as follows:

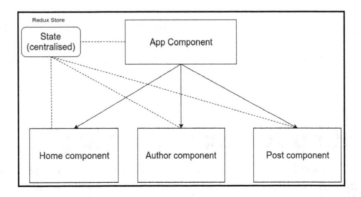

As you can see in the preceding image, Redux will create a *single store* that holds the state, which can then be supplied to the required components as props. Since the entire application has a single state, it becomes easy to maintain and the application state becomes more predictable for developers.

So, let's take a look at how Redux manages its store. The Redux implementation has three important parts:

- Store
- Actions
- Reducers

Store

A store is a centralized state that contains the entire application state. Like normal states, the store is also a simple JavaScript object, which contains only plain data (a store object should not contain any methods). Also, the state is read-only, which means that other parts of the application cannot directly make changes to the state. The only way to modify the state is to emit an action.

Actions

Actions are functions that are designed to perform a task. Whenever a component needs to modify the state, it will have to call an action. Actions are supplied to the component as props. The return type of an action function should be a plain object. The object returned by an action is supplied to the reducers.

Reducers

Reducers are simple methods whose function is to update the store. Since the store is a JavaScript object, organized as key-value pairs, each key will have its own reducer. The reducer function accepts two arguments, the object returned from the action and the current state, and it will return a new state.

Implementing Redux in the blog

Now that you have a good idea of why Redux is being used, let's get started with implementing Redux in our Blog application. This chapter uses the same server that you used in the preceding chapter, hence, you will have to keep the server running while working on this chapter too.

The starter files for this chapter are the same as the completed code file from the preceding chapter, except the `package.json` file, which has the following new libraries included in its dependencies:

- `redux`
- `react-redux`
- `redux-thunk`
- `redux-persist`
- `localforage`

We'll see what each of these libraries does while building our application. We will use the same `.env` file that we used in the preceding chapter with the `REACT_APP_SERVER_URL` environment variable, whose value is the URL of the running server. Navigate to the project root folder in your terminal and execute `npm install` followed by `npm start` to start the development server of the application.

The folder structure

The first thing we will need to do before we start with Redux is to define a proper folder structure for the Redux components. Currently, this is how our `src/` directory looks:

```
.
├──── App.css
├──── App.js
├──── App.test.js
├──── assets
├──── Components
├──── index.css
├──── index.js
├──── logo.svg
├──── registerServiceWorker.js
├──── routes.js
└──── services
```

We will need to create a new directory called `redux`, which will hold our `store`, `actions`, and `reducers`. Now, the directory structure will look as follows:

```
.
├──── App.css
├──── App.js
├──── App.test.js
├──── assets
├──── Components
├──── index.css
├──── index.js
├──── logo.svg
├──── redux
├──── registerServiceWorker.js
├──── routes.js
└──── services
```

Inside the `redux` directory, you will need to create four different directories, namely `actions`, `actionTypes`, `reducers`, and `store`. Your `redux` directory will now look like this:

```
.
├──── actions
├──── actionTypes
├──── reducers
└──── store
```

You might be wondering about the `actionTypes` directory. In Redux, all the actions should be predefined. You don't want an uninformed action to happen. Hence, we will create the `actionTypes` folder, which will hold constants for all the actions that our application can do.

Now that we have the required folder structure, let's start with creating our initial state.

Initial state

We always define the initial state in our React components in the constructor, where we create the state variables. Similarly, we will need to create an initial state for our Redux too. The only difference is that the Redux state will have to hold the state for the entire app.

Let's strategize how the initial state will look:

- The data that is used on the home page of our blog is an array of posts, hence we will need a posts array
- The data used for showing a list of authors is also an array
- We also need to maintain states for the AJAX calls and their success or error status

In your `store` directory, create a new file--`initialState.js`--and add the following code containing the `initialState` object:

```
const initialState = {
  posts: [

  ],
  authors: [

  ],
  ajaxCalls: {
    getAllPosts: {
      loading: false,
      hasError: false,
    },
    getAuthors: {
      loading: false,
      hasError: false,
    },
    addPost: {
      loading: false,
      hasError: false,
    }
  }
};

export default initialState;
```

As you can see, the `initialState` constant contains an empty array for posts and authors and an object that has the status information for the three network requests (AJAX calls) that we will use in this application.

Once we add Redux, our application will have to make only three network requests--one to get all the posts, one to get all the authors, and the third one to add a new post. If we want to see a post in the post details page, we can easily use the posts array we got in the first network request.

Your `redux` folder should now look like this:

```
.
├── actions
├── actionTypes
├── reducers
└── store
    └── initialState.js
```

Action types

Now that we have got our initial state ready, let's define all the actions our Blog application can do. Actions in our blog are nothing but the network requests we make to retrieve data. Each network request will have four actions associated with it.

Consider the request where we get all the blog posts from the server. The actions associated with this network request will be as follows:

- Start the AJAX call
- Network request success
- Network request failure
- Get posts data

So, in your `redux/actionTypes` directory, create an `actionTypes.js` file that will hold a constant value for all the actions that will happen in our application. In the `actionTypes.js` file, add the following code:

```
const actions = {

  GET_POSTS_AJAX_CALL_START : 'GET_POSTS_AJAX_CALL_START',
  GET_POSTS_AJAX_CALL_SUCCESS: 'GET_POSTS_AJAX_CALL_SUCCESS',
  GET_POSTS_AJAX_CALL_FAILURE: 'GET_POSTS_AJAX_CALL_FAILURE',
  GET_POSTS: 'GET_POSTS',

  GET_AUTHORS_AJAX_CALL_START: 'GET_AUTHORS_AJAX_CALL_START',
  GET_AUTHORS_AJAX_CALL_SUCCESS: 'GET_AUTHORS_AJAX_CALL_SUCCESS',
  GET_AUTHORS_AJAX_CALL_FAILURE: 'GET_AUTHORS_AJAX_CALL_FAILURE',
  GET_AUTHORS: 'GET_AUTHORS',

  ADD_POST_AJAX_CALL_START: 'ADD_POST_AJAX_CALL_START',
  ADD_POST_AJAX_CALL_SUCCESS: 'ADD_POST_AJAX_CALL_SUCCESS',
  ADD_POST_AJAX_CALL_FAILURE: 'ADD_POST_AJAX_CALL_FAILURE',
  ADD_POST: 'ADD_POST',
```

```
};

export default actions;
```

Your `redux` folder should have the following structure now:

```
.
├── actions
├── actionTypes
│   └── actionTypes.js
├── reducers
└── store
    └── initialState.js
```

We have created the `actionTypes`, which we can use throughout the application, so let's create the actions that the application should use to update the state.

Actions

Actions are dispatched from the React components when they need to modify the state of the application. We need two actions for our application, one for the posts page and one for the authors page. However, as in the preceding chapter, I'll only focus on the posts page; you can work on the authors page once you are done with this chapter. The completed code files have the actions completed for the authors page too, so you can use it as your reference.

Let's get started. In the `actions` directory, create two files, `authorActions.js` and `postActions.js`. Your `redux` folder should look like this:

```
.
├── actions
│   ├── authorActions.js
│   └── postActions.js
├── actionTypes
│   └── actionTypes.js
├── reducers
└── store
    └── initialState.js
```

Here, leave the `authorActions.js` file empty, and we'll work on the `postActions.js` file. This is how a standard action function should look:

```
const sumAction = (a, b) => {
  return {
    type: 'SUM_TWO_NUMBERS',
    payload: { answer: a+b }
  }
};
```

As you can see, the action returns an object with two properties, namely, `type` and `payload`. The type property is used by the *reducers* to identify the type of action that happened and the `payload` delivers the result of that action. `payload` is optional, since some actions do not produce a direct result, but type property should be present in all the objects returned by actions.

This works great for simple actions such as the sum of two numbers that we saw in the preceding example code, which is synchronous. However, most of the time, actions we do in our application are asynchronous, and we cannot simply return a JSON object from those actions.

To overcome this problem and do asynchronous actions, Redux has a concept called **middleware**. Middleware are libraries that can affect the way Redux works, especially for cases such as having asynchronous functions in the actions. The middleware that we will use in this application for this purpose is the `redux-thunk` library. This library is already included in the `package.json` file of this chapter's starter files and would have already been installed when you did `npm install`.

So, here's how `redux-thunk` works. `redux-thunk` allows actions to dispatch other actions instead of returning a plain JavaScript object. This is useful because we can call any number of actions we need when the asynchronous event is running. The actions that return other actions have the following weird syntax:

```
const ajaxRequestAction = () => {           // Action
  return dispatch => {                      // dispatcher
    makeAjaxRequest()                       // asynchronous code
    .then(response => {
      dispatch(successAction(response));    // dispatch successAction
    })
    .catch(error => {
      dispatch(errorAction(error));         // dispatch errorAction
    });
  }
}
```

```
const successAction = (response) => {
  return {
    type: 'REQUEST_SUCCESS',
    payload: { response },
  };
}

const errorAction = (error) => {
  return {
    type: 'REQUEST_FAILURE',
    payload: { error },
  };
}
```

The preceding syntax is quite hard to understand at first, but if you look closely, the ajaxRequestAction will return another function instead of returning an object. That function will have dispatch as its argument.

Let's call the function returned by ajaxRequestAction the *dispatcher* (*just for our reference*). Once we are inside the dispatcher, we can do any asynchronous actions we need. A dispatcher need not return any values. However, the dispatcher has the ability to dispatch other actions.

Let's create the actions for the posts of our blog in the postActions.js file. In your postActions.js file, you will first need to add two import statements:

```
import actions from '../actionTypes/actionTypes';
import apiCall from '../../services/api/apiCall';
```

The first one is the actions object that we created in the actionTypes folder. This contains all the actions that can be performed in our application. The second one is the apiCall service, which will make the network request.

There are two types of actions that need to be performed on the posts in our blog:

- Get all posts
- Add a new post

Get all posts

Usually, our React component will have to trigger only a single action--getAllPosts()-- which will make the network request and return the post data. This action will be our dispatcher. This action will start the network request and dispatch all the other actions based on the result of the network request. In your postActions.js file, add the following code:

```
export const getAllPosts = () => {

  return dispatch => {                      // Create the dispatcher

    dispatch(postsApiCallStart());          // Dispatch - api call started

    apiCall('posts', {}, 'GET')
      .then(posts => {
        dispatch(postsApiCallSuccess());    // Dispatch - api call success
        dispatch(getPosts(posts));          // Dispatch - received posts array
      })
      .catch(error => {
        dispatch(postsApiCallFailure());    // Dispatch - api call failed
        console.error(error);
      });

  };

};
```

Note the export keyword before the getAllPosts function. This is because all the actions will be used from inside the React components, hence, we are prefixing them with export keywords so that they can be imported later.

Our dispatcher, getAllPosts, will make the network request and dispatch all the other normal actions, which will be used by the reducers of our app. Add the following code to your postActions.js file, which contains the code for all the actions dispatched by the getAllPosts action:

```
export const postsApiCallStart = () => {
  return {
```

```
    type: actions.GET_POSTS_AJAX_CALL_START,
  };
};

export const postsApiCallSuccess = () => {
  return {
    type: actions.GET_POSTS_AJAX_CALL_SUCCESS,
  };
};

export const postsApiCallFailure = () => {
  return {
    type: actions.GET_POSTS_AJAX_CALL_FAILURE,
  };
};

export const getPosts = (posts) => {
  return {
    type: actions.GET_POSTS,
    payload: { posts },
  };
};
```

The actions for tracking the status of the API calls do not need to return a `payload`. Since its status will be a boolean value, it only returns the action's type. However, the `getPosts` action, which should return the post details, returns a `payload` along with the action type, which is the posts array.

This looks like a lot of code for a simple network request, but, trust me, once your application scales up, these are the only actions you'll ever need whenever you need to get all the posts.

 You should always specify the type of the action using the actions object you created in the `actionTypes` file. This way, you can prevent other developers in the team from accidentally creating unexpected actions in your application.

Adding a new post

Since adding a post is an action related to posts, we will add the actions in the same `postActions.js` file. Add the following code for `addNewPost` action, which also acts as the dispatcher for adding a new post in your `postActions.js` file:

```
export const addNewPost = (body) => {
  return dispatch => {
```

```
      dispatch(addPostApiCallStart());

      apiCall(`post`, body)
      .then(() => {

        dispatch(addPostApiCallSuccess());
        dispatch(getAllPosts());                    // Dispatch - getAllPosts action

      })
      .catch(error => {

        dispatch(addPostApiCallFailure());

      });
   };
};
```

The addNewPost action is pretty much similar to our preceding getAllPosts action. However, it requires a body argument, which will contain the post details needed for adding the post to the server. You should also note that, once the success response from the server is received that the post has been added, the addNewPost action will dispatch the getAllPosts action, which will retrieve all the posts, including the newly created post. This saves our React component the trouble of dispatching multiple actions.

The code for the remaining actions, which are dispatched by the addNewPost action, is as follows:

```
export const addPostApiCallStart = () => {
  return {
    type: actions.ADD_POST_AJAX_CALL_START
  };
};

export const addPostApiCallSuccess = () => {
  return {
    type: actions.ADD_POST_AJAX_CALL_SUCCESS
  };
};

export const addPostApiCallFailure = () => {
  return {
    type: actions.ADD_POST_AJAX_CALL_FAILURE
  };
};
```

That's all for the actions part. We currently have the following three parts in our blog application:

However, they are connected with each other at the moment. Our next step is to create the reducers, which provide the ability to update the application state.

Reducers

Reducers are simple functions that receive the action object returned from the actions and then update the state using them. Generally, since our application state is represented as an object which is a key-value pair, we will need to create a reducer for each key (or property). This is the structure of our application state, which we created in the initial state section:

```
{
  posts: [],
  authors: [],
  ajaxCalls: {
    ...
  },
}
```

We have got three properties in our state, hence, we will need three reducers, namely, `postsReducer.js`, `authorsReducer.js`, and `ajaxCallsReducer.js`. These reducers will represent our application state in the store. We also need another reducer, which will be used to combine these three reducers into a single object that will be used as our state.

In your `redux` directory, create the four files highlighted in the following structure; your `redux` folder structure should now look as follows :

```
.
├── actions
│   ├── authorActions.js
│   └── postActions.js
├── actionTypes
│   └── actionTypes.js
├── reducers
│   ├── ajaxCallsReducer.js
│   ├── authorsReducer.js
│   ├── postsReducer.js
│   └── rootReducer.js
└── store
    └── initialState.js
```

This is how the reducer function works:

- The reducer function accepts two parameters; the first one is the old state and the second one is the action object returned by an action.
- It will return a new state, which will completely overwrite the old state. This is because, just like updating state in React components, updating state in Redux should also be immutable.

Consider the following example. This is how Redux stores states; the value of states are the results of the reducers:

```
{
  posts: postsReducer(oldPosts, action),
}
```

If an action happens that receives new posts, the reducer will return all the new posts, which will update the post's state without mutating it. Remember that all reducers will be listening to all the actions. Hence, we will need to properly filter the required action inside the reducer, and if none of the actions affect the reducer, it should simply return the old state.

Open your `postsReducer.js` file, and add the following import statements:

```
import initialState from '../store/initialState';
import actions from '../actionTypes/actionTypes';
```

Once you have added these `import` statements, add the following code for the posts reducer:

```
const postsReducer = (state = initialState.posts, action) => {
  switch(action.type) {
    case actions.GET_POSTS:
      return action.payload.posts;

    default:
      return state;
  }
};

export default postsReducer;
```

The `postsReducer` function will accept two parameters, as mentioned earlier:

- `state`: It contains the old value of the `posts` state. At first load, however, the old state will be null, hence, `initialState.posts` is passed as a default parameter for the state.

- `action`: It is the action object returned by the actions.

Since the reducer gets called for every action, we will simply need to add a switch case statement with which we can determine the type of action and whether it will affect our state. In our switch case statement, we have added two cases for the following conditions:

- If the action's type is `GET_POSTS`, we know that it contains all the posts, hence, we can simply return the posts from the action's `payload`.
- If it is not, then the `default` case will be executed, which will simply return the old state.

The `authorsReducer.js` file is for you to try out, but it can't be left empty. In this file, add the following code:

```
import initialState from '../store/initialState';
import actions from '../actionTypes/actionTypes';

const authorsReducer = (state = initialState.authors, action) => {
  switch(action.type) {

    default:
      return state;
  }

};

export default authorsReducer;
```

It will simply return the `initialState` for all the actions. You can work on this reducer to try out Redux in the author list page.

For `ajaxCallsReducer.js`, the code is too long to be specified in the book, so you should copy the contents of the file from the completed code files. The exact code will work fine. The working of `ajaxCallsReducer` is very simple. It toggles the value of the `loading` and `hasError` properties to `true` or `false` based on the result of the network request. Since the state cannot be mutated, it uses the spread operator (`...state`) to perform this operation.

Consider the case in which `GET_POSTS_AJAX_CALL_START` happens:

```
case actions.GET_POSTS_AJAX_CALL_START:
  return {
    ...state,
    getAllPosts: {
      loading: true,
      hasError: false,
```

```
    },
  };
```

Here, a new state object is created with the loading property inside the `getAllPosts` property set to `true`. This state can be useful for showing the loading indicator in the application.

The Root Reducer

The last item we have left in the reducers part is the root reducer. In this file, all the reducers are combined together to be used as a state for the application. Redux provides a method called `combineReducers`, which can be used for this purpose. In your `rootReducer.js` file, add the following import statements:

```
import { combineReducers } from 'redux';
import postsReducer from './postsReducer';
import authorsReducer from './authorsReducer';
import ajaxCallsReducer from './ajaxCallsReducer';
```

This will import the `combineReducers` function along with other reducers. To combine all reducers into a single root reducer, you will simply need to add the following code:

```
const rootReducer = combineReducers({
  posts: postsReducer,
  authors: authorsReducer,
  ajaxCalls: ajaxCallsReducer,
});

export default rootReducer;
```

We will import this reducer to create our store in the next section. At the moment, this is how data flows between actions and reducers:

Store

The last stage of working with the Redux part is to create the store object using the root reducer. Inside the `redux/store` directory, create the `configureStore.js` file, which will create our store object. We will also need to apply our `redux-thunk` middleware in this file, which will allow us to use actions that will dispatch other actions.

Redux provides the `createStore` function to create the store object and the `applyMiddleware` function to add middleware. In your `configureStore.js` file, add the following code:

```
import { createStore, applyMiddleware } from 'redux';
import thunk from 'redux-thunk';
import rootReducer from '../reducers/rootReducer';
```

To create a store, you will simply need to call the `createReducer` function with `rootReducer`, the preceding state, and the `applyMiddleware` method as parameters. The first parameter is compulsory, whereas the others are optional. In the `configureStore.js` file, add the following code after the `import` statements:

```
const configureStore = (preloadedState) => {
  return createStore(
    rootReducer,
    preloadedState,
    applyMiddleware(thunk)
  );
};

export default configureStore;
```

The `configureStore` function will be used to create the store object for our React components. The final folder structure of our `redux` directory will look as follows:

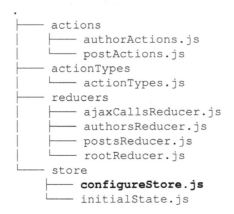

```
.
├── actions
│   ├── authorActions.js
│   └── postActions.js
├── actionTypes
│   └── actionTypes.js
├── reducers
│   ├── ajaxCallsReducer.js
│   ├── authorsReducer.js
│   ├── postsReducer.js
│   └── rootReducer.js
└── store
    ├── configureStore.js
    └── initialState.js
```

That's all for now in the `redux` part. We will now work with the React components of our blog and connect Redux with React using the `react-redux` library. Now, this is how data flows in the `redux` part:

Connecting Redux with React components

We wrapped the entire `App` component of our blog inside the `BrowserRouter` component of React router to implement routing in the `index.js` file. Redux follows a similar approach. We need to wrap the `App` component, which is already wrapped inside the router within a `Provider` component of the `react-redux` library.

Open your `src/index.js` file, and add the following import statements after the `import` statements that are already present in the file:

```
import { Provider } from 'react-redux';
import configureStore from './redux/store/configureStore';
```

This will import the `Provider` component of `react-redux` and the `configureStore` function that we created in the preceding section. We will need to create a `store` object from the `configureStore` function. After the preceding `import` statements, add the following line to create the store object:

```
const store = configureStore();
```

Currently, this is how your `ReactDOM.render()` method looks:

```
ReactDOM.render(
  <Router>
    <App />
  </Router>
  ,
  document.getElementById('root')
);
```

You need to replace it with the following lines:

```
ReactDOM.render(
  <Provider store={store}>
    <Router>
      <App />
    </Router>
```

```
    </Provider>
    ,
    document.getElementById('root')
);
```

We have now wrapped the entire `App` component inside the `Provider`, which provides the React components with the ability to connect with Redux. We'll now see how to connect an individual component with the state present in the Redux store and its actions.

The App component

The first component that we will connect with Redux is the `App` component, which acts as the parent component to all the other components in our application. This means that, regardless of the URL we visit in our application, the `App` component will be executed. This makes the `App` Component the best place to do actions, such as `getAllPosts`, which will retrieve the posts array.

This section is the most confusing part in Redux, hence, you will have to pay close attention to how we pass the Redux store and actions to the React component as props. Also, make sure that you refer to the completed code files if you face any errors at this stage.

You will need to add a few `import` statements in your `App.js` file. The first thing you will need to import is the `connect` component provided by `react-redux` library:

```
import { connect } from 'react-redux';
```

This will provide a wrapper to connect your React component with Redux. This works in the same way as the `withRouter` component of the React router, which supplies history, location, and match props to the React component.

You will also need to import the `bindActionCreators` function of Redux, which will convert the action functions into simple objects that can be used by React components:

```
import { bindActionCreators } from 'redux';
```

Another important thing we will need to import is the `postActions`, which will be used by our `App` component. Since `postActions` contains a lot of functions exported individually, we can import all of them together as a single object using the following `import` statement:

```
import * as postActions from './redux/actions/postActions';
```

We now have all the required `import` statements in place. Our next step is the actual implementation part. Currently, this is how the export statement of the `App` component looks:

```
export default withRouter(App);
```

Our `App` component is wrapped inside `withRouter`. To connect this with Redux, we will need to wrap the `App` component inside the `connect` function we imported from `react-redux`, and the result should be inside the `withRouter` component.

However, the connect function itself requires two functions--`mapStateToProps` and `mapDispatchToProps`--as parameters. In these two functions, `mapStateToProps` will convert the state from the store and `mapDispatchToProps` will convert the actions into props, which can be used by React components. Now, pay close attention, because we will be seeing another weird syntax soon.

Replace the export code of your `App` component with the following lines of code:

```
function mapStateToProps() {
  return {
    // No states needed by App Component
  };
}

function mapDispatchToProps(dispatch) {
  return {
    postActions: bindActionCreators(postActions, dispatch),
  };
}

export default withRouter(
  connect(
    mapStateToProps,
    mapDispatchToProps
  )(App)
);
```

Take a look at the preceding code snippet carefully. If the export statement makes no sense to you, no worries, we'll sort that out. Let's see what `connect` does. The `connect` function will accept two parameters--`mapStateToProps` and `mapDispatchToProps`--which are functions, and it will return a function:

```
connectFunction = connect(mapStateToProps, mapDispatchToProps);
```

The `App` component is wrapped inside the `connectFunction` as `connectFunction(App)`. The entire component is then wrapped inside the `withRouter()` function. So, basically, this is what the export statement works like:

```
export default withRouter(connectFunction(App));
```

Which is what we have combined together and writing as:

```
export default withRouter(
  connect(
    mapStateToProps,
    mapDispatchToProps
  )(App)
);
```

The `App` component does not use any states, hence, the `mapStateToProps` function will return an empty object. The `mapDispatchToProps` function, however, will return `postActions` as an object using the `bindActionCreators` function, which will then be supplied to the `App` component as a prop.

We will now have the `App` component make the API call for getting all the posts by adding the following line of code in the `componentWillMount()` method:

```
this.props.postActions.getAllPosts();
```

Also, since `postActions` is passed as a prop to our `App` component, add the following property to the `propType` validation we added in the `App` component:

```
postActions: PropTypes.object.isRequired
```

Refer to the completed code files if you face any problems in including the preceding code snippets in the `App.js` file. Once you have completed this step, keep the server running from the `Chapter06\Server` directory and open your application in Chrome.

You should see the blog running with the same 3 second loading time whenever we click on the menu items in the navigation bar icon or on the **Read More** button in the post. We will fix this in the next section.

Home component

In the preceding section, we used the `App` component to retrieve the data from the server and store it in the Redux store. This means that we no longer need to make any network requests in our Home component. We will simply need to retrieve data from the Redux store.

The Home component does not trigger any Redux actions, hence, we only need to import the connect component from `react-redux`. In your `Home.js` file, add the following `import` statement:

```
import { connect } from 'react-redux';
```

Replace the `export` statement of our `Home.js` file with the following code:

```
function mapStateToProps(state) {
  return {
    posts: state.posts,
    loading: state.ajaxCalls.getAllPosts.loading,
    hasError: state.ajaxCalls.getAllPosts.hasError,
  };
}

export default connect(mapStateToProps)(Home);
```

Since the Home component will not do any actions, we can safely ignore the `mapDispatchToProps` function in connect. However, we got some work for the `mapStateToProps` function, which simply returned an empty object in the preceding chapter.

The `mapStateToProps` function has one argument, which is a state that contains the entire Redux state of the applications. In the return statement, we will simply need to mention which part of the state we need to deliver to the React component as props. The best part about connect is that, whenever reducers update the states, it will update these props using the `mapStateToProps` function.

We have now got some new props for our Home component. So, in your Home component, add the following `propType` validation:

```
static propTypes = {
  posts: PropTypes.array.isRequired,
  loading: PropTypes.bool.isRequired,
  hasError: PropTypes.bool.isRequired,
}
```

Also, we no longer need any states or API calls in our Home component, hence, you can *delete both* the *constructor* and the `componentWillMount` methods. Instead, in the JSX of your render method, replace `this.state.posts` with `this.props.posts`. Do the same for both the `loading` and `hasError` states. Now our Home component depends directly on the Redux store. Refer to the completed code files if you face any problems.

Here's the cool part--if you click on any other section in the navigation bar and return to Home, you will see that the posts load instantly. This is because all the posts are stored and ready for use inside our Redux store. If you click on the **Read More** button in the posts list of the home page, you should see a loading indicator again, since it is retrieving post details from the server. Let's also connect that component with Redux.

Post component

Open your `src/Components/Post.js` file in VSCode. Our first step is to add the required `import` statements:

```
import { connect } from 'react-redux';
import { bindActionCreators } from 'redux';
```

Let's strategize how we will connect this component with Redux:

- We will need to get the Post ID, which is present in the URL
- Once we have the ID, we should find the post with the ID in our store's posts array using the `Array.find()` method
- Finally, we can send the required post as props

Now, replace your `export` statement in `Post.js` with the following code:

```
function mapStateToProps(state, ownProps) {

  return {
    post: state.posts.find(post => post.id === ownProps.match.params.id),
    loading: state.ajaxCalls.getAllPosts.loading,
    hasError: state.ajaxCalls.getAllPosts.hasError,
  };
}

export default withRouter(
  connect(mapStateToProps)(Post)
);
```

The `mapStateToProps` function has a second argument, which is `ownProps`. It contains all the props of the Post component. From `ownProps`, we can obtain the post ID, which is present in the match object supplied by the `withRouter` component of the React router. We will then use the find method to find the post and return the required data in the return statement.

Your `propType` validation inside the Post component should look as follows:

```
static propTypes = {
  history: PropTypes.object.isRequired,
  location: PropTypes.object.isRequired,
  match: PropTypes.object.isRequired,
  post: PropTypes.object,
  loading: PropTypes.bool.isRequired,
  hasError: PropTypes.bool.isRequired,
}
```

You can delete the constructor and the `componentWillMount` methods just as we did for our Home component, and then, in your render method, replace `this.state.loading` with `this.props.loading` and `this.state.hasError` with `this.props.hasError`.

However, before you replace `this.state.post` with `this.props.post`, we should make sure that `this.props.post` has a value, since, during loading, the posts array will be empty, and the value of `this.props.post` will be undefined. In your render method, replace the three lines where you have used `this.state.post` with the following code:

```
{
  this.props.post
  ?
    <div>
      <h2>{this.props.post.title}</h2>
      <p>{this.props.post.author}</p>
      <p>{this.props.post.content}</p>
    </div>
  :
    null
}
```

Now try reloading the page. It will take three seconds for the first load, but once your data is loaded, you will see that navigating to other pages (except the author page) will be a breeze. Clicking on the **Read More** button in the home page will take you to the post details page instantly.

It's your turn to try this out in the `AuthorList` and `AuthorPosts` components. The last component in which we need to connect Redux is the NewPost component.

The NewPost component

The NewPost component requires both state and actions from Redux. It needs the loading and `hasError` data from state and will have to use `postActions` to submit a post to the server. So, let's start by including the required `import` statements in the `src/Components/NewPost/NewPost.js` file:

```
import { connect } from 'react-redux';
import { bindActionCreators } from 'redux';
import * as postActions from '../../redux/actions/postActions';
```

Now, replace your `export` statement in the `NewPost.js` file with the following code:

```
function mapStateToProps(state) {
  return {
    loading: state.ajaxCalls.addPost.loading,
    hasError: state.ajaxCalls.addPost.hasError,
  };
}

function mapDispatchToProps(dispatch) {
  return {
    postActions: bindActionCreators(postActions, dispatch),
  };
}

export default connect(
  mapStateToProps,
  mapDispatchToProps
)(NewPost);
```

Since we have got props in our `NewPost` component, add the following `propType` validation code inside the `NewPost` class:

```
static propTypes = {
  postActions: PropTypes.object.isRequired,
  loading: PropTypes.bool.isRequired,
  hasError: PropTypes.bool.isRequired,
}
```

Unlike the `Home` and `Post` components, the `NewPost` component requires both state and props to render the JSX elements. We can delete the loading and `hasError` states and replace them with props. You should refer to the completed code files (if needed), and replace the loading and `hasError` states inside the JSX of the render method with props.

You should then replace your entire `apiCall().then().catch()` chain inside the submit method with this following single line of code:

```
this.props.postActions.addNewPost(body);
```

Your `submit` method will now look as follows:

```
submit() {
  if(this.state.author && this.state.content && this.state.title) {
    this.setState({loading: true});

    const date = new Date();
    const epoch = (date.getTime()/1000).toFixed(0).toString();
    const body = {
      id: uuidv4(),
      author: this.state.author,
      title: this.state.title,
      content: this.state.content,
      datetime: epoch,
    };

    this.props.postActions.addNewPost(body);

  } else {
    alert('Please Fill in all the fields');
  }
}
```

The `submit` method will now trigger an action--`addNewPost`, which contains the required network request. However, we need to show a success message once the network request is complete. To detect the completion of a network request, since all our updates to the store are immutable, if the status of loading or `hasError` properties in the `ajaxCalls` property of the Redux's state changes, it will lead to the creation of a new object, which will automatically be delivered to the `NewPost` component by `react-redux`.

This means that new props will be received by the `NewPost` React component at the end of the network request. In this case, we can use the `componentWillReceiveProps` `lifecycle` method of React to show the success message and clear the input fields once the post is submitted. Add the following code of `componentWillReceiveProps` to the `NewPost` class:

```
componentWillReceiveProps(nextProps) {
  if(this.props !== nextProps) {
    if(nextProps.loading === false && nextProps.hasError === false) {
      this.setState({
        success: true,
```

```
        author: '',
        title: '',
        content: '',
      });
    } else if(nextProps.loading === false && nextProps.hasError === true)
  {
      this.setState({success: false});
    }
  }
}
```

componentWillReceiveProps will have the new props that are supplied to the component (in our case, from react-redux) as its parameter, which we will call nextProps. In the componentWillReceiveProps method, a simple this.props !== nextProps check is done to make sure that current props and new props are not the same objects. If they both hold the same object, we can skip the operation. We then only need to check whether loading is complete and whether there are any errors using if else statements, as used in the preceding code snippet.

Once you have included the preceding code snippet, try to add a post (make sure that the server is running). It should add the post and display the success message. Now, click on the Home menu option. You will see the new post that you added appear instantly with no loading time required. The secret to this is that the addNewPost action will automatically call the getAllPosts action, which will update your Redux store in the background. With the store updated using the new post, your Home component can get the updated posts state directly from Redux, which makes things appear instantly.

This provides a great user experience for users, as they will find that every update happens instantly instead of having to wait for the loading indicator.

The Redux data flow

After connecting your Redux code with the React components, you will find that Redux follows the same one-way data flow as React. This is the data flow of Redux:

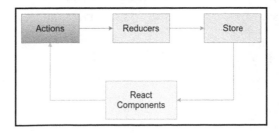

This is how data flow happens in a React component:

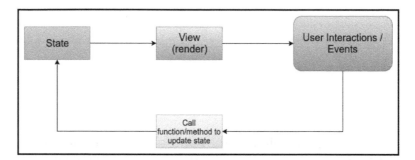

Also, both the state in a React component and the state in a Redux store should be immutable. This immutability is essential for React and Redux to work properly. However, since JavaScript does not strictly implement any immutable data types at the moment, we need to be careful not to mutate the states. In React components, we will use the `this.setState()` method, and we use spread operators (`...`) inside reducers for Redux to update states without mutating them.

This can prove troublesome for large projects with a huge amount of data. Facebook has introduced a library called `Immutable.js`, available at: `https://facebook.github.io/immutable-js/`, which can solve this problem by creating immutable data types in JavaScript. This library is out of the scope of this book, but ensure that you give it a try later.

Persisting Redux store

Our blog is fast to load since we have integrated Redux into it, however, our users still have to wait three seconds for the initial load. What if we could persist the Redux store offline and show it to users while the new data is loading?

Sounds good, and it's very simple too! I have already added two libraries to the dependencies list for this purpose:

- `redux-persist`: `https://github.com/rt2zz/redux-persist`
- `localForage`: `https://github.com/localForage/localForage`

`redux-persist` provides a simple way to persist your Redux store and rehydrate it whenever needed. This makes your store available offline when your users visit your page for the second time.

`localForage` is a simple storage library that lets you use `indexDB` using an API similar to `localStorage`. `redux-persist` works well with `localStorage`, but it recommends using `localForage` as its default storage engine for web browsers.

Now, persisting the Redux store isn't that complicated; you just need to add a few lines of code in the Redux store to persist it and make the reducers listen for a *rehydration* action to rehydrate data from the persisted store. It's as easy as changing just the following three files:

The first file: Open your `configureStore.js` file and add the following import statement:

```
import { autoRehydrate } from 'redux-persist';
```

Then, change the `return` statement inside your `configureStore` method to the following:

```
return createStore(
  rootReducer,
  preloadedState,
  applyMiddleware(thunk),
  autoRehydrate()
);
```

Now, this adds the `autoRehydrate()` function while creating the store that will emit the rehydrate actions.

The second file: Open your `index.js` file and add the following `import` statements:

```
import { persistStore } from 'redux-persist';
import localForage from 'localforage';
```

This will import the `persistStore()` function that can persist your store and the `localForage` library that will be used as the storage engine. Now, you will need to add a single line of code after the line where you created your store:

```
const store = configureStore();          // Store gets created here
persistStore(store, {storage: localForage}); // next line which will
persist your store
```

The third file: Open your `postsReducer.js` file. In this posts reducer, we will listen for another action, which is the rehydrate action emitted while rehydrating your persisted Redux store. Redux Persist maintains a set of constants, which has defined the rehydrate action similar to how we have defined our actions in the `actionTypes.js` file.

In the reducers file, add the following `import` statement:

```
import * as constants from 'redux-persist/constants';
```

This will import the constants from `redux-persist`. You should then add an additional case statement inside the `postsReducer` function, which will hydrate the Redux store:

```
case constants.REHYDRATE:
  if(action.payload.posts) {
    return action.payload.posts;
  }
  return state;
```

This case will check whether the rehydrate action has occurred, and then it uses an `if` condition to check whether the rehydrate action contains the `posts` property in the action's payload. Refer to the completed code files if you face any issues with it.

Now, once it is complete, open the application in Chrome and try reloading the page. You should see that the posts are available even while the data is loading from the server, just like in the following image:

This allows the users to use the application offline even while the posts are loading. We have completely removed the 3 second loading issue from the blog.

Redux is a great library for managing states in a separate state container. It's centralized state management with React proved to be very useful and efficient, that many libraries were created for centralized state management in other frameworks too, such as `@ngrx/store` for Angular and `vuex` for Vue.js. In this chapter, we only covered the basics of Redux--refer to the Redux documentation and its tutorial videos to learn Redux in-depth. Also, check out **Redux DevTools** at `https://github.com/gaearon/redux-devtools`, which provides cool features, such as hot reloading and time travel debugging for your Redux application.

The author page hasn't been connected to Redux yet. So, do give it a try and complete the blog.

Summary

Congratulations! You have successfully completed the Redux chapter and also completed the book. In this chapter, we covered what Redux is and how we can use it to improve state management. We then created a Redux store with the actions and reducers needed to manage the store data. We used the `react-redux` library to connect our Redux code with the React components and used props instead of states to render the JSX elements.

Finally, we used `redux-persist` with `localforage` as the storage engine to persist our Redux store and make our application work offline. This chapter has made the blog faster and more user-friendly for users.

You has now completed your journey through this book, but you have just got started with your journey in exploring the world of JavaScript. There's still a lot to learn and a lot more to come. So, be prepared to learn and explore, no matter what you want to do.

Index